Oxford English for

Information Technology

Eric H. Glendinning | John McEwan

Contents

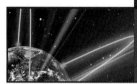

Computer Users

STARTER	**1**	Work in groups. Share information on how you use computers in your free time. Compare answers with other groups and make a list of uses for your class.

LISTENING	**2**	You are going to hear four people talk about how they use computers. Before you listen, try to predict the uses they describe.

User	Possible use
primary school teacher	
Open University student	
girl (Louise), aged 6	
artist	

3 🎧 Now listen to the recordings and note the actual uses described.

User	Actual use
primary school teacher Open University student girl (Louise), aged 6 artist	

4 🎧 Now listen to the recordings again to find the answers to these questions:

1 How does the story-telling program encourage children to work together?
2 In what way is the children's reaction to this program different from other uses they make of computers?
3 What is the OU student studying?
4 What opportunity has she to meet other students?
5 What can you do with Pets 3?
6 What does Louise do with clipart?
7 How did the artist display work to dealers in the past?
8 What is the difficulty in selling through a website?

LANGUAGE WORK **Revision: Past simple and Present perfect**

Study these examples of the Present perfect from the recording of the artist.

1 *I've scanned* in about a third of these photographs.
2 *I've organised* the paintings into themes.
3 *I've added* a sound track.

Why doesn't the speaker use the Past simple?

4 *I scanned* in about a third of these photographs.
5 *I organised* the paintings into themes.
6 *I added* a sound track.

We use the Present perfect to describe past actions with present relevance. The artist uses the Present perfect because he is describing a CD he has just made and what he is going to do with it in the near future.

We use the Past simple to describe completed actions in the past. It is often used with time expressions such as *last year, before PCs were introduced, in 1998.* Note these examples from the recording:

7 I made one for Mary's birthday *last week.*
8 We tried it out *last term.*

5   The artist is being interviewed. Make questions to match his answers. Use the correct form of the Past simple or Present perfect, whichever is correct. For example:

Question: What *did you do yesterday*?
Answer: Worked on the computer.

1 Q What ...
   A Worked on a CD of my paintings.
2 Q How many ...
   A About a third.
3 Q What ...
   A I destroyed them.
4 Q How ...
   A I scanned them in.
5 Q How ...
   A I've organised them into themes.
6 Q Have ...
   A Yes, I've added a sound track.
7 Q How long ...
   A It's taken me about a week.
8 Q When ...
   A I started about ten years ago.
9 Q What ...
   A Before I had a computer, I had to use slides.
10 Q Have ...
   A Yes, I've sold a few.

6   Put the tenses in this dialogue in the correct form: Past simple or Present perfect.

1 A What (do) today?

2 B I (work) on my project. I (search) the Web for sites on digital cameras.

3 A (find) any good ones?

4 B I (find) several company sites – Sony, Canon, ... but I (want) one which (compare) all the models.

5 A Which search engine (use)?

6 B Dogpile mostly. (ever use) it?

7   A   Yes, I (try) it but I (have) more luck with AskJeeves. Why don't you try it?

8   B   I (have) enough for one night. I (spend) hours on that project.

9   A   I (not start) on mine yet.

10 B   Yeh? I bet you (do) it all.

PROBLEM-SOLVING   7   How do you think these professions might use computers? Compare answers with others in your group.

architects
interior designers
farmers
landscape gardeners
musicians
rally drivers
sales people

SPEAKING   8   Work in pairs. Find out this information from your partner. Make sure you use the correct tense in your questions. For example:

download music from the Internet   [what site]
A   *Have you ever downloaded music from the Internet?*
B   *What site did you use?*

1   send a video email attachment   [who to, when]
2   fit an expansion card   [which type]
3   replace a hard disk   [what model]
4   fix a printer fault   [what kind]
5   make your own website   [how]
6   have a virus   [which virus]
7   watched TV on the Internet   [which station]
8   write a program   [which language]

WRITING   9   Describe how you use computers in your study and in your free time.

A Find the answers to these questions in the following text.

1 Name some types of devices that use 'computers on a chip'.
2 What uses of handheld computers are mentioned in the text?
3 What are the benefits of using computers with the following items?
   a Security systems
   b Cars
   c Phones
4 What smart devices are mentioned in the text?
5 What are smart cards used for?
6 What are the advantages of multimedia?
7 What can medical expert systems do?
8 How can computers help the disabled?
9 What types of computing systems are made available to people in remote locations using electronic classrooms or boardrooms?
10 What aspects of computing can people power determine?

Computers Make the World Smaller and Smarter

The ability of tiny computing devices to control complex operations has transformed the way many tasks are performed, ranging from scientific research to producing
5 consumer products. Tiny 'computers on a chip' are used in medical equipment, home appliances, cars and toys. Workers use handheld computing devices to collect data at a customer site, to generate forms, to control
10 inventory, and to serve as desktop organisers.

Not only is computing equipment getting smaller, it is getting more sophisticated. Computers are part of many machines and devices that once required continual human
15 supervision and control. Today, computers in security systems result in safer environments, computers in cars improve energy efficiency, and computers in phones provide features such as call forwarding, call monitoring, and
20 call answering.

These smart machines are designed to take over some of the basic tasks previously performed by people; by so doing, they make life a little easier and a little more pleasant.
25 Smart cards store vital information such as health records, drivers' licenses, bank balances, and so on. Smart phones, cars, and appliances with built in computers can be programmed to better meet individual needs.
30 A smart house has a built-in monitoring system that can turn lights on and off, open and close windows, operate the oven, and more.

With small computing devices available for
35 performing smart tasks like cooking dinner, programming the VCR, and controlling the flow of information in an organization, people are able to spend more time doing what they often do best – being creative. Computers can
40 help people work more creatively.

Multimedia systems are known for their educational and entertainment value, which we call 'edutainment'. Multimedia combines

45 text with sound, video, animation, and graphics, which greatly enhances the interaction between user and machine and can make information more interesting and appealing to people. Expert systems software enables computers to 'think' like experts.

50 Medical diagnosis expert systems, for example, can help doctors pinpoint a patient's illness, suggest further tests, and prescribe appropriate drugs.

Connectivity enables computers and software

55 that might otherwise be incompatible to communicate and to share resources. Now that computers are proliferating in many areas and networks are available for people to access data and communicate with others,

60 personal computers are becoming interpersonal PCs. They have the potential to significantly improve the way we relate to each other. Many people today telecommute – that is, use their computers to stay in touch

65 with the office while they are working at home. With the proper tools, hospital staff can get a diagnosis from a medical expert hundreds or thousands of miles away. Similarly, the disabled can communicate more

70 effectively with others using computers.

Distance learning and videoconferencing are concepts made possible with the use of an electronic classroom or boardroom accessible to people in remote locations. Vast databases

75 of information are currently available to users of the Internet, all of whom can send mail messages to each other. The information superhighway is designed to significantly expand this interactive connectivity so that

80 people all over the world will have free access to all these resources.

People power is critical to ensuring that hardware, software, and connectivity are effectively integrated in a socially responsible

85 way. People – computer users and computer professionals – are the ones who will decide which hardware, software, and networks endure and how great an impact they will have on our lives. Ultimately people power

90 must be exercised to ensure that computers are used not only efficiently but in a socially responsible way.

[Adapted from 'Computing in the Information Age', 2nd edition, Nancy Stern & Robert A. Stern, (Wiley), pages 19–22]

B   Re-read the text to find the answers to these questions:

1   Match the terms in Table A with the statements in Table B.

Table A

a	Edutainment
b	Multimedia
c	Expert system
d	Telecommute
e	Information superhighway

Table B

i	Software that enables computers to 'think' like experts
ii	Use computers to stay in touch with the office while working at home
iii	Internet system designed to provide free, interactive access to vast resources for people all over the world
iv	Multimedia materials with a combination of educational and entertainment content
v	A combination of text with sound, video, animation, and graphics

2   Mark the following statements as True or False:

a   Desktop organisers are programs that require desktop computers.

b   Computers are sometimes used to monitor systems that previously needed human supervision.

c   Networking is a way of allowing otherwise incompatible systems to communicate and share resources.

d   The use of computers prevents people from being creative.

e   Computer users do not have much influence over the way that computing develops.

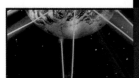

Computer Architecture

STARTER **1** Name these different types of computers. Then match the possible users below to each type. Justify your choice.

Fig 1

1 Marketing research person collecting data from the general public
2 large company processing payroll data
3 travelling salesperson giving marketing presentations
4 large scientific organisation processing work on nuclear research
5 businessperson keeping track of appointments while travelling
6 graphic designer
7 secretary doing general office work

2 What do these abbreviations mean? Use the Glossary if necessary.

1 CD-ROM   5 AGP
2 RDRAM   6 SDRAM
3 MB   7 SVGA
4 GHz

Now study the text below to find this information:

1 What is the memory size of this PC?
2 Which input devices are supplied?
3 What size is the monitor?
4 How fast is the processor?
5 What is the capacity of the hard drive?
6 Which operating system does it use?
7 What multimedia features does the computer have?

HOW TO READ A COMPUTER AD.

Fig 2
Dell computer

1 Intel Pentium IV 1.7GHz Processor
2 Mini Tower Chassis
3 256MB Rambus RDRAM
4 60GB Hard Drive
5 Embedded Intel 3D Direct AGP video with 64MB SDRAM
6 64-voice wavetable sound
7 48 X CD-ROM Drive
8 19" (17.9" VIS) Colour SVGA monitor
9 Microsoft Windows XP
10 1.44MB 3.5" Floppy Drive
11 Microsoft Intellimouse
12 105-key keyboard

1 The main processing chip that operates at a clock speed of 1.7 thousand million cycles per second.

2 A small size of tall and narrow style of case containing the computer system.

3 256 megabytes of Rambus dynamic type of main memory chips that constitute the computer RAM.

4 A hard drive internal storage device with a capacity of approx. 60 thousand million bytes.

5 A video controller for controlling the monitor screen that is built on to the computer motherboard. It can process 3D images using the AGP type of video bus interface. It also contains approx. 64 million bytes of synchronous dynamic random access memory that is used as video memory.

6 A soundcard that has 64 voices and generates sounds using the wavetable system.

7 A CD-ROM storage device that operates at 48 times the speed of the original CD-ROM devices.

8 A colour monitor for displaying output on a screen at resolutions determined by the SVGA standard. The diagonal measurement of the whole screen is 19 inches but the diagonal measurement of the actual viewable area of the screen is only 17.9 inches.

9 The operating system that is used to control the system.

LANGUAGE WORK   Function of an item

We can describe the function of an item in a number of ways. Study these examples.

Using the Present simple

1 ROM *holds* instructions which are needed to start up the computer.

*Used to-*infinitive, *Used for* + *-ing* form

2 ROM is *used to hold* instructions which are needed to start up the computer.

3 ROM is *used for holding* instructions which are needed to start up the computer.

Emphasising the function

4 *The function of ROM is* to hold instructions which are needed to start up the computer.

4 Match each item in Column A with its function in Column B. Then describe its function in two ways.

A Item	B Function
RAM	controls the cursor
processor	inputs data through keys like a typewriter
mouse	displays the output from a computer on a screen
clock	reads DVD-ROMs
3.5" floppy drive	reads and writes to removable magnetic disks
monitor	holds instructions which are needed to start up the computer
keyboard	
DVD-ROM drive	holds data read or written to it by the processor
cache	provides extremely fast access for sections of a program and its data
ROM	controls the timing of signals in the computer
	controls all the operations in a computer

5 With the help of the Glossary if necessary, describe the functions of these items.

1	scanner	6	supercomputer
2	printer	7	mainframe computer
3	ATM	8	barcodes
4	PDA	9	swipe cards
5	hard disk drive	10	memory

LANGUAGE WORK   Prepositions of place

Study these examples of prepositions of place.

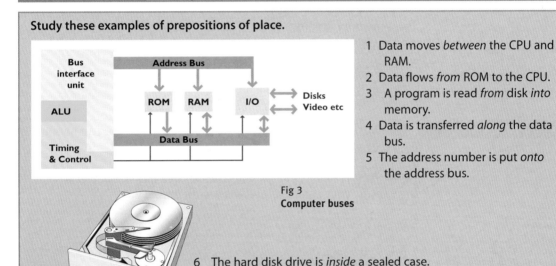

Fig 3
Computer buses

1 Data moves *between* the CPU and RAM.
2 Data flows *from* ROM to the CPU.
3 A program is read *from* disk *into* memory.
4 Data is transferred *along* the data bus.
5 The address number is put *onto* the address bus.

Fig 4
Hard disk

6 The hard disk drive is *inside* a sealed case.
7 Heads move *across* the disk.
8 Tracks are divided *into* sectors.

6 Complete each sentence using the correct preposition.

1 The CPU is a large chip .... the computer.
2 Data always flows .... the CPU .... the address bus.
3 The CPU can be divided .... three parts.
4 Data flows .... the CPU and memory.
5 Peripherals are devices .... the computer but linked .... it.
6 The signal moves .... the VDU screen .... one side .... the other.
7 The CPU puts the address .... the address bus.
8 The CPU can fetch data .... memory .... the data bus.

PROBLEM-SOLVING   7   Study these 'System upgrades and options' for the computer described in Task 3. Which upgrades and/or options would improve these aspects of this computer?

1   capacity
2   speed
3   protection from damage due to power failure
4   network connections

Upgrades and options
3Com 10/100 Ethernet controller
CD-RW Drive
Extra memory module
APC 1400 Smart-UPS
3 Year Next-Business-Day On-site Service

SPEAKING   8   Work in pairs, A and B. Find out as much as you can about your partner's computer and complete this table.

Student A your computer details are on page 184.
Student B your computer details are on page 190.

Feature	A	B
processor type		
processor speed		
bus speed		
memory (RAM)		
memory type		
hard disk capacity		
hard disk type		
monitor size		
monitor resolution		
CD-ROM drive speed		

WRITING **9** Put these instructions for opening a computer in the correct sequence.

a Release the two catches underneath and lift up to remove panel.

b Shut down your computer by choosing Shut Down from the Apple menu or the Special menu.

c If there are security screws on the vertical plate on the back of the computer, remove them with a Philips screwdriver.

d Unplug all the cables except the power cord from your computer.

e Pulling gently, slide the tray out.

10 Match these figures to the instructions.

Fig 5
Opening a computer

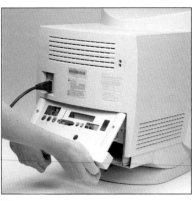
i

ii

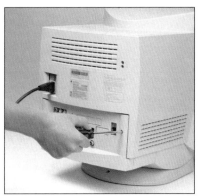
iii

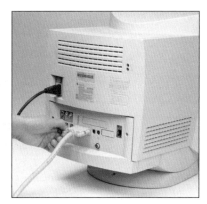
iv

11 Add these sequence words to your instructions: *first, then, next, after that, finally.*

Find the answers to these questions in the following texts.

1   What is one of the main causes of a PC not running at its highest potential speed?

2   What word in the text is used instead of 'buffer'?

3   What device looks after cache coherency?

4   What is the main alternative to 'write-through cache'?

5   When does a write-back cache write its contents back to main memory?

6   When is data marked as 'dirty' in a write-back cache?

7   What determines what data is replaced in a disk cache?

CACHE MEMORY

Most PCs are held back not by the speed of their main processor, but by the time it takes to move data in and out of memory. One of the most important techniques for getting around this
5 bottleneck is the memory cache.

The idea is to use a small number of very fast memory chips as a buffer or cache between main memory and the processor. Whenever the processor needs to read data it looks in this cache
10 area first. If it finds the data in the cache then this counts as a 'cache hit' and the processor need not go through the more laborious process of reading data from the main memory. Only if the data is not in the cache does it need to access main
15 memory, but in the process it copies whatever it finds into the cache so that it is there ready for the next time it is needed. The whole process is controlled by a group of logic circuits called the cache controller.

20 One of the cache controller's main jobs is to look after 'cache coherency' which means ensuring that any changes written to main memory are reflected within the cache and vice versa. There are several techniques for achieving this, the most obvious

25 being for the processor to write directly to both the cache and main memory at the same time. This is known as a 'write-through' cache and is the safest solution, but also the slowest.

The main alternative is the 'write-back' cache
30 which allows the processor to write changes only to the cache and not to main memory. Cache entries that have changed are flagged as 'dirty', telling the cache controller to write their contents back to main memory before using the space to
35 cache new data. A write-back cache speeds up the write process, but does require a more intelligent cache controller.

Most cache controllers move a 'line' of data rather than just a single item each time they need to
40 transfer data between main memory and the cache. This tends to improve the chance of a cache hit as most programs spend their time stepping through instructions stored sequentially in memory, rather than jumping about from one
45 area to another. The amount of data transferred each time is known as the 'line size'.

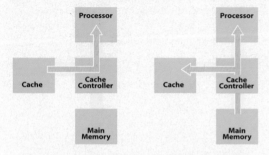

If there is a cache hit then the processor only needs to access the cache. If there is a miss then it needs to both fetch data from main memory and update the cache, which takes longer. With a standard write-through cache, data has to be written

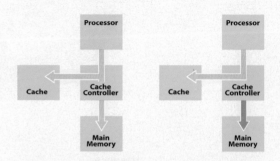

both to main memory and to the cache. With a write-back cache the processor needs only write to the cache, leaving the cache controller to write data back to main memory later on.

[Adapted from Cache Memory, PC Plus, February 1994, Future Publishing Ltd.]

How a Disk Cache Works

Disk caching works in essentially the same way whether you have a cache on your disk controller or you are using a software-based solution. The CPU requests specific data from
5 the cache. In some cases, the information will already be there and the request can be met without accessing the hard disk.

If the requested information isn't in the cache, the data is read from the disk along with a large
10 chunk of adjacent information. The cache then makes room for the new data by replacing old. Depending on the algorithm that is being applied, this may be the information that has been in the cache the longest, or the
15 information that is the least recently used. The CPU's request can then be met, and the cache already has the adjacent data loaded in anticipation of that information being requested next.

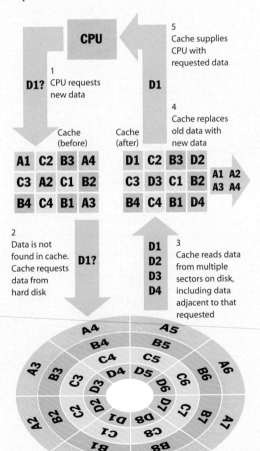

[Adapted from How a Disk Cache Works, PC Magazine, September 1990]

B Re-read the texts to find the answers to these questions.

1   Match the terms in Table A with the statements in Table B.

Table A
a   Cache hit
b   Cache controller
c   Cache coherency
d   Write-through cache
e   Write-back cache
f   Line size

Table B
i   The process of writing changes only to the cache and not to main memory unless the space is used to cache new data
ii   The amount of data transferred to the cache at any one time
iii The process of writing directly to both the cache and main memory at the same time
iv   The processor is successful in finding the data in the cache
v   Ensuring that any changes written to main memory are reflected within the cache and vice versa
vi   The logic circuits used to control the cache process

2   Mark the following as True or False:

a   Cache memory is faster than RAM.
b   The processor looks for data in the main memory first.
c   Write-through cache is faster than write-back cache.
d   Write-back cache requires a more intelligent cache controller.
e   Most programs use instructions that are stored in sequence in memory.
f   Most cache controllers transfer one item of data at a time.
g   Hardware and software disk caches work in much the same way.

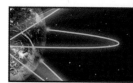

Computer Applications

Work in groups. List as many uses as you can for computers in one of these areas.

1 supermarkets
2 hospitals
3 airports
4 police headquarters

Study this diagram. Using only the diagram, try to list each stage in the operation of this computerised speed trap to make an explanation of how it operates. For example:

1 Camera 1 records the time each vehicle passes.

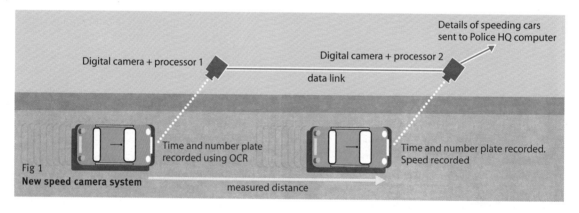

Details of speeding cars sent to Police HQ computer

Digital camera + processor 1

Digital camera + processor 2

data link

Time and number plate recorded using OCR

Time and number plate recorded. Speed recorded

Fig 1
New speed camera system

measured distance

3 Part 1 of the text describes the system which predates the one shown in Fig 1. Does it contain any information that may help complete your explanation? Read it quickly to find out. Ignore any information which is not helpful to you.

Part 1

In the last ten years, police have installed speed trap units on many busy roads. These contain a radar set, a microprocessor and a camera equipped with a flash. The radar sends out a beam of radio waves at a frequency of 24 gigahertz. This is equivalent to a wavelength of 1.25 cms. If a car is moving towards the radar, the reflected signal will bounce back with a slightly smaller wavelength. If away from the radar, the waves will reflect with a slightly longer wavelength. The microprocessor within the unit measures the difference in wavelength between outgoing and returning signals and calculates the speed of each vehicle. If it is above the speed pre-set by the police, the camera takes a picture of the vehicle. The information is stored on a smart card for transfer to the police computer. The owner of the vehicle can then be traced using the Driver and Vehicle Licensing Centre database.

4 Part 2 describes the new system. Read it to complete the stages in your explanation.

Some drivers have now got used to these traps. They slow down when they approach one to ensure that the camera is not triggered. They speed up again as soon as they have passed. This is known as 'surfing'. One way of outwitting such motorists is a new computerised system. This consists of two units equipped with digital cameras positioned at a measured distance apart. The first unit records the time each vehicle passes it and identifies each vehicle by its number plates using optical character recognition software. This information is relayed to the second unit which repeats the exercise. The microprocessor within the second unit then calculates the time taken by each vehicle to travel between the units. The registration numbers of those vehicles exceeding the speed limit are relayed to police headquarters where a computer matches each vehicle with the DVLC database. Using mailmerge a standard letter is then printed off addressed to the vehicle owner.

LANGUAGE WORK   Present passive

Study these sentences.

1   The radar sends out a beam of radio waves.
2   The information is stored on a smart card.

In 1 the verb is active and in 2 it is passive, the Present passive. Why is this so? What difference does it make? In 1 the agent responsible for the action is included – the radar. In 2 the agent is not included although we know what it is – the microprocessor. The passive is often used to describe the steps in a process where the action is more important than the agent and where the agent is already known to the reader. If we need to add the agent, we can do so like this:

3   The information is stored on a smart card *by the microprocessor.*

5 Describe the operation of the new speed trap by converting each of these statements to the Present passive. Add information on the agent where you think it is necessary.

1   The first unit records the time each vehicle passes.
2   It identifies each vehicle by its number plates using OCR software.
3   It relays the information to the second unit.
4   The second unit also records the time each vehicle passes.
5   The microprocessor calculates the time taken to travel between the units.
6   It relays the registration numbers of speeding vehicles to police headquarters.
7   A computer matches each vehicle with the DVLC database.
8   It prints off a letter to the vehicle owners using mailmerge.

6   With the help of this diagram, sequence these steps in the operation of an EPOS till. Then write a description of its operation in the Present passive.

a   The scanner converts the barcode into electrical pulses.
b   The branch computer sends the price and description of the product to the EPOS till.
c   The scanner reads the barcode.
d   The branch computer records the sale of the product.
e   The till shows the item and price.
f   The checkout operator scans the item.
g   The scanner sends the pulses to the branch computer.
h   The till prints the item and price on the paper receipt.
i   The branch computer searches the stock file for a product matching the barcode EAN.

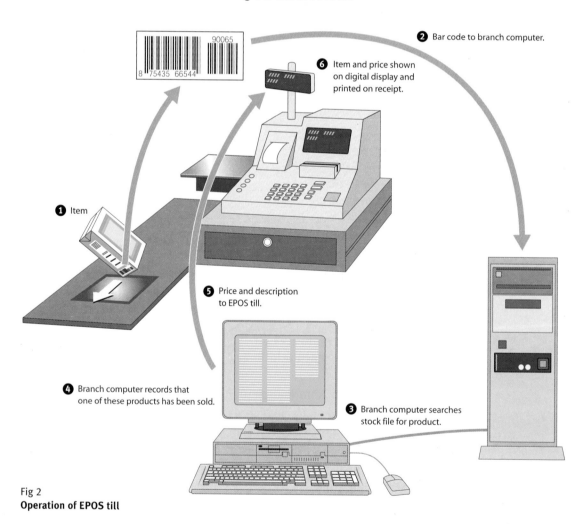

Fig 2
Operation of EPOS till

PROBLEM-SOLVING **7** Assuming cost is not a problem, what computer applications would make today's cars safer, more comfortable, more secure and more efficient? List your ideas; then compare ideas with others in your group.

SPEAKING **8** Work in pairs, A and B. Be prepared to describe the process shown in your diagram to your partner. Take notes on the process described to you. Ask your partner to repeat or explain further if you do not understand any of the steps in his/her description. If you prefer, you may describe another computing process you are familiar with.

Student A Your process is on page 184.
Student B Your process is on page 190.

WRITING **9** Write a description of the process you described in Task 8.

A Find the answers to these questions in the following text.

1   What tool is often used in data mining?
2   What AI method is used for the following processes?
   a   Separate data into subsets and then analyse the subsets to divide them into further subsets for a number of levels.
   b   Continually analyse and compare data until patterns emerge.
   c   Divide data into groups based on similar features or limited data ranges.
3   What term is used for the patterns found by neural networks?
4   When are clusters used in data mining?
5   What types of data storage can be used in data mining?
6   What can an analyst do to improve the data mining results?
7   Name some of the ways in which data mining is currently used.

DATA MINING

Data mining is simply filtering through large amounts of raw data for useful information that gives businesses a competitive edge. This information is made up of meaningful patterns
5   and trends that are already in the data but were previously unseen.

The most popular tool used when mining is artificial intelligence (AI). AI technologies try to work the way the human brain works, by making
10   intelligent guesses, learning by example, and using deductive reasoning. Some of the more popular AI methods used in data mining include neural networks, clustering, and decision trees.

Neural networks look at the rules of using data,
15   which are based on the connections found or on a sample set of data. As a result, the software continually analyzes value and compares it to the other factors, and it compares these factors repeatedly until it finds patterns emerging. These
20   patterns are known as rules. The software then looks for other patterns based on these rules or sends out an alarm when a trigger value is hit.

Clustering divides data into groups based on similar features or limited data ranges. Clusters
25   are used when data isn't labelled in a way that is favourable to mining. For instance, an insurance company that wants to find instances of fraud wouldn't have its records labelled as fraudulent or not fraudulent. But after analyzing patterns
30   within clusters, the mining software can start to figure out the rules that point to which claims are likely to be false.

Decision trees, like clusters, separate the data into subsets and then analyze the subsets to
35   divide them into further subsets, and so on (for a few more levels). The final subsets are then small enough that the mining process can find interesting patterns and relationships within the data.

40   Once the data to be mined is identified, it should be cleansed. Cleansing data frees it from duplicate information and erroneous data. Next, the data should be stored in a uniform format within relevant categories or fields. Mining tools
45   can work with all types of data storage, from large data warehouses to smaller desktop databases to flat files. Data warehouses and data

Data stores
You must first have data to mine. Data stores include one or several databases or data warehouses.

Cleanse data
Data must be stored in a consistent format and free from errors and redundancies.

Search data
Actual mining occurs when data is combed for patterns and trends. Rules for patterns are noted.

Analyze reports
Someone must analyze mining results for validity and relevance.

Report findings
The mining results can then be reviewed and interpreted, and a plan of action determined.

marts are storage methods that involve archiving large amounts of data in a way that makes it easy
50 to access when necessary.

When the process is complete, the mining software generates a report. An analyst goes over the report to see if further work needs to be done, such as refining parameters, using other
55 data analysis tools to examine the data, or even scrapping the data if it's unusable. If no further work is required, the report proceeds to the decision makers for appropriate action.

The power of data mining is being used for
60 many purposes, such as analyzing Supreme Court decisions, discovering patterns in health care, pulling stories about competitors from newswires, resolving bottlenecks in production processes, and analyzing sequences in the human
65 genetic makeup. There really is no limit to the type of business or area of study where data mining can be beneficial.

B Re-read the text to find the answers to these questions.

1   Match the terms in Table A with the statements in Table B.

Table A		
a Data mining	c	Cleansed data
b AI	d	Data warehouse

Table B
i   Storage method of archiving large amounts of data to make it easy to access
ii   Data free from duplicate and erroneous information
iii A process of filtering through large amounts of raw data for useful information
iv   A computing tool that tries to operate in a way similar to the human brain

2   Mark the following as True or False:

a   Data mining is a process of analysing known patterns in data.
b   Artificial intelligence is commonly used in data mining.
c   In data mining, patterns found while analysing data are used for further analysing the data.
d   Data mining is used to detect false insurance claims.
e   Data mining is only useful for a limited range of problems.

3   Complete the following description of the data mining process using words from the text:

Large amounts of data stored in data .... are often used for data .... The data is first .... to remove .... information and errors. The .... is then analysed using a tool such as .... An analysis report is then analysed by an .... who decides if the .... need to be refined, other data .... tools need to be used, or if the results need to be discarded because they are .... The analyst passes the final results to the .... makers who decide on the .... action.

Peripherals

1   Identify the peripherals in this computer application. Divide them into input and output devices.

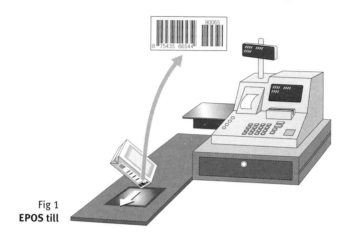

Fig 1
EPOS till

2   Link the inputs on the left and the outputs on the right with the appropriate peripherals in the centre.

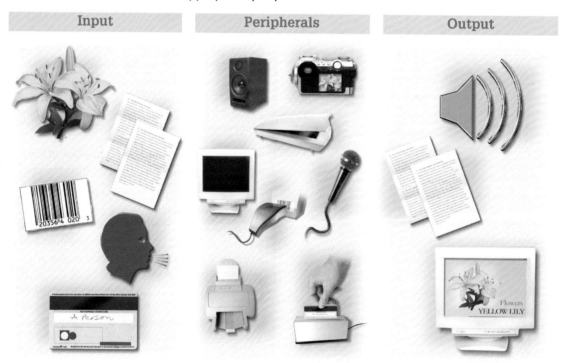

Input	Peripherals	Output

Fig 2
Input and output devices

LISTENING   **3**   Study this description and answer these questions.

1 How do digital cameras differ from conventional cameras?
2 How do they work?
3 What are their advantages and disadvantages compared to conventional cameras?

How a digital camera works

Digital cameras store images on memory cards so pictures can be transferred easily to a computer.

A lens focuses the image on to a CCD unit or Charge-Coupled Device where the film would normally be.

So you can aim the camera accurately, there is an optical viewfinder.

So you can play back the images and decide which to keep and which to re-shoot, the image is passed to a small LCD screen on the back of the camera.

Fig 3
Canon PowerShot, G1

4   🎧 Listen to Part 1 of this discussion between A and B and complete this table of similarities and differences between conventional and digital cameras. Tick (✓) or cross (✗) the boxes.

Feature	Digital	Conventional
lens		
viewfinder		
requires chemical processing		
film		
transfer images directly to PC		
can delete unsatisfactory images		

5   🎧 Listen to Part 2 of the dialogue to list the disadvantages of digital cameras.

6   🎧   Now listen to both parts again to find the answers to these questions:

1   What does a CCD contain?
2   What is a pixel?
3   How can you view pictures before they are downloaded to a PC?
4   When you have downloaded the images, what can you do with them?
5   Is special software required?
6   Why is the resolution important?
7   What does the capacity of a digital camera depend on?
8   Why is it worth getting a rechargeable battery?

LANGUAGE WORK   **Revision: Comparison and contrast**

Study this comparison of digital and conventional cameras.

FEATURE	DIGITAL	CONVENTIONAL
lens	✓	✓
viewfinder	✓	✓
requires chemical processing	✗	✓
film	✗	✓
transfer images directly to PC	✓	✗
can delete unsatisfactory images	✓	✗

Note how we can compare and contrast these types of cameras.

Comparing features which are similar:

1   *Both* cameras have lenses.
2   *Like* the conventional camera, the digital camera has a viewfinder.

Contrasting features which are different:

3   The conventional camera requires chemical processing *whereas* the digital camera does not.
4   The conventional camera uses film *unlike* the digital camera.
5   With a digital camera you can transfer images directly to a PC *but* with a conventional camera you need to use a scanner.
6   With digital cameras you can delete unsatisfactory images; *however* with conventional cameras you cannot.

7 Study this data about storage devices. Then complete the blanks in the following sentences comparing and contrasting the different types.

Device	Read/Write	Speed	Media Capacity	Media Removable	Cost
Floppy disk	Read and write	Slow	Very low	Yes	Low
Fixed hard disk	Read and write	Fast	Very high	No	Medium
Removable hard disk	Read and write	Medium to fast	High	Yes	Medium
CD-ROM	Read only	Medium	High	Yes	Low
CD-R	Recordable	Slow	High	Yes	Medium
CD-RW	Read and write	Medium	High	Yes	Medium
CD-MO	Read and write	Medium	High	Yes	High
DVD-ROM	Read only	Medium	High	Yes	Medium
DVD-RAM	Read and write	Medium	Very high	Yes	High
Magnetic Tape	Read and write	Very slow	High	Yes	Medium

1 You can write to hard disks .... optical disks.

2 Floppy disks have a .... capacity .... other devices.

3 CD-ROMs and floppy disks are .... low priced.

4 DVD-RAM has a .... capacity .... other optical disks.

5 CD-ROMs cannot be re-recorded .... some other optical disks can be.

6 .... hard disks, you can read from and write to CD-MO drives.

7 .... CD-ROMs, CD-Rs are recordable.

8 Magnetic tape is much .... other devices.

9 .... DVD-RAM and fixed hard disks have very high media capacity.

10 Floppy disks are cheap .... DVD-RAM is expensive.

8 Write your own comparison of printer types.

Type	Speed	Text Quality	Graphics Capability	Colour Quality	Cost
Dot-matrix	Slow to medium	Fair to good	Limited	Fair if you add a colour option	Low
Ink-Jet	Medium to fast	Good to excellent	Good to excellent	Good to Very Good	Low to high
Laser	Medium to very fast	Excellent	Good to excellent	Good in colour laser printers	Medium to high
Thermal Transfer	Medium to fast	Excellent	Good to excellent	Good to superior	Medium to high
Solid Ink	Medium to fast	Excellent	Good to excellent	Good	Medium to high
Electro-static	Slow to fast	Fair to good	Fair to good	Fair to good	Low to high

PROBLEM-SOLVING **9** Study this list of needs. Which type of peripheral would you advise in each case?

1 inputting printed graphics
2 building cars
3 controlling the screen cursor in a fast action game
4 making choices on a screen in a public information terminal
5 recording moving images
6 recording a book loan in a library
7 printing very high quality text and graphics
8 creating drawings
9 printing building plan drawings
10 recording sound
11 listening to music without disturbing others
12 storing programs and data
13 inputting a lot of text
14 backing up large quantities of data

WRITING **10** Describe the EPOS till shown in Fig 1. Explain the function of each peripheral using the structures studied in Unit 2.

11 Check these websites for the latest digital cameras. Compare the newest cameras with the one described in Fig 3. You will find its specifications on www.canon.com.

www.minolta.com

www.fujifilm.com

www.pentax.com

www.olympus.com

www.samsungcamera.com

www.ricohcamera.com

www.sony.com

www.canon.com

A Find the answers to these questions in the following text.

1 What is Currie Munce's main aim?
2 How quickly did the possible areal density of hard disks increase in the 1990s?
3 How long does Munce think magnetic recording technology will continue to make rapid advances in capacity?
4 What problem does he predict for magnetic storage?
5 What is the predicted limit for discrete bit magnetic storage capacity?
6 What storage technologies might replace current magnetic systems?
7 What is the advantage of holographic storage being three-dimensional?
8 What improvements are predicted due to the fast access rates and transfer times of holographic storage?
9 What is predicted to be the most important high capacity removable storage media in the next 10 years?
10 What method of software distribution is likely to replace optical disks?

Ready for the Bazillion-Byte Drive?

Thinking about writing your memoirs – putting your life story down on paper for all eternity? Why not skip the repetitive strain injury and just capture your whole life on full-motion video,
5 putting it all in a device the size of a sugar cube? It might not be as far off as you think.

Currie Munce, director of IBM's Advanced HDD Technology Storage Systems Division, has one avowed goal: Build bigger storage. Recently
10 Munce and his fellow Ph.Ds restored Big Blue's lead in the disk space race with a new world record for areal (bit) density: 35.3 gigabits per square inch – roughly three times as dense as any drive shipping at press time.

15 During the 1990s, areal density doubled every 18 months, keeping pace with the transistor density gains predicted by Moore's Law. But increasingly daunting technical challenges face those who would push the storage envelope further. 'I think
20 magnetic recording technology has another good 5 to 10 years,' says Munce. 'After that, we'll see substantial difficulties with further advances at the pace people are accustomed to.'

From here on, a phenomenon called
25 superparamagnetism threatens to make densely-packed bits unstable. Provided that new developments continue to thwart superparamagnetic corruption, scientists speculate that the theoretical limit for discrete bit
30 recording is 10 terabits per square inch (1 terabit = 1,000 gigabits).

Approaching this limit will require new technologies. Two possible contenders are atomic force microscopy (AFM) and holographic storage.

35 AFM would use a spinning plastic disk, perhaps inside a wristwatch, and a tiny, 10-micron cantilever with a 40-angstrom tip (an angstrom represents the approximate radius of an atom) to write data. In theory, AFM will allow densities of
40 300 to 400 gigabits per square inch.

While AFM is still in the lab, holographic storage is closer to reality. According to Rusty Rosenberger, optical program manager for Imation, 'We are targeting a $5\frac{1}{4}$-inch disk with
45 125GB of storage and a 40MB-per-second transfer rate.' Future iterations of holographic systems should improve substantially.

The three-dimensional nature of holography makes it an appealing storage medium because
50 'pages' of data can be superimposed on a single volume – imagine transferring a whole page of text at once as opposed to reading each letter in sequence. Hans Coufal, manager of IBM's New Directions in Science and Technology Research
55 division, predicts that the fast access rates and transfer times of holographic storage will lead to improved network searches, video on demand, high-end servers, enterprise computing, and supercomputing.

60 Meanwhile, also-ran technologies are thriving. Tape, first used for data storage in 1951 with the Univac I, has been revitalized by the corporate hunger for affordable archiving solutions. In the consumer arena, says Dataquest analyst Mary
65 Craig, recordable CD-ROMs and DVDs will remain the dominant high-capacity removable storage media for the next decade. Despite their failure to match the areal density gains of hard disks, optical disks are cheap to produce, making
70 them ideal for software distribution (until a mature digital rights management system facilitates online delivery). Finally, solid state options such as flash cards can't yet match the pricing of hard disks at high capacities.

75 Further out, scientists salivate over the prospect of data manipulation and storage on an atomic level. Because consumer demand for capacity is lagging behind what technology can deliver, bringing new storage options to the masses will
80 depend on seeding the need for more space.

[Adapted from 'Ready for the Bazillion-Byte Drive?' by Thomas Claburn, PC Magazine, March 2000]

B Re-read the text to find the answers to these questions.

1 Match the terms in Table A with the statements in Table B.

Table A	
a	Big Blue
b	Areal density
c	Moore's Law
d	Superparamagnetism
e	Terabit
f	AFM
g	Angstrom

Table B	
i	Atomic force microscopy
ii	The approximate radius of an atom
iii	IBM
iv	The data capacity of a storage device measured in bits per square inch
v	Prediction that the number of transistors that can be incorporated into a processor chip will double every 18 months
vi	A phenomenon that threatens to make densely packed bits unstable in magnetic storage devices
vii	One thousand gigabits

2 Mark the following statements as True or False:

a The development of AFM is more advanced than holographic storage.
b The predicted maximum storage density of AFM is 400 gigabits per square inch.
c Holography works in 3D.
d Univac I was the first computer to use tape storage devices.
e Users want higher capacity storage devices than technology can provide.

Former Student

Paul is 24. He has a Higher National Certificate in Computing and a Higher National Diploma in Computing Support which he completed two years ago. He has been working for a company providing support services for the last eighteen months.

STARTER   **1**   Study this list of some of the subjects included in his Diploma course. In which of these subject areas would he study the topics which follow?

1   Computer Architecture
2   HW Installation & Maintenance
3   Info Tech Applications (1)
4   Info Tech Applications (2)
5   Multi-user Operating System
6   Network Technology
7   Software Development Life Cycle
8   Standalone Computer System Support
9   Software Development Procedural Lang.
10   Data Communications
11   Information Systems & Services
12   Systems Development
13   Communication
14   Project Management
15   Mathematics for Computing

a   LAN Topologies
b   PC Bus Architectures
c   Modems
d   How to connect printers
e   Unix Operating System
f   Pascal
g   Writing a program
h   Creating a database
i   Maintenance of desktops
j   Wordprocessing and
    other office applications
k   Binary system
l   Making presentations

LISTENING   **2**   🎧 Listen to Part 1 of the recording to find the answers to these questions:

1   Which of the subject areas listed in Task 1 does Paul mention?
2   Which additional subjects does he mention?
3   Why did he choose to do his Diploma in support?
4   What practical work was included in the course?
5   Which subject did he particularly enjoy?

3   🎧 Listen to Part 2 of the recording and answer these questions:

1   What suggestions does Paul have for improving the course? Note a) his suggestions for improvement and b) the reasons he gives.

2   Which of the subjects he studied has he found useful in his work? Note a) the subjects and b) examples in the work situation.

4   🎧 Listen to Part 3 of the recording to answer these questions:

1   In which situations does Paul have to learn fast?
2   What sources does he use for help?
3   What advice did the college provide on sources of information?
4   What was the problem with the set book?
5   How does he feel about going back to college?

LANGUAGE WORK   **Revision: Past simple questions**

Study these examples of questions about the past.	**Asking about people:** Who taught you Maths? Whose classes did you most enjoy?
Asking about quantity: How many days a week did you study? How much programming did you do?	**Asking about things:** What made you choose computing support? What did you like most?
Asking about time: When did you study Communication?	**Asking about actions:** What did you do on Fridays? What happened on Monday mornings?

5   Study this description of a student's first term. What questions might the interviewer have asked to obtain the information in italics?

> In her first term Pauline studied *6 subjects*[1]. She had classes on *four days*[2] each week. On Monday morning *she had IT and Information Systems*[3]. *Tuesday*[4] was a free day for home study. On Wednesday she had Systems Analysis *in Room 324*[5]. She studied *Computer Architecture*[6] on Thursdays. *Programming*[7] happened on Friday mornings. Communication took place *once a week*[8] on Friday afternoons. She liked *Mr Blunt's classes*[9] most. She had a 15-minute coffee break each day and a lunch break *from 12.00 to 1.00*[10].

WORD STUDY   **6**   *up-* and *-up* verbs   Complete each gap in these sentences with the appropriate form of the correct verb from this list:

back up	keep up	update
build up	set up	upgrade
catch up	start up	upload
free up		

1   To avoid losing data, you should .... your files regularly.

2   You can .... your PC by adding a new motherboard.

3   Delete some files to .... space on your hard disk.

4   Data is .... from regional PCs to the company's mainframe each night.

5   The operating system boots when you .... your computer.

6   She's taking a course to .... her knowledge of computing.

7   The computer checks the memory when it ....

8   He .... a website to advertise his travel company.

9   You can .... with developments by reading PC magazines.

10   If you miss a class, you can study the hand-outs to ....

11   The image in a digital camera is .... from a red, green and blue image.

| SPEAKING | 7 | **Role Play** Work in pairs. Using the tapescript for Part 1 of the interview, on page 198, play the parts of the Interviewer and Paul. |

| WRITING | 8 | Study this description of a computer course. Then write a description of your own computing course, or one of its components, in the same way. |

Computer Use and Applications

AIMS:

1 To introduce complete beginners to computer systems.

2 To give a basic foundation in computer technology and to introduce appropriate terminology.

3 To give a description of the major components (hardware and software) which make up a computer system.

4 To show how computer systems are used in commerce and industry.

5 To give practical experience in using various systems.

DESCRIPTION:

The course is in four parts.

Part 1 Introduction to college computer science facilities, including how to access the computers, the Unix filestore, using email, the editor and simple network commands.

Part 2 The basic structure of computer hardware and systems software. Topics include compilers vs interpreters and memory management.

Part 3 Introduces some more advanced software tools, documentation tools and language processors.

Part 4 Discusses various uses of computers including spreadsheets, databases, communications and impacts on society.

STAFF:

Dr Peter Jones

METHOD AND FREQUENCY OF CLASS:

Two lectures per week with practical exercises once every two weeks.

ASSESSMENT:

Three formal coursework assignments.

UNIT 6

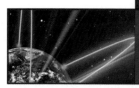

Operating Systems

STARTER

1 Study this screen display and answer these questions.

1 How do you enter Unix commands?
2 Which Unix commands does it show?
3 What is the output of each command?
4 What will happen when the last command is entered?
5 Which other Unix commands do you know?

```
$ date
Mon Sep 24 12:45:38 BST 2001
$ passwd
passwd: Changing password for dsea03
Enter login password:
New password:
$ ls
home   local   mnt   packages   scratch
$ logout >
```

Fig 1
Unix screen display

READING

2 Match the labels to the four layers of this diagram with the help of the diagram caption.

1 applications programs
2 user
3 hardware
4 operating system

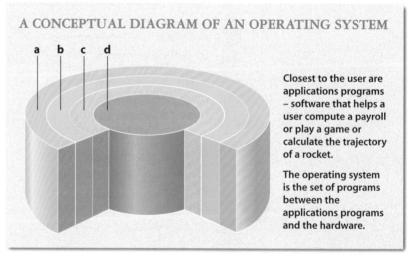

A CONCEPTUAL DIAGRAM OF AN OPERATING SYSTEM

Closest to the user are applications programs – software that helps a user compute a payroll or play a game or calculate the trajectory of a rocket.

The operating system is the set of programs between the applications programs and the hardware.

Fig 2
Conceptual diagram of an operating system

3 Study this text title. What do you think it means?

Operating Systems: Hidden Software

Now read this text to check your answer and to find the answers to these questions:

1 What difference is there between applications software and operating systems?
2 Why is the supervisor program the most important operating system program?
3 What is the difference between resident and non-resident programs?
4 What are the main functions of an operating system?

When a brand new computer comes off the factory assembly line, it can do nothing. The hardware needs software to make it work. Are we talking about applications software such as wordprocessing or spreadsheet software? Partly. But an applications software package does not communicate directly with the hardware. Between the applications software and the hardware is a software interface – an operating system. An operating system is a set of programs that lies between applications software and the computer hardware.

The most important program in the operating system, the program that manages the operating system, is the supervisor program, most of which remains in memory and is thus referred to as resident. The supervisor controls the entire operating system and loads into memory other operating system programs (called nonresident) from disk storage only as needed.

An operating system has three main functions: (1) manage the computer's resources, such as the central processing unit, memory, disk drives, and printers, (2) establish a user interface, and (3) execute and provide services for applications software. Keep in mind, however, that much of the work of an operating system is hidden from the user. In particular, the first listed function, managing the computer's resources, is taken care of without the user being aware of the details. Furthermore, all input and output operations, although invoked by an applications program, are actually carried out by the operating system.

4 Complete the gaps in this summary of the text on operating systems using these linking words and phrases:

although	*in addition*
because	*such as*
but	*therefore*

The user is aware of the effects of different applications programs .... operating systems are invisible to most users. They lie between applications programs, ... wordprocessing, and the hardware. The supervisor program is the most important. It remains in memory, ... it is referred to as resident. Others are called non-resident .... they are loaded into memory only when needed. Operating systems manage the computer's resources, ... the central processing unit. ...., they establish a user interface, and execute and provide services for applications software. .... input and output operations are invoked by applications programs, they are carried out by the operating system.

LANGUAGE WORK   *-ing* form (1) as a noun; after prepositions

We can use the *-ing* form of the verb as a noun. It can be the subject, object, or complement of a sentence. For example:

1 *Managing* the computer's resources is an important function of the operating system.
2 The operating system starts *running* the user interface as soon as the PC is switched on.
3 Another function of the operating system is *executing* and *providing* services for applications software.

The *-ing* form is also used after prepositions. This includes *to* when it is a preposition and not part of the infinitive. For example:

4 *Without* the user *being* aware of the details, the operating system manages the computer's resources.
5 We begin *by focusing* on the interaction between a user and a PC operating system.
6 We look forward *to having* cheaper and faster computers.

5 Rewrite each of these sentences like this:

An important function of the operating system is to manage the computer's resources.

Managing the computer's resources is an important function of the operating system.

1 One task of the supervisor program is to load into memory non-resident programs as required.

2 The role of the operating system is to communicate directly with the hardware.

3 One of the key functions of the operating system is to establish a user interface.

4 An additional role is to provide services for applications software.

5 Part of the work of mainframe operating systems is to support multiple programs and users.

6 The task in most cases is to facilitate interaction between a single user and a PC.

7 One of the most important functions of a computer is to process large amounts of data quickly.

8 The main reason for installing more memory is to allow the computer to processs data faster.

6 Complete these sentences with the correct form of the verb: infinitive or *-ing* form.

1 Don't switch off without (close down) your PC.
2 I want to (upgrade) my computer.
3 He can't get used to (log on) with a password.
4 You can find information on the Internet by (use) a search engine.
5 He objected to (pay) expensive telephone calls for Internet access.
6 He tried to (hack into) the system without (know) the password.
7 You needn't learn how to (program) in HTML before (design) webpages.
8 I look forward to (input) data by voice instead of (use) a keyboard.

PROBLEM-SOLVING **7** Try to find the commands from the lists below which will have these actions.

VMS	Unix
help	write
directory	cp
search	lpr
copy	ls
rename	mkdir
print	date
show users	rm
show time	man
create/directory	grep
phone	rwho
delete	mv

Action	VMS command	Unix command
List all the files in a directory		
Delete a file		
Rename a file		
Copy a file		
Send a file to a printer		
Obtain help		
Create a directory		
Show date and time		
Show users on system		
Talk to other users on system		
Search for a string in a file		

SPEAKING **8** Work in pairs, A and B. Each of you has information about some popular operating systems. Find out from the information you have and by asking each other, the answers to these questions:

Student A Your information is on page 184.
Student B Your information is on page 190.

1 Which operating system is used on Apple Macintosh microcomputers?
2 What is Penpoint designed for?

3 Name one system used on IBM mainframes.
4 Which operating system is Linux related to?
5 Name an IBM operating system similar to MS-DOS.
6 Which operating system replaced MS-DOS?
7 Which systems are in fact graphically orientated shells for MS-DOS?
8 How many versions of Windows 9X were developed?
9 Which operating systems are designed for networks?
10 Which operating system is used by DEC VAX minicomputers?

WRITING   9   This description of the Mac OS X is drawn from the table below. Write a similar description of Linux.

Mac OS X is a Unix-based operating system designed for use on Apple Mac computers. It includes memory-protection, pre-emptive multitasking and symmetric multiprocessing support. Graphics are provided by a graphics engine known as Quartz. It has advanced-PDF standards support, OpenGL and Quicktime integrated into the OS. The operating system features are accessed through a graphical user interface called Aqua.

	Mac OS X	Linux
type	Unix-based	Unix-based
computer	Apple Mac	wide variety
features	memory-protection, pre-emptive multi-tasking, symmetric multiprocessing support	variety of distribution kits available
graphics engine	Quartz	XFree86
standard support	advanced-PDF, OpenGL, Quicktime	
user interface type	GUI	command line, GUI
user interface	Aqua	KDE, Gnome
source code availability	not available	freely available

A Find the answers to these questions in the following text.

1 What did Linus Torvalds use to write the Linux kernel?
2 How was the Linux kernel first made available to the general public?
3 What is a programmer likely to do with source code?
4 Why will most software companies not sell you their source code?
5 What type of utilities and applications are provided in a Linux distribution?
6 What is X ?
7 What graphical user interfaces are mentioned in the text?

LINUX

Linux has its roots in a student project. In 1992, an undergraduate called Linus Torvalds was studying computer science in Helsinki, Finland. Like most computer science courses, a
5 big component of it was taught on (and about) Unix. Unix was the wonder operating system of the 1970s and 1980s: both a textbook example of the principles of operating system design, and sufficiently robust to be the standard OS in
10 engineering and scientific computing. But Unix was a commercial product (licensed by AT&T to a number of resellers), and cost more than a student could pay.

Annoyed by the shortcomings of Minix (a
15 compact Unix clone written as a teaching aid by Professor Andy Tannenbaum) Linus set out to write his own 'kernel' – the core of an operating system that handles memory allocation, talks to hardware devices, and makes
20 sure everything keeps running. He used the GNU programming tools developed by Richard Stallman's Free Software Foundation, an organization of volunteers dedicated to fulfilling Stallman's ideal of making good software that
25 anyone could use without paying. When he'd written a basic kernel, he released the source code to the Linux kernel on the Internet.

Source code is important. It's the original from which compiled programs are generated. If you
30 don't have the source code to a program, you can't modify it to fix bugs or add new features. Most software companies won't sell you their source code, or will only do so for an eye-watering price, because they believe that if they

35 make it available it will destroy their revenue stream.

What happened next was astounding, from the conventional, commercial software industry point of view – and utterly predictable to 40 anyone who knew about the Free Software Foundation. Programmers (mostly academics and students) began using Linux. They found that it didn't do things they wanted it to do – so they fixed it. And where they improved it, 45 they sent the improvements to Linus, who rolled them into the kernel. And Linux began to grow.

There's a term for this model of software development; it's called Open Source (see www.opensource.org/ for more information). 50 Anyone can have the source code – it's free (in the sense of free speech, not free beer). Anyone can contribute to it. If you use it heavily you may want to extend or develop or fix bugs in it – and it is so easy to give your fixes back to 55 the community that most people do so.

An operating system kernel on its own isn't a lot of use; but Linux was purposefully designed as a near-clone of Unix, and there is a lot of software out there that is free and was designed 60 to compile on Linux. By about 1992, the first 'distributions' appeared.

A distribution is the Linux-user term for a complete operating system kit, complete with the utilities and applications you need to make 65 it do useful things – command interpreters, programming tools, text editors, typesetting tools, and graphical user interfaces based on the X windowing system. X is a standard in academic and scientific computing, but not 70 hitherto common on PCs; it's a complex distributed windowing system on which people implement graphical interfaces like KDE and Gnome.

As more and more people got to know about 75 Linux, some of them began to port the Linux kernel to run on non-standard computers. Because it's free, Linux is now the most widely-ported operating system there is.

[Adapted from 'Smooth Operator' by Charles Stross, Computer Shopper magazine, November 1998]

B Re-read the text to find the answers to these questions.

1 Match the terms in Table A with the statements in Table B.

Table A

a	Kernel
b	Free Software Foundation
c	Source code
d	Open Source
e	A distribution
f	X

Table B

i	A type of software development where any programmer can develop or fix bugs in the software
ii	The original systems program from which compiled programs are generated
iii	A complete operating system kit with the utilities and applications you need to make it do useful things
iv	A standard distributed windowing system on which people implement graphical interfaces
v	An organization of volunteers dedicated to making good software that anyone could use without paying
vi	the core of an operating system that handles memory allocation, talks to hardware devices, and makes sure everything keeps running

2 Mark the following statements as True or False:

a Linux was created in the 1980s.
b Minix was created by a university student.
c Linux is based on Unix.
d Minix is based on Unix.
e Linux runs on more types of computer than any other operating system.

Graphical User Interfaces

1 Study this diagram of a graphical user interface (GUI). Identify these features:

1	window	5	taskbar
2	icon	6	submenu
3	menu	7	desktop
4	system tray	8	button

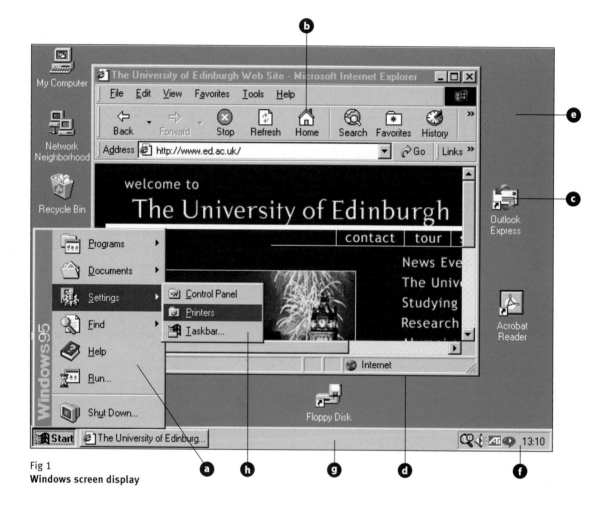

Fig 1
Windows screen display

2 Study this second example of a GUI.

1 How does it differ from Fig 1?
2 In what ways is it the same?

Folder
This is a folder icon, and these all tend to look the same – like a kind of 3D view of a suspension file. Sometimes they're adorned with other graphics, but they're usually pretty easy to spot. Double-clicking on a folder icon displays that folder's contents in another window, which is what we've done here.

Menu bar
Just about all programs display a menu bar across the top of the screen, including the 'Finder'. The menu bar will change, depending on the program you're running at the time.

Document
This is a text file which tells us something about the contents of this CD-ROM. You can read it by simply double-clicking on it – your iMac will then automatically find the program needed to open it.

Application
This is an application, or program icon. Double-clicking on it will start the program. It's not always obvious whether an icon is for a document or a program, but you soon get to be able to spot these things.

Hard Disk icon
Folders, files, documents and other items are displayed as little icons like this. This one, in fact, represents your iMac's internal hard disk.

CD-ROM icon
Your hard disk icon (and Wastebasket icon) may be the only ones you see on your desktop. If you insert a CD-ROM, though, it will appear as an icon on your desktop too. We've double-clicked on it to display its contents. To eject a CD, by the way, you have to drag its icon onto the Wastebasket – you can't just press the CD-ROM drive button. If you do, you'll be waiting an awful long time.

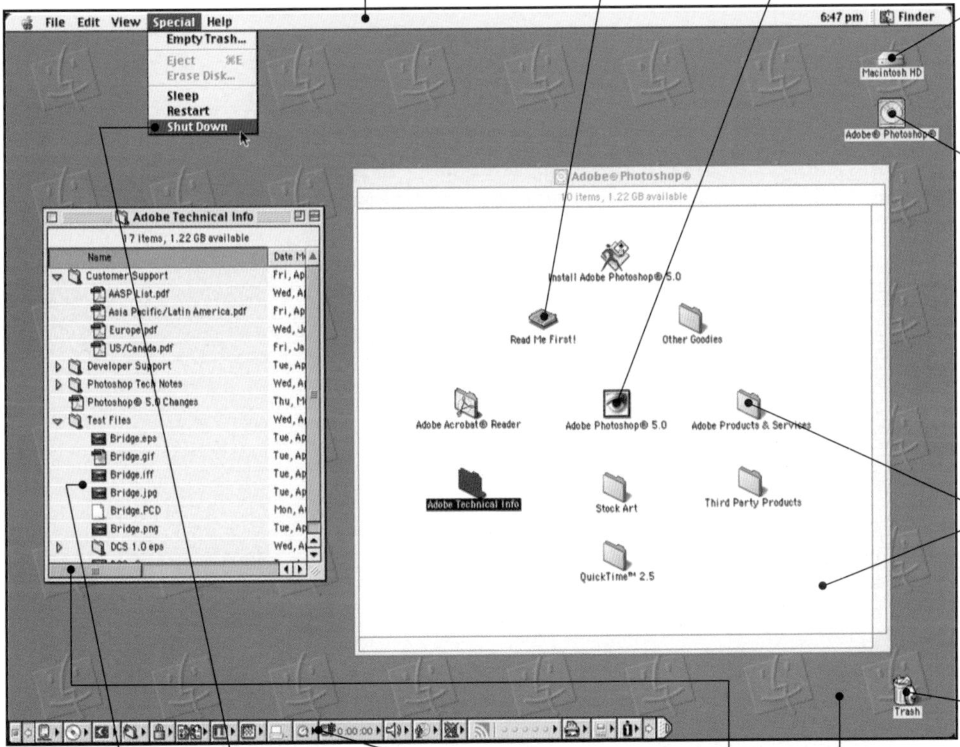

Folder window
When you double-click on a folder or a disk drive, its contents are displayed in a window like this one. These contents can be documents, programs or other folders.

Wastebasket icon
The Wastebasket is where you throw things you no longer need. It doesn't empty straight away, (though as you can see, ours is so full the lid's fallen off), so you can change your mind if you have to. When you want to eject a disk, be it a CD-ROM or a floppy disk (if you've got a floppy disk drive attached), you drag its icon on to the Wastebasket and the iMac will spit it out automatically.

Fig 2
Mac GUI

List view
This is another folder window, but this time we're looking at the contents in 'List' view. Otherwise, it's the same as the window next to it – a 'window' on a folder, basically. You can nest folders many layers deep, in case you're wondering, and you're likely to get confused long before your iMac does – try to keep your filing system as simple as possible.

Menu/menu option
To open a menu, click on its name in the menu bar. This displays a drop-down list like the one you see here. To choose one of the menu options, just click on it (the options are highlighted as the mouse pointer moves over them to help you get the right one). Don't forget to always shut down your iMac via this menu, NOT by simply switching the power off.

Control Strip
The Control Strip offers quick access to many of your iMac's settings like the speaker volume, sound input and CD player controls. Until you've found out what these gadgets do, you can 'hide' it by clicking on the small ribbed area to the far right. This reduces it to a little handle in the bottom left-hand corner of the screen. Click this handle if you want to display the Control Strip again.

Scrollbar
You'll see these gadgets whenever the contents of a folder won't fit in the window. You click on either the horizontal or vertical scroll arrows to display more of the contents – either that, or drag on the little blue 'scrollbox'.

Desktop pattern
This background image can be swapped for many more via the Appearance control panel. You can use a repeating 'pattern' like this, or a single image – a scanned photograph for example.

READING **3** Study this diagram of the Windows Desktop and answer these questions about its features.

1 What does Outlook Express let you do?
2 Which feature shows you current programs?
3 How do you read the date?
4 What is *My Briefcase* for?
5 Which background colour is most common?
6 Which feature shows other computers networked with yours?
7 Which feature lets you see which files are stored on your PC?
8 What is the program that helps you get on the Internet?
9 How do you delete files permanently?

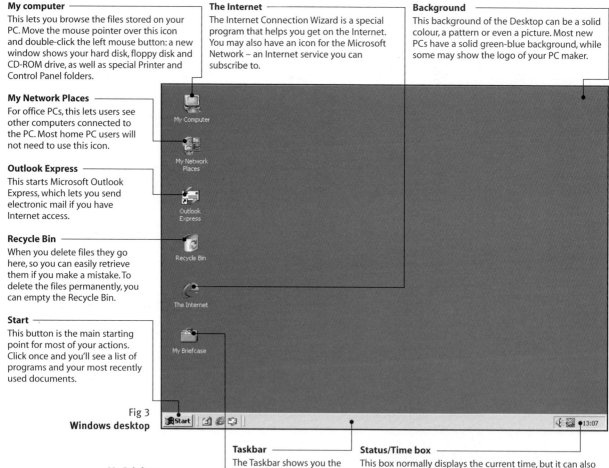

My computer
This lets you browse the files stored on your PC. Move the mouse pointer over this icon and double-click the left mouse button: a new window shows your hard disk, floppy disk and CD-ROM drive, as well as special Printer and Control Panel folders.

My Network Places
For office PCs, this lets users see other computers connected to the PC. Most home PC users will not need to use this icon.

Outlook Express
This starts Microsoft Outlook Express, which lets you send electronic mail if you have Internet access.

Recycle Bin
When you delete files they go here, so you can easily retrieve them if you make a mistake. To delete the files permanently, you can empty the Recycle Bin.

Start
This button is the main starting point for most of your actions. Click once and you'll see a list of programs and your most recently used documents.

Fig 3
Windows desktop

The Internet
The Internet Connection Wizard is a special program that helps you get on the Internet. You may also have an icon for the Microsoft Network – an Internet service you can subscribe to.

Background
This background of the Desktop can be a solid colour, a pattern or even a picture. Most new PCs have a solid green-blue background, while some may show the logo of your PC maker.

My Briefcase
If you often take files and documents to and from a PC at work, My Briefcase helps you to keep them organized and up to date.

Taskbar
The Taskbar shows you the programs that you are currently running and the windows you have open. To switch between different windows, click on their buttons on the Taskbar.

Status/Time box
This box normally displays the current time, but it can also display other information. Pause the mouse pointer over the time for a moment and a pop-up box tells you the date. The box is also used very often by programs to show the status of tools such as the printer, modem or – on a notebook (a portable computer) – it might display the amount of battery power you have left.

LANGUAGE WORK   Verbs + object + infinitive; Verbs + object + to-infinitive

New developments in computing are often designed to make something easier. These verbs are often used to describe such developments:

allow   let
enable   permit
help

Study these examples:

1   A GUI *lets you point* to icons and click a mouse button to execute a task.
2   A GUI *allows you to use* a computer without knowing any operating system commands.
3   The X Window System *enables Unix-based computers to have* a graphical look and feel.
4   Voice recognition software *helps disabled users (to) access* computers.

Allow, enable and *permit* are used with this structure:

verb + object + to-infinitive

Let is used with this structure:

verb + object + infinitive

Help can be used with either structure.

4   Complete the gap in each sentence with the correct form of the verb in brackets.

1   The Help facility enables users .... (get) advice on most problems.

2   Adding more memory lets your computer .... (work) faster.

3   Windows allows you .... (display) two different folders at the same time.

4   The Shift key allows you .... (type) in upper case.

5   The MouseKeys feature enables you .... (use) the numeric keypad to move the mouse pointer.

6   ALT + TAB allows you .... (switch) between programs.

7   The StickyKeys feature helps disabled people .... (operate) two keys simultaneously.

8   ALT + PRINT SCREEN lets you .... (copy) an image of an active window to the Clipboard.

5   Describe the function of these features using 'enabling' verbs.

1   In a window, the vertical scroll bar
2   The Find command
3   The Undo command
4   Cut and paste
5   Print Screen
6   Menus
7   Recycle bin
8   Tooltips

PROBLEM-SOLVING   **6**   Study this version of a GUI. Which part of the screen would you touch if you want to:

1   make a phone call
2   send an email
3   access a keyboard
4   record an appointment
5   get help
6   write new mail

What do you think happens if you touch these areas of the screen?
g, h, i, j, k, l

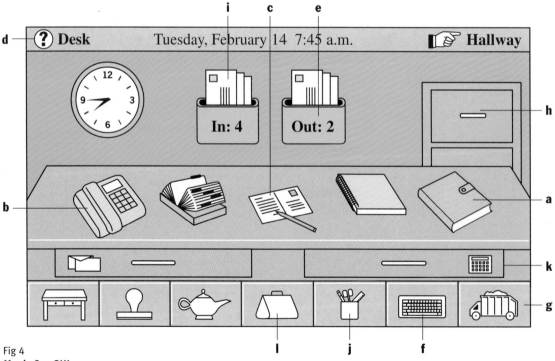

Fig 4
Magic Cap GUI

SPEAKING   **7**   Work in groups. Complete this questionnaire for yourself. Then take turns in your group to explain how to perform each of these actions. You may need these verbs:

choose
right/left/double-click on
hover
drag and drop
select

Do you know how to:	Yes	No
1 create a folder?		
2 start a program?		
3 shut down the system?		
4 adjust the speaker volume?		
5 arrange the icons?		
6 display the date?		
7 in Windows, show Tooltips?		

WRITING   **8**   Study these instructions for moving a file from one folder to another using Windows Explorer. Then write your own instructions for one of the actions in Task 7. Compare your instructions with those given in the Help facility on your computer.

TO MOVE A FILE

1 If you want to move a file that was saved in a different folder, locate and open the folder.

2 Right-click the file you want to move; then click Cut on the shortcut menu.

3 Locate and open the folder where you want to put the file.

4 Right-click the folder; then click Paste on the shortcut menu.

A Find the answers to these questions in the following text.

1   What developments are driving the development of completely new interfaces?

2   What has inspired a whole cottage industry to develop to improve today's graphical user interface?

3   In what way have XML-based formats changed the user interface?

4   What type of computers are certain to benefit from speech technology?

5   Name a process where a mouse is particularly useful and a process where it is not so useful.

6   What facilities are multimodal interfaces likely to offer in the future?

7   What type of input device will be used to give vision to the user interface?

8   What development has led to an interest in intelligent agents?

9   List ways in which intelligent agents can be used.

USER INTERFACES

Cheaper and more powerful personal computers are making it possible to perform processor-intensive tasks on the desktop. Break-throughs in technology, such as speech recognition, are enabling new ways of interacting with computers. And the convergence of personal computers and consumer electronics devices is broadening the base of computer users and placing a new emphasis on ease of use. Together, these developments will drive the industry in the next few years to build the first completely new interfaces since SRI International and Xerox's Palo Alto Research Center did their pioneering research into graphical user interfaces (GUIs) in the 1970s.

True, it's unlikely that you'll be ready to toss out the keyboard and mouse any time soon. Indeed, a whole cottage industry – inspired by the hyperlinked design of the World Wide Web – has sprung up to improve today's graphical user interface. Companies are developing products that organize information graphically in more intuitive ways. XML-based formats enable users to view content, including local and network files, within a single browser interface. But it is the more dramatic innovations such as speech recognition that are poised to shake up interface design.

Speech will become a major component of user interfaces, and applications will be completely redesigned to incorporate speech input. Palm-size and handheld PCs, with their cramped keyboards and basic handwriting recognition, will benefit from speech technology.

Though speech recognition may never be a complete replacement for other input devices, future interfaces will offer a combination of input types, a concept known as multimodal input. A mouse is a very efficient device for desktop navigation, for example, but not for

changing the style of a paragraph. By using both a mouse and speech input, a user can first point to the appropriate paragraph
50 and then say to the computer, 'Make that bold.' Of course, multimodal interfaces will involve more than just traditional input devices and speech recognition. Eventually, most PCs will also have handwriting
55 recognition, text to speech (TTS), the ability to recognize faces or gestures, and even the ability to observe their surroundings.

At The Intelligent Room, a project of Massachusetts Institute of Technology's
60 Artificial Intelligence Lab, researchers have given sight to PCs running Microsoft Windows through the use of video cameras. 'Up to now, the PC hasn't cared about the world around it,' said Rodney A. Brooks,
65 the Director of MIT's Artificial Intelligence Lab. 'When you combine computer vision with speech understanding, it liberates the user from having to sit in front of a keyboard and screen.'

70 It's no secret that the amount of information – both on the Internet and within intranets – at the fingertips of computer users has been expanding rapidly. This information onslaught has led
75 to an interest in intelligent agents, software assistants that perform tasks such as retrieving and delivering information and automating repetitive tasks. Agents will make computing significantly easier. They
80 can be used as Web browsers, help-desks, and shopping assistants. Combined with the ability to look and listen, intelligent agents will bring personal computers one step closer to behaving more like humans.
85 This is not an accident. Researchers have long noted that users have a tendency to treat their personal computers as though they were human. By making computers more 'social,' they hope to also make them
90 easier to use.

As these technologies enter mainstream applications, they will have a marked impact on the way we work with personal computers. Soon, the question will be not
95 'what does software look like' but 'how does it behave?'

[Adapted from 'User-Interfaces' by John Morris, PC Magazine, June 9, 1998]

B Re-read the text to find the answers to these questions.

1 Match the terms in Table A with the statements in Table B.

Table A
a GUI
b Multimodal interface
c Intelligent agent
d TTS
e The Intelligent Room

Table B
i Software assistant that performs tasks such as retrieving and delivering information and automating repetitive tasks
ii Text to speech
iii Graphical user interface
iv A project of the Massachusetts Institute of Technology's Artificial Intelligence Lab
v A system that allows a user to interact with a computer using a combination of inputs such as speech recognition, hand-writing recognition, text to speech, etc.

2 Mark the following statements as True or False:

a Fewer people are using computers because computer functions are becoming integrated into other electronic devices.
b Keyboards and mice will soon not be required for using personal computers.
c There have been no improvements in interface design since the development of the GUI.
d Speech recognition is likely to completely replace other input devices.
e Computer speech and vision will free the user from having to sit in front of a keyboard and screen.
f Intelligent agents will make computers seem more like humans.

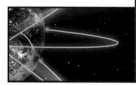

Applications Programs

STARTER | **1** | Identify these applications programs.

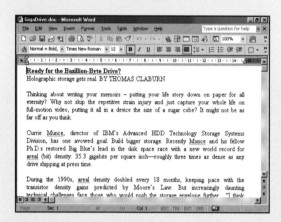

a

b

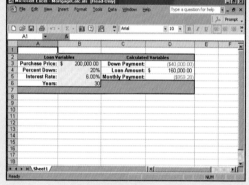

c

d

e

Fig 1
Screen displays

2 Conduct a survey to find out who in your class:

1 can name a spreadsheet program
2 has used a spreadsheet
3 can name a database program
4 has used a database
5 knows how to insert graphics into a document
6 can name a wordprocessing program
7 can centre a line of text
8 can disable the autocorrect

3 Study this diagram of a medical centre. Which applications programs will be used by the following?

1 Reception
2 Practice Manager
3 Doctors

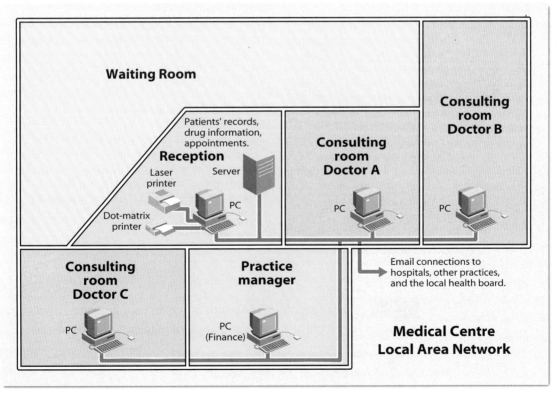

Fig 2
Medical centre LAN

READING   **4**   Work in groups. Read paragraph A and additional paragraphs selected by your teacher. Complete this note-taking frame for each text you read.

	B	C	D
Users			
Use			
Program types			
Data input			
Output			

A The system consists of 5 networked PCs, one in each of the consulting rooms, one in the Practice Manager's office and the other in Reception alongside the file server. (Each PC has its own laser printer.) There is also a dot-matrix printer in Reception for prescriptions as these are printed on special paper. All users have access to Microsoft Office.

B Doctors use the system to access a number of databases. The most important holds the records of all the patients in the practice. These files contain personal details and the medical history of the patient. The doctor can call up the appointments book prior to the consultation. By clicking on the patient's name, they have immediate access to that patient's records. At the end of each consultation, the doctor enters brief case notes including the diagnosis and treatment. This database can also be used to produce statistics for research and reports.

Doctors can also access a drugs database on CD-ROM which provides prescribing information on thousands of drugs including their suitability for different categories of patients. This is updated every month. Another database is a conditions dictionary which provides information on a wide range of problems.

C Reception staff use specially tailored software developed from a database to enter all appointment dates and times for each doctor. The program generates daily lists of appointments and can be accessed by the doctors. Reception use the patient database to identify children and old people who are due to have vaccinations. They then use mailmerging to create letters asking for appointments to be made.

D The Practice Manager uses a payroll package based on a spreadsheet to calculate salaries for each employee of the health centre. She enters all income and expenditure to produce practice accounts. She uses a database to produce a monthly rota of which doctors are on call in evenings and at weekends. This rota is available over the network to all users.

5   Exchange information with others in your group to complete notes for all the texts. Ask and answer questions like these:

1   How do Reception use the system?
2   What type of program do they use?
3   What kind of data do they enter?
4   What is the output from the program?

Study this extract from an instruction manual for software for doctors in a health centre.

PATIENT BROWSER

Patient Browser allows you to find specific patients and open their records. It also allows you to identify different categories of patients.

Maximise, minimise, and close buttons

Click here to display or remove search criteria

Title Bar   Menu Bar   Tool Bar

1 To find patients, first click on the appropriate tab (Personal, Address or Registration).

2 Enter the search criteria. A combination of tabs may be used (e.g. enter a surname under the Personal tab and select a doctor in the Registration tab).

3 Select the Defaults button if you wish to clear the criteria boxes of any existing entries, or to search for all patients, but the list may be a long one.

4 Start the search by clicking on the Find button.

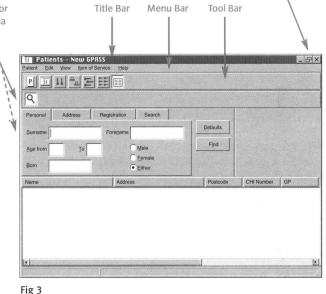

Fig 3
GPASS

We make simple instructions using the infinitive:

Click on the appropriate tab.
Enter the search criteria.

We can add an explanation using the to-infinitive or *by + -ing*:

To find patients, click on the appropriate tab.
Click on the Find button *to start* the search.
Start the search *by clicking* on the Find button.

We can put the instructions in order using sequence words:

First click on the appropriate tab.
Then enter the selection criteria.
Finally click on the Find button.

We can link two instructions and emphasise their order like this:

Having entered the selection criteria, click on the Find button.
Once the selection criteria *have been entered*, click on the Find button.

---

6 Write simple instructions for identifying all male patients called Smith in the 16 to 50 age group registered with Doctors Warner and Roberts.

7 Complete the gaps in these instructions for finding the records of all members of the Green family living in postcode WX14 3PH and registered with any doctor in the practice.

1 First enter the search criteria by ....
2 To .... , enter Green in the Surname box.
3 Ensure both male and female members of the family are found by ....
4 .... select the Address tab.
5 Having .... , enter the postcode.
6 .... choose the Registration tab.
7 Once .... , select All doctors.
8 .... , click on Find to ....

PROBLEM-SOLVING **8** Study these versions of OfficeSuite and decide which version provides the best value for the following users. The versions are listed from cheapest to most expensive.

OfficeSuite Standard

- wordprocessor
- spreadsheet
- presentation program
- email
- PIM

OfficeSuite Small Business Edition

- wordprocessor
- spreadsheet
- DTP
- email
- PIM
- small business tools

OfficeSuite Professional

- wordprocessor
- spreadsheet
- database
- DTP
- presentation program
- email
- small business tools

OfficeSuite Premium

- wordprocessor
- spreadsheet
- database
- DTP
- presentation program
- email
- PIM
- small business tools
- website editor
- image editor

OfficeSuite Developer

- wordprocessor
- spreadsheet
- database
- DTP
- presentation program
- email
- PIM
- small business tools
- website editor
- image editor
- developer tools

1   A salesperson who wants to make presentations at conferences.
2   An administrative assistant who needs to write office correspondence and send and receive emails.
3   A programmer who wants to develop applications tailored to a company's needs.
4   A company wanting to produce its own in-house newsletter.
5   A company wishing to develop its own website.
6   A company which wants to analyse all its sales records.
7   A promotions person who wants to be able to edit complex graphics and incorporate them in brochures.
8   A company which wants to share documents on a local area network.

SPEAKING   **9**   Work in pairs, A and B. Each of you has a review of a computer game. Find out from each other this information:

1   The name of the game.
2   The company who produce it.
3   The platform on which it's played.
4   The bad points.
5   The good points.
6   The star rating.

Student A your game details are on page 185.
Student B your game details are on page 191.

WRITING   **10**   Work in groups. Decide which applications programs would be used and for what purpose, by the following:

1   a museum
2   publishers of a subscription-only magazine
3   police headquarters

11   Write your recommendations for one of the users in Task 10. Give reasons for each applications program you recommend.

Find the answers to these questions in the text below.

1 How do you pay for the applications provided by an ASP?
   a no charge
   b charged according to use
   c single payment

2 What two main services does an ASP provide?

3 How does an ASP ensure that they have enough storage space for the changing needs of customers?

4 What types of applications are available from ASPs?

5 Why is it useful for a small business to be able to rent specialist tools from an ASP?

6 What is one of the best established areas of ASP use?

Application Service Providers

If your hard disk is packed to bursting point, the IT department is far too busy to fix your email problems, and your business can't afford to buy the tools that you'd like to develop the company
5 website, then it's time to think about using an application service provider (ASP). Rather than installing software on each machine or server within your organisation, you rent applications from the ASP, which provides remote access to
10 the software and manages the hardware required to run the applications.

There are a lot of advantages to this approach. The havoc caused by viruses makes the idea of outsourcing your email and office suite services
15 an attractive option. It also gives you more flexibility – you pay for applications as and when you need them, rather than investing in a lot of costly software which you're then tied to for years. Not having to worry about upgrading
20 to the latest version of your office suite or about battling with the complexities of managing an email system, leaves businesses with more time. Time to focus on what they do best.

However, there are some potential pitfalls. To
25 use applications remotely requires a lot of bandwidth, which is only really available from a broadband connection or a leased line to the ASP itself. It is also important to ensure that the ASP will be able to provide a secure, reliable
30 service which will be available whenever you need it.

Providing applications and storage space for vast numbers of users requires some powerful technology on the part of the ASP. This includes
35 security controls and data storage as well as providing the physical links to customers. For

the most part, ASPs don't own the data centres that store the information. Instead, they lease space from data storage specialists. In this way,
40 they can be confident of meeting customers' increasing storage requirements by buying more space as it's needed.

There's a wide variety of applications available for use via ASPs. Office suite applications and
45 email services are two of the most generic applications available through ASPs. Large, complex business applications such as enterprise resource planning tools like SAP are another popular candidate for delivery through
50 an ASP. Other business services, such as payroll and accounting systems are also available. This is particularly beneficial to small businesses which are likely to grow quickly and don't want to deal with the problems caused by
55 outgrowing their existing system and having to move to a high-end package. ASPs also offer a means of using specialist tools that would otherwise prove prohibitively expensive. Small businesses have the opportunity to use such
60 tools for short periods of time as and when they need them, rather than having to buy the software as a permanent investment.

One of the major barriers for small businesses which want to make a start in e-commerce is
65 ensuring that they have sufficient resources to cope with sudden large increases in customers. This means not only having adequate storage for all your customers' details, but ensuring that you have the technology in place to handle
70 stock levels, efficient delivery and large volumes of traffic. It's very rare for an e-commerce business to handle all of these elements by itself, making this one of the best-established areas of ASP use. Being able to respond
75 rapidly to changes in the size of your customer base and the type of product that they want to order from your business, demands more flexibility than traditional software can provide.

[Adapted from 'ASP and you shall receive' by Maggie Williams, PC Direct Magazine, November 2000]

B Re-read the text to find the answers to these questions.

1 Note the advantages and disadvantages of using an ASP.

2 Match the items in Table A with the statements in Table B.

Table A
a Website
b ASP
c Virus
d Office suite
e Bandwidth
f Broadband
g Data centre
h SAP

Table B
i Set of standard programs used in an office
ii Facility for storing large amounts of information
iii Capacity of a network connection
iv High capacity Internet connection
v Self-replicating program
vi Common enterprise resource planning tool
vii Application service provider
viii Collection of related webpages

3 Using information from the text, mark the following as True or False:

a Software from an ASP must be installed locally on a user's computer.
b You need a high bandwidth connection to use an ASP service.
c ASPs usually use their own storage space for customers.
d Using an ASP gives you more flexibility.
e An e-commerce business usually provides all of the required technology itself.

Multimedia

STARTER **1**   Match the multimedia terms in Column A to the activities in Column B. More than one match is possible.

Column A	Column B
MIDI	watching movies
MP3	composing music on a PC
DVD	downloading music from the Internet
MPEG	using reference works like encyclopaedias

2   Study this diagram which explains MP3. Answer these questions:

1   How does MP3 reduce the size of music files?
2   What can you obtain from www.mp3.com?
3   How can you listen to MP3 files?

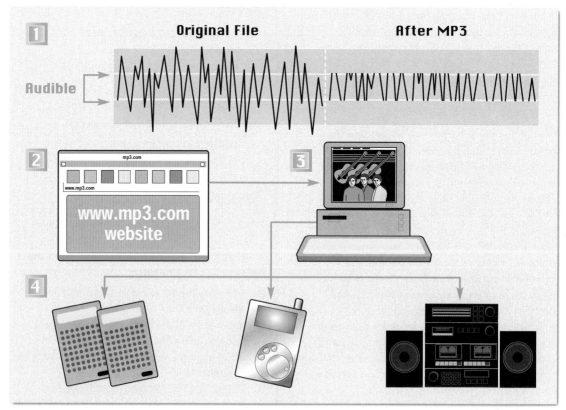

Fig 1
How MP3 will transform music

3 Match these captions to the pictures in Fig 1. Consider again your answers to Task 2.

a Once you've paid by credit card (unless it's one of the millions of free files), music is downloaded to your PC.

b The original music file is stripped of anything that is inaudible to the human ear. After MP3 has done its work, the file is reduced to roughly one twelfth that of the original recording.

c MP3 files can be listened to on your PC, a dedicated MP3 player, or your hi-fi.

d MP3 files are put on a website, where browsers can listen to samples and buy a single track or album ... or even create their own compilation.

READING 4 Read this text to find the answers to these questions.

1 What does MP3 stand for?
2 What is the difference between MP3 and WAV files?
3 What kind of sound does MP3 strip out?
4 What kind of information is included in the tag?

Understanding MP3

The name comes from MPEG (pronounced EM-peg), which stands for the Motion Picture Experts Group. MPEG develops standards for audio and video compression. MP3 is actually MPEG Audio Layer 3.

MP3 competes with another audio file format called WAV. The key difference is that MP3 files are much smaller than WAV files. An MP3 file can store a minute of sound per megabyte, while a WAV file needs 11 or 12 megabytes to hold the same amount. How does MP3 achieve this compression? CDs and audio files don't reproduce every sound of a performance. Instead, they sample the performance and store a discrete code for each sampled note. A CD or WAV file may sample a song 44,000 times a second, creating a huge mass of information.

By stripping out sounds most people can't hear, MP3 significantly reduces the information stored. For instance, most people can't hear notes above a frequency of 16kHz, so it eliminates them from the mix. Similarly, it eliminates quiet sounds masked by noise at the same frequency. The result is a file that sounds very similar to a CD, but which is much smaller. An MP3 file can contain spoken word performances, such as radio shows or audio books, as well as music. It can provide information about itself in a coded block called a tag. The tag may include the performer's name, a graphic such as an album cover, the song's lyrics, the musical genre, and a URL for more details.

5 Read the rest of this text to find the answers to these questions:

1 How do you play MP3 files?
2 What does the Windows Media Player file do with an MP3 file?
3 What is a standalone player?
4 What special features can players offer?
5 What information can you obtain by clicking on the track info button?
6 What does a skin enable you to do?
7 How do you play music from a CD-ROM on an MP3 player?
8 What hardware and software do you need to make your own audio CDs?

Play MP3 Files

Most machines today have enough processing power and memory to play MP3s immediately. Simply download an MP3 file like any other and click on it in Windows Explorer. The Windows Media Player will decode the file and route the signals to your soundcard and then to your speakers.

Other MP3 features include:

Players.

Most standalone players have many features beyond Windows' default Media Player. To control what music you play, players let you group songs into playlists and randomize the selections. To control how the music sounds, they offer spectrum analyzers, graphic equalizers, and frequency displays.

Track info.

A track info button gives you the information on the MP3 file's tag. Other buttons may take you to a music library where you can organize your MP3 files by performer or genre.

Skins or themes.

These programs are designed to change the appearance of the most popular players. They're akin to the wallpaper that alters the look of the Windows desktop. With a skin, a player can become a jukebox, a car dashboard, or a Star Trek tricorder. Think of them as easily interchangeable faceplates.

Rippers and encoders.

A ripper is a program that rips songs from a CD in your CD-ROM drive and turns them into WAV files. An encoder converts WAV files into MP3 files or vice versa. Many MP3 players incorporate rippers and encoders and can do both steps in one.

Recorders.

With a writeable CD-ROM drive, a recorder program lets you create your own audio CDs.

LANGUAGE WORK   -ing clauses (2) cause and effect

Study this sentence.

1   Using MIDI, computers can communicate with synthesizers.

It contains two clauses. An -ing clause:

Using MIDI

and a main clause:

computers can communicate with synthesizers

We can use an -ing clause, as in example 1, to explain how something happens. The -ing

clause explanation can be placed before, or after the main clause as in example 2.

2   DVD drives read DVD disks *(by) using blue laser light.*

We can also use -ing clauses to link a cause and effect.

3   A WAV file may sample a song 44,000 times a second, [cause] *creating a huge mass of information.* [effect]

---

6   Match each cause and effect. Then link them with an *-ing* clause.

Cause	Effect
1 Computers with MIDI interface boards can be connected to MIDI instruments.	a This permits extra information to be stored on the performer and other track details.
2 Each side of a DVD can have two layers.	b You can create your own compilation.
3 MP3 removes sounds we can't hear.	c This allows you to sample a new group before buying their CD.
4 You can download single tracks.	d This gives an enormous storage capacity.
5 Each MP3 file has a tag.	e This allows the music being played to be stored by the computer and displayed on the monitor.
6 MP3 players contain several devices.	f This enables you to change the appearance of your player.
7 You can download a skin program.	g These allow you to control the way the music sounds.
8 You can legally download some music.	h This produces much smaller files.

7 Explain how each of these actions happen. The explanations are available in Tasks 2, 3 and 4.

1 MP3 reduces the information stored.
2 You can alter the look of your MP3 player.
3 You can 'rip' the audio information from a CD.
4 You can convert a WAV file to MP3 format.
5 You can view the lyrics, notes and author data.
6 You can control how the music sounds.
7 You can access many free and legal music files for downloading.
8 You can play MP3 files through your sound system.

SPEAKING **8** Work in pairs, A and B. With the help of the notes provided, explain to your partner one aspect of multimedia.

Student A Your notes are on page 185.
Student B Your notes are on page 191.

Link your notes into a text describing one aspect of multimedia. Choose either the Student A or the Student B notes.

WRITING **9** Study the diagram, Fig 2, which illustrates how MIDI operates. Then link each set of sentences into one complex sentence to form a continuous paragraph. You may add, omit and change words.

1 Most modern music is mixed.
   This uses computers.

2 Musicians record their music into a computer system.
   This system is called a Musical Instrument Digital Interface (MIDI).

3 MIDI was developed as a standard interface.
   MIDI is for linking music synthesizers and instruments together.

4 Computers can be connected to MIDI instruments.
   These computers are fitted with MIDI interface boards.
   This allows the music to be stored on computer.
   This allows the music to be displayed on the monitor.
   The music is being played.

5 The music can be displayed as a musical score.
   The music can be edited.
   This uses all the features of a mixing desk.

The PC Setup

What goes where in a typical PC music set-up

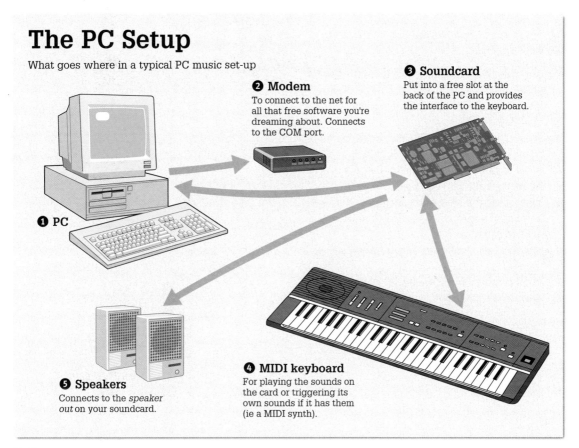

❷ Modem
To connect to the net for all that free software you're dreaming about. Connects to the COM port.

❸ Soundcard
Put into a free slot at the back of the PC and provides the interface to the keyboard.

❶ PC

❺ Speakers
Connects to the *speaker out* on your soundcard.

❹ MIDI keyboard
For playing the sounds on the card or triggering its own sounds if it has them (ie a MIDI synth).

Fig 2
What is MIDI?

6 The music can also be printed out from the computer.
The music is being played.

7 MIDI doesn't transmit any sound.
It transmits simple binary information.

8 The information is called a MIDI message.
The message encodes sound as 8-bit bytes of digital information.

9 The most common messages consist of instructions.
These instructions tell the receiving instrument to play a note for a specific duration of time.

10 The instructions also contain details of how loud to play that note.
The instructions contain a number.
The number indicates which instrument to play.
Number 67 is a saxophone.

A Find the answers to these questions in the following text.

1   Into what two components is the data stream split?
2   What information does an Intra frame contain?
3   What is stored in the P-frames following an I-frame?
4   What is stored in a P-frame in the case of a bouncing ball?
5   What gives the massive reduction in the amount of information needed to reproduce a video sequence?
6   Why is a new I-frame used after a few P-frames?
7   What is stored in a B-frame?
8   Why do B-frames not propagate errors?

THE TRICKS TO MPEG'S SUCCESS

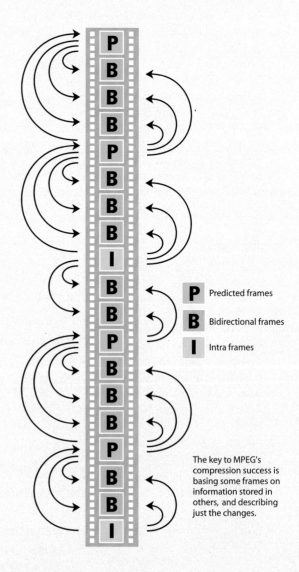

P Predicted frames

B Bidirectional frames

I Intra frames

The key to MPEG's compression success is basing some frames on information stored in others, and describing just the changes.

The most common system for the compression of video is MPEG. It works like this. The single data stream off the CD-ROM is split into video and audio components, which are then decompressed
5 using separate algorithms. The video is processed to produce individual frames as follows. Imagine a sequence of frames depicting a bouncing ball on a plain background. The very first is called an Intra Frame (I-frame). I-frames are compressed
10 using only information in the picture itself just like conventional bitmap compression techniques like JPEG.

Following I-frames will be one or more predicted frames (P-frames). The difference between the P-
15 frame and the I-frame it is based on is the only data that is stored for this P-frame. For example, in the case of a bouncing ball, the P picture is stored simply as a description of how the position of the ball has changed from the previous I-frame.
20 This takes up a fraction of the space that would be used if you stored the P-frame as a picture in its own right. Shape or colour changes are also stored in the P-frame. The next P-frame may also be based on this P-frame and so on. Storing
25 differences between the frames gives the massive reduction in the amount of information needed to reproduce the sequence. Only a few P-frames are allowed before a new I-frame is introduced into the sequence as a new reference point, since a
30 small margin of error creeps in with each P-frame.

Between I and P-frames are bi-directional frames (B-frames), based on the nearest I or P-frames both before and after them. In our bouncing ball example, in a B-frame the picture is stored as the
35 difference between the previous I or P-frame and the B-frame and as the difference between the B-frame and the following I or P-frame. To recreate the B-frame when playing back the sequence, the MPEG algorithm uses a combination of two
40 references. There may be a number of B-frames between I or P-frames. No other frame is ever based on a B-frame so they don't propagate errors like P-frames.

Typically, you will have two or three Bs between
45 Is or Ps, and perhaps three to five P-frames between Is.

[Adapted from 'The Tricks to MPEG's Success', Windows Magazine, March 1994]

B Re-read the text to find the answers to these questions.

1 Mark the following statements as True or False:

a JPEG is the most common compression system used for video.

b P-frames only store the changes in the image.

c There is always at least one P-frame between two I-frames.

d B-frames store the complete picture information.

e There can only be one B-frame between each I and P-frame.

f There are typically about four P-frames between each I-frame.

2 Match the words in Table A with the statements in Table B.

Table A
a Algorithm
b I-frame
c JPEG
d P-frame
e B-frame
f MPEG

Table B
i A common type of compression used for video data
ii A compressed video frame known as a predicted frame
iii A compressed video frame that stores changes between the frame before it and the frame after it.
iv A formula used for decompressing components of a data stream
v A type of compression used for bitmap images
vi A compressed video frame that contains the complete image information

Computing Support Officer

STARTER | **1** | Study this screen display of Windows Explorer. Add these titles to the texts:

1. Toggle-box
2. Explorer pane
3. Selected icon
4. Divider
5. Guidelines
6. Navigation pane

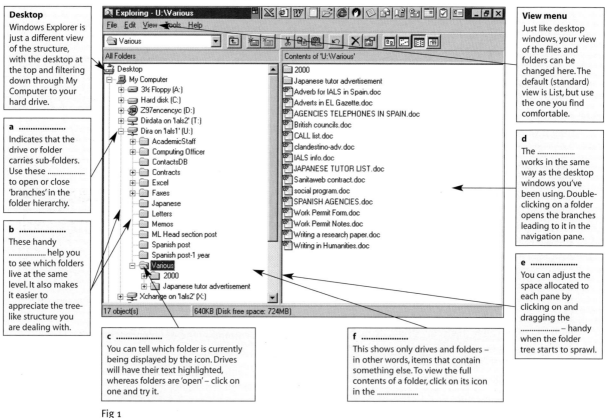

Desktop
Windows Explorer is just a different view of the structure, with the desktop at the top and filtering down through My Computer to your hard drive.

a ....
Indicates that the drive or folder carries sub-folders. Use these .... to open or close 'branches' in the folder hierarchy.

b ....
These handy .... help you to see which folders live at the same level. It also makes it easier to appreciate the tree-like structure you are dealing with.

c ....
You can tell which folder is currently being displayed by the icon. Drives will have their text highlighted, whereas folders are 'open' – click on one and try it.

View menu
Just like desktop windows, your view of the files and folders can be changed here. The default (standard) view is List, but use the one you find comfortable.

d
The .... works in the same way as the desktop windows you've been using. Double-clicking on a folder opens the branches leading to it in the navigation pane.

e ....
You can adjust the space allocated to each pane by clicking on and dragging the .... – handy when the folder tree starts to sprawl.

f ....
This shows only drives and folders – in other words, items that contain something else. To view the full contents of a folder, click on its icon in the ....

Fig 1
Windows Explorer

LISTENING | **2** | 🎧 Barbara is a Computing Support Officer in a large company. She's advising Clive, the Sales Director. Listen to Part 1 of the recording to find the answers to these questions:

1. What is Clive's problem?
2. What does he want to do?

3   🎧   These screen displays show some of the steps in Barbara's explanation. Listen to Part 2 of the recording and put them in the correct sequence.

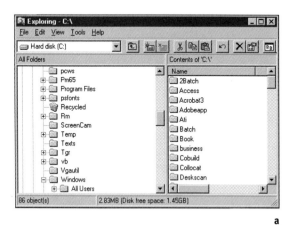

a

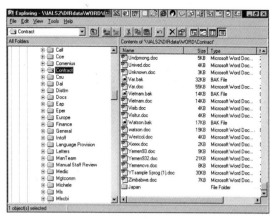

b

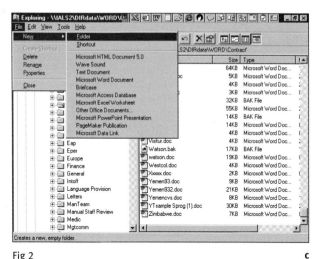

Fig 2   c
4 screen displays

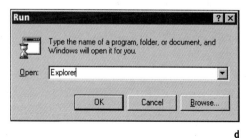

d

4   🎧   Listen to Part 3 to answer these questions:

1   What additional task does Clive need help with?
2   What indication is there that Contract now contains subfolders?
3   What are the subfolders called?
4   What operation is used to move files into the new subfolders?
5   What does Barbara refer to as a 'handy tool'?

LANGUAGE WORK   **Revision:** *If-sentences*

Study these uses of *if*-sentences.

Action and effect

We can use an *if*-sentence to link an action and its effect. For example:

1   If you click on that [action], that'll just compact your C drive [effect].
2   If you click on that [action], that opens it up and shows you all your folders [effect].

The action is in the Present simple and the effect is in the Present simple or described using *will, can,* or *may* depending how certain it is to follow.

Polite instructions

We use the action part of *if*-sentences, especially in spoken English, to give instructions in a polite way. The effect part is assumed.

3   If you bring your cursor down to the very bottom [*you'll find the Start button*].
4   If you just hit Enter [*that will activate the program*].

Imagined action and effect

We can use an *if*-sentence to describe the possible effect of an imagined action. For example:

5   If you spilled coffee on your keyboard [imagined action], you could damage it [possible effect].
6   If there were no other folders there [imagined action], you wouldn't have a little box in there [possible effect].

To show this describes imagined, not real, events, the action is in the Past simple and the effect is described using *would, could,* and *might* depending how certain it is to follow.

5   Match the actions in Column A with appropriate effects from Column B. Then join each action and effect using an if-sentence.

Column A	Column B
1 you press Print Screen	a you can drag it across the screen
2 you press Ctrl + Alt + Del in Windows 98	b it would speed up the computer
	c you may lose data
3 you added more memory	d you would have more space at your desk
4 you installed a modem	
5 you used a better search engine	e you would be able to connect to a telephone line
6 you forget to save regularly	
7 you hold down the mouse button over an icon	f you can make a copy of the screen
	g you would find more relevant results
8 you used an LCD display	h it displays a list of active programs

6 Describe the effects of these actions using an *if*-sentence.

1   you don't virus-check floppies
2   there was a power cut while you were using your computer
3   you install a faster processor
4   you forgot your password
5   you press the delete key
6   you use a search engine
7   you double-click on an icon
8   you use power-saving options

WORD STUDY **7** **Noun + Noun compounds** Match each word from Column A with its partner from Column B to make a computing term. All these terms are from previous units.

Column A		Column B	
1	barcode	a	tray
2	mainframe	b	program
3	laser	c	bus
4	expansion	d	pane
5	floppy	e	computer
6	control	f	reader
7	supervisor	g	bar
8	task	h	card
9	system	i	drive
10	explorer	j	printer

SPEAKING **8** Work in pairs, A and B. Instruct each other how to perform these computer operations in Windows or Mac OS. Take notes from your partner's instructions.

Student A Copying a file.
Student B Saving a file.

Networks

1 With the help of this diagram, try to describe the function of these components of a typical network system:

1	a file server	5	a LAN
2	a bridge	6	a gateway
3	a router	7	a modem
4	a backbone		

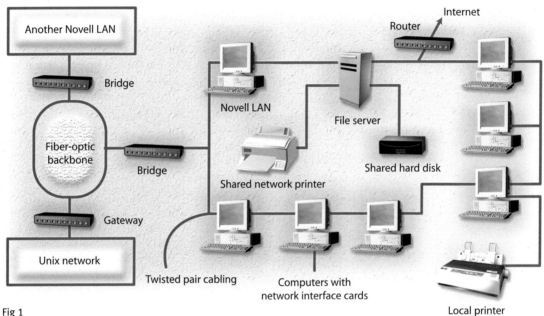

Fig 1
Components of a typical LAN

2 Now read these definitions to check your answers. You may also refer to the Glossary.

A bridge is a hardware and software combination used to connect the same type of networks. Bridges can also partition a large network into two smaller ones and connect two LANs that are nearby each other.

A router is a special computer that directs communicating messages when several networks are connected together. High-speed routers can serve as part of the Internet backbone.

A gateway is an interface that enables dissimilar networks to communicate, such as two LANs based on different topologies or network operating systems.

A backbone is the main transmission path, handling the major data traffic, connecting different LANs together.

A LAN is a network contained within a small area, for example a company department.

A modem is a device for converting digital signals to analogue signals and vice versa to enable a computer to transmit and receive data using an ordinary telephone line.

READING **3** Now study this text and the diagram of a simple home network setup. Match the diagram key to the components of the network.

The technology needed to set up a home network is here today. It is just a matter of connecting a number of PCs equipped with Ethernet adapters to a hub using twisted-pair cabling which uses sockets rather like phone sockets. Special isolation adapters can be fitted to allow existing mains lines to be used instead of twisted-pair cabling. Most future home networks, however, are likely to be wireless network systems, using tuned transmitter and receiver devices. The simplest networks allow basic file-sharing and multi-player gaming as well as sharing of peripherals such as printers. Most advanced home networks are likely to have a client/server structure, with low-cost terminals, or 'thin' clients, connected to a central server which maintains the system's storage capacity and, depending on whether the terminals are dumb or processor-equipped network computers, its processing power. To make the most of such a network, it must become part of an integrated home entertainment and control system. To the user, the desktop becomes just one of many features accessible throughout the house. Tired of working in the study? Pop down to the living room and reload it into the terminal there. Before you start work, call up the hi-fi control program and have the music of your choice pumped through the living room speakers. Computer and entertainment networks can be separate but linked by the server to allow control of the latter from the terminals. Future home networks are more likely to have the entire system based on a single loop.

KEY TO THE DIAGRAM

1. Line receiver delivering home entertainment audio to speakers within the room.

2. TV set relaying digital TV broadcasts relayed from the receiver by the home entertainment system.

3. Network modem allowing clients to access the Internet simultaneously. Ideally this would be replaced by an ISDN adapter or DSL modem fitted inside the server.

4. Thin client comprising a display, keyboard, mouse, floppy and CD-ROM drive. If the client is NetPC-based, it will have its own processor and memory. A dumb terminal will simply act as an interface to the real computer, the server.

5. Network printer connected to any client.

6. Line driver connected to the home entertainment system: the cable TV player, DVD player, etc.

7. Home server. It contains roughly 5Gb of storage per terminal and one or more processors, depending on whether it is connected to network computers or to cheaper dumb terminals.

8. Entertainment system delivery network. This also hooks up to the server to control the system and receive digital audio and video from it.

9. Entertainment network control pad. While the system can be controlled by a PC, there would be one of these per connected room to ensure that the client does not need to be activated to use the system.

10. Data line linking clients to server.

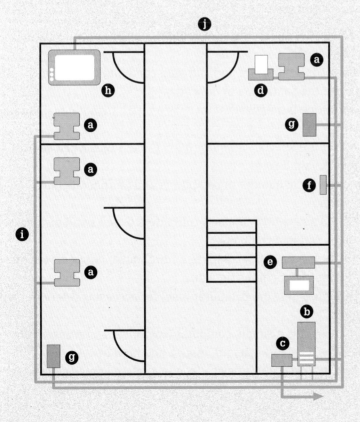

Fig 2
Simple home network

LANGUAGE WORK   Relative clauses with a participle

Relative clauses with a participle are often used in technical descriptions. They allow you to provide a lot of information about a noun using as few words as possible.

Study these examples from the Task 3 text.

1 The technology *needed to set up a home network*
2 PCs *equipped with Ethernet adapters*
3 Network modem *allowing clients to access the Internet simultaneously*
4 Data line *linking client to server*

We can use the passive participle as in examples 1 and 2.

1 The technology needed to set up a home network.
   = technology *which is needed*
2 PCs equipped with Ethernet adapters
   = PCs *which are equipped*

We can use an active participle as in examples 3 and 4.

3 Network modem allowing clients to access the Internet simultaneously
   = modem *which allows clients to access the Internet simultaneously*
4 Data line linking client to server
   = data line *which links client to server*

4   Complete these definitions with the correct participle of the verb given in brackets.

1 A *gateway* is an interface (enable) dissimilar networks to communicate.
2 A *bridge* is a hardware and software combination (use) to connect the same type of networks.
3 A *backbone* is a network transmission path (handle) major data traffic.
4 A *router* is a special computer (direct) messages when several networks are linked.
5 A *network* is a number of computers and peripherals (link) together.
6 A *LAN* is a network (connect) computers over a small distance such as within a company.
7 A *server* is a powerful computer (store) many programs (share) by all the clients in the network.
8 A *client* is a network computer (use) for accessing a service on a server.
9 A *thin client* is a simple computer (comprise) a processor and memory, display, keyboard, mouse and hard drives only.
10 A *hub* is an electronic device (connect) all the data cabling in a network.

5   Link these statements using a relative clause with a participle.

1   a   The technology is here today.
    b   It is needed to set up a home network.
2   a   You only need one network printer.
    b   It is connected to the server.
3   a   Her house has a network.
    b   It allows basic file-sharing and multi-player gaming.
4   a   There is a line receiver in the living room.
    b   It delivers home entertainment audio to speakers.
5   a   Eve has designed a site.
    b   It is dedicated to dance.
6   a   She has built in links.
    b   They connect her site to other dance sites.
7   a   She created the site using a program called Netscape Composer.
    b   It is contained in Netscape Communicator.
8   a   At the centre of France Telecom's home of tomorrow is a network.
    b   It is accessed through a Palm Pilot-style control pad.
9   a   The network can simulate the owner's presence.
    b   This makes sure vital tasks are carried out in her absence.
10 a   The house has an electronic door-keeper.
    b   It is programmed to recognise you.
    c   This gives access to family only.

PROBLEM-SOLVING   **6**   Work in two groups, A and B. Group A, list all the advantages of a network. Group B, list all the disadvantages. Then together consider how the disadvantages can be minimised.

Group A Advantages of a network	Group B Disadvantages of a network

SPEAKING   **7**   **Transmission modes** Work in pairs, A and B. Explain to your partner how one mode of transmission between computers operates with the help of the text provided. Your explanation should allow your partner to label his/her diagram.

Student A

Your text is on page 186. Your explanation should allow your partner to label this diagram.

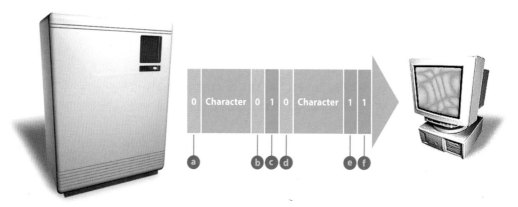

Fig 3
Asynchronous transmission

Student B

Your text is on page 192. Your explanation should allow your partner to label this diagram.

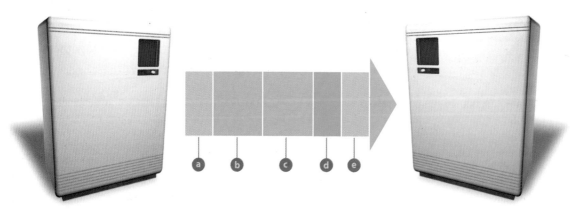

Fig 4
Synchronous transmission

WRITING   **8**   Using the lists you compiled in Task 6, describe the advantages and disadvantages of networks. Try to link some of the advantages and disadvantages as in these examples.

Advantages	Disadvantages
Allow data to be shared.	Permit viruses to spread quickly.
Users can share software on the server.	Server failure means no one can work.

1   Although networks allow data to be shared, they permit viruses to spread quickly.
2   Users can share software on the server; however server failure means that no one can work.

WHEN YOU HAVE FINISHED THE READING SECTION ON THE FOLLOWING PAGES, COME BACK TO THESE ADDITIONAL EXERCISES

3   Identify which layer attaches the following headers to a network transmission:

a   Specifying the language, the compression and encryption schemes
b   Identifying each segment's checksum and its position in the message
c   Containing the sequence of packets and the address of the receiving computer
d   Marking the beginning and end of the message and specifying whether the messages will be sent half-duplex or full-duplex
e   Identifying the sending and receiving computers

4   Fill in the missing words in the following sentences then put the sentences in the correct order:

a   The checksum is recalculated by the .... layer which also reassembles the message ....
b   The message is .... and .... by the presentation layer.
c   The message is reconverted into .... by the physical layer.
d   The session layer then sends the message to the next ....
e   The application layer converts the bits into .... characters, and directs the data to the correct ....
f   The incoming .... are recounted by the network layer for .... and billing purposes.
g   The .... layer confirms the arrival of the packets, ... them in, and calculates the .... for each packet.
h   The parts of the message are .... by the .... layer until the message is ....

A **Find the answers to these questions in the following text.**

1 Into what units is data subdivided by the following layers?
   a transport layer
   b network layer
2 What is the purpose of a transmission checksum test?
3 How long does the data-link layer keep a copy of each packet?
4 What processes can be carried out at intermediate nodes?
5 Which network communications layer is described by each of the following statements?
   a Makes sure that the message is transmitted in a language that the receiving computer can understand
   b Protects the data being sent
   c Encodes and sends the packets
   d Supervises the transmission
   e The part of a communications process that a user sees
   f Starts communications and looks after communications among network nodes
   g Chooses a route for the message
   h Makes backup copies of the data if required
   i Confirms the checksum, then addresses and duplicates the packets

Network Communications

1 The application layer is the only part of a communications process that a user sees, and even then, the user doesn't see most of the work that the application does to prepare a message
5 for sending over a network. The layer converts a message's data from human-readable form into bits and attaches a header identifying the sending and receiving computers.

2 The presentation layer ensures that the
10 message is transmitted in a language that the receiving computer can interpret (often ASCII). This layer translates the language, if necessary, and then compresses and perhaps encrypts the data. It adds another header specifying the
15 language as well as the compression and encryption schemes.

3 The session layer opens communications and has the job of keeping straight the communications among all nodes on the network.
20 It sets boundaries (called bracketing) for the beginning and end of the message, and establishes whether the messages will be sent half-duplex, with each computer taking turns sending and receiving, or full-duplex, with both
25 computers sending and receiving at the same time. The details of these decisions are placed into a session header.

4 The transport layer protects the data being sent. It subdivides the data into segments,
30 creates checksum tests – mathematical sums based on the contents of data – that can be used later to determine if the data was scrambled. It can also make backup copies of the data. The transport header identifies each segment's
35 checksum and its position in the message.

5 The network layer selects a route for the message. It forms data into packets, counts them, and adds a header containing the sequence of packets and the address of the receiving
40 computer.

6 The data-link layer supervises the transmission. It confirms the checksum, then addresses and duplicates the packets. This layer keeps a copy of each packet until it receives
45 confirmation from the next point along the route that the packet has arrived undamaged.

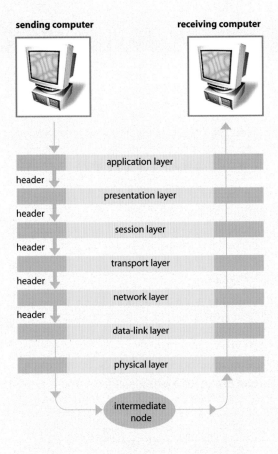

sending computer   **receiving computer**

application layer

header

presentation layer

header

session layer

header

transport layer

header

network layer

header

data-link layer

physical layer

intermediate node

7 The physical layer encodes the packets into the medium that will carry them – such as an analogue signal, if the message is going across a
50 telephone line – and sends the packets along that medium.

8 An intermediate node calculates and verifies the checksum for each packet. It may also reroute the message to avoid congestion on the network.

55 9 At the receiving node, the layered process that sent the message on its way is reversed. The physical layer reconverts the message into bits. The data-link layer recalculates the checksum, confirms arrival, and logs in the
60 packets. The network layer recounts incoming packets for security and billing purposes. The transport layer recalculates the checksum and reassembles the message segments. The session layer holds the parts of the message until the
65 message is complete and sends it to the next layer. The presentation layer expands and decrypts the message. The application layer converts the bits into readable characters, and directs the data to the correct application.

B Re-read the text to find the answers to these questions.

1 Match the term in Table A with the statement in Table B.

Table A
a Bracketing
b Half-duplex
c Full-duplex
d Checksum

Table B
i   Transmission mode in which each computer takes turns sending and receiving
ii Mathematical calculations based on the contents of data
iii Set boundaries for the beginning and end of a message
iv Transmission mode in which both computers send and receive at the same time

2 Mark the following statements as True or False:

a   Most of the work that an application does to prepare a message for sending over a network is not seen by the user.

b   ASCII is always used to transmit data.

c   The encryption layer compresses the message.

d   The network layer keeps track of how many packets are in each message.

e   The network layer keeps a copy of each packet until it arrives at the next node undamaged.

f   Analogue signals are used on ordinary telephone lines.

g   When a message arrives at its destination, it passes through the same seven network communications layers as when it was sent, but in reverse order.

▶ Additional exercises on page 77

['How Computers Work' by Ron White and Timothy Edward Downs (Ziff-Davis Press) – Extract in PC Magazine, February 1993]

The Internet

1 Match each of the Internet services in Column A with the uses in Column B.

Column A	Column B
1 IRC	a logging on to your computer at a distance
2 MOOs	b sending and receiving messages
3 email	c downloading a file from a server
4 FTP	d chatting to other users in real-time
5 WWW	e accessing newsgroups
6 Telnet	f browsing webpages
7 Usenet	g taking part in simulations in a shared environment

READING **2** **Computer-Mediated Communication (CMC)** Work in groups of three, A, B, and C. Read one of these examples of CMC and complete this table.

Extract	A	B	C
Type of CMC			
Number of participants			
Topics			
Synchronous or asynchronous			
Special features of this type of CMC			

Extract A

```
Inside the lounge of the House of Language.
There is a television in the corner.
You see the following exits: east and north
Hank, Spartacus, Diana, Tony (resting)

Hank says, 'have any of you guys tried batmud? :)'
Diana says, 'no'
Spartacus says, 'what is it?'
Hank says, 'it's a virtual reality game. you'll find it at: bat.org'
Diana groans.
Diana says, 'these things are addictive. You spend *hours*on them.'
Rupert appears with a flash of lightning.
Spartacus says, 'we have a new participant. welcome Rupert!'
Rupert says, 'Thanks. How do you get to the kitchen?'
Hank says, 'type 'go kitchen'. You can find the instructions on 'help topics' '
Rupert says, 'Do you use Telnet?'
Diana says, 'use tf...it's much better.'
```

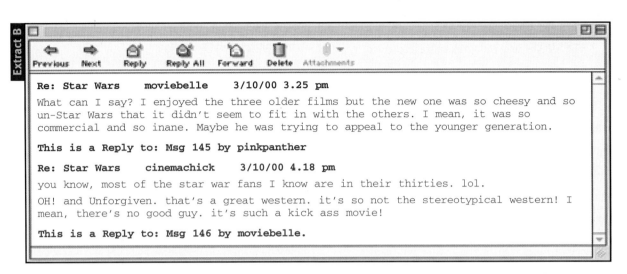

Extract B

⇦ Previous   ⇨ Next   Reply   Reply All   Forward   Delete   Attachments

Re: Star Wars   moviebelle   3/10/00 3.25 pm

What can I say? I enjoyed the three older films but the new one was so cheesy and so un-Star Wars that it didn't seem to fit in with the others. I mean, it was so commercial and so inane. Maybe he was trying to appeal to the younger generation.

This is a Reply to: Msg 145 by pinkpanther

Re: Star Wars   cinemachick   3/10/00 4.18 pm

you know, most of the star war fans I know are in their thirties. lol.

OH! and Unforgiven. that's a great western. it's so not the stereotypical western! I mean, there's no good guy. it's such a kick ass movie!

This is a Reply to: Msg 146 by moviebelle.

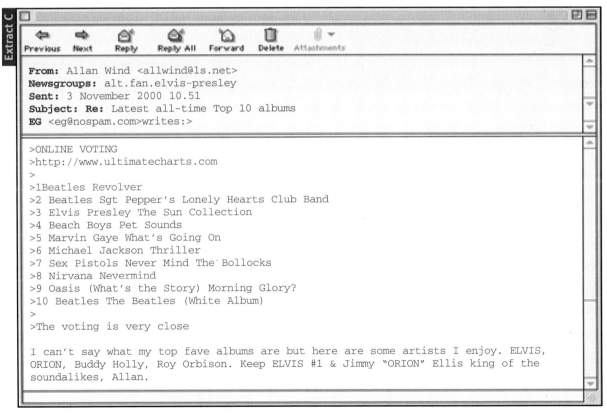

Extract C

⇦ Previous   ⇨ Next   Reply   Reply All   Forward   Delete   Attachments

From: Allan Wind <allwind@ls.net>
Newsgroups: alt.fan.elvis-presley
Sent: 3 November 2000 10.51
Subject: Re: Latest all-time Top 10 albums
EG <eg@nospam.com>writes:>

>ONLINE VOTING
>http://www.ultimatecharts.com
>
>1Beatles Revolver
>2 Beatles Sgt Pepper's Lonely Hearts Club Band
>3 Elvis Presley The Sun Collection
>4 Beach Boys Pet Sounds
>5 Marvin Gaye What's Going On
>6 Michael Jackson Thriller
>7 Sex Pistols Never Mind The Bollocks
>8 Nirvana Nevermind
>9 Oasis (What's the Story) Morning Glory?
>10 Beatles The Beatles (White Album)
>
>The voting is very close

I can't say what my top fave albums are but here are some artists I enjoy. ELVIS, ORION, Buddy Holly, Roy Orbison. Keep ELVIS #1 & Jimmy "ORION" Ellis king of the soundalikes, Allan.

3   Compare results orally with the others in your group. Complete a table for each of the other extracts using the information the others provide.

LANGUAGE WORK   Warnings

Where might you see these warnings?

1 Never give out your home address or phone number.
2 This appliance must be earthed.
3 Avoid turning off main power while computer is running.
4 It is an offence to make unauthorised access to computer material.
5 No smoking, eating or drinking at the computer.
6 A machine which has been exposed to a moist atmosphere should be given time to dry out before being put into use.

Warnings are used to ensure safety, to prevent damage to equipment and breaches of security, and to ensure the law is not broken. The simplest warnings are basic instructions NOT to do something:

Don't do X.   Avoid Xing.
No Xing.   Never do X.

Sometimes the warning is twinned with matching good practice:

Always do Y; never do X.
Do Y rather than doing X.

Warnings may be made stronger by using *must/must not* and in some cases *should/should not*. For example:

The wire linking a static earthing band to earth must contain a resistor of at least 1megohm.

If there is any reason to fear the warning may not be understood, a reason for the warning may be added. For example:

Never remove ICs with a screwdriver. *The pins are very fragile.*

4 Rewrite each of these warnings according to the prompt. Add a reason to the warning where you think it appropriate.

1

> Don't give open access to PCs.

Avoid ...

2

> **You must not use your own floppies on these machines.**

Never ...

3

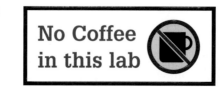

No Coffee in this lab

... must not ...

4

> ### Avoid giving financial information in a chat room.

Don't ...

5

> ### NEVER GIVE OUT YOUR PASSWORD.

Always ...

6

> ⚠ Don't use out-of-date anti-virus software.

Use ...

7

> Never use a computer that has been standing for a long time in a cold environment without waiting until it has reached normal room temperature.

Always ...

8

> Cards must not be removed from their anti-static packing until required.

Never ...

9

> Use an IC extraction tool; don't use a screwdriver.

... rather than ...

10

> Always ensure the power is switched off when working on a computer.

... must not ...

5 Translate some of the rules for computer use in your own college or university into English. Compare your translations with others in your group and agree on the best English versions.

PROBLEM-SOLVING   6   Choosing a free ISP Read these hints on choosing a free ISP. Then decide which of the options available offer the best deal to these users. Be prepared to defend your choice.

1 a household with a young family
2 a small home-based business
3 someone who enjoys online gaming
4 someone who doesn't want a lot of spam in their email

Using a free ISP requires no new technology – all you need is a computer, a modem, a telephone line, and the appropriate software (which is available free of charge when you sign up with the service). Once installed on your PC you can access the Internet as normal, but your connection costs only the price of a local call, and you pay nothing else – not even for features such as an unlimited number of email addresses, unlimited Web space and original content.

Most of the services are very similar, but it is still worth looking around for a service that offers at least the following features:

CD-ROM or Online sign up
Many free ISPs require you to sign up for their service online (which obviously means you already need to have an Internet connection and some experience with setting up a dial-up networking connection). If you are a complete beginner, you'll need a free ISP which can provide its sign-up software on CD-ROM that will automatically configure your computer to access the Internet.

Local rate calls
Although using the ISP is free, you still have to pay for your online time. Nearly all ISPs however provide local call access numbers. Any free ISP that uses a national rate number or charges an initial set-up or administration fee should be avoided.

Email
Having several email accounts is very useful – you can separate business and personal email for example, or provide an address for each member of your family. Many free ISPs also offer only Web-based mail which is great if you need to get into your computer on the move as you can access it from any computer with Internet access. POP3 email however is faster and more efficient and can be downloaded to your PC to read offline – a combination of the two is ideal.

Free Web space
A decent amount of free Web space would be around 25-50Mb. This would be sufficient for most of your own personal website developments. Also check to see if there are any restrictions on your use of Web space, since some free ISPs will not let you use the space for commercial purposes.

Newsgroups
Newsgroups are huge discussion forums on the Internet that are an amazingly rich resource of information and a brilliant way to communicate with other Internet users. Unfortunately they are also the home to some of the most unsavoury content on the Internet (they are largely unmoderated) and as a result many free ISPs restrict access to some or all newsgroups.

Customer Support
Check support line charges; many free ISPs use their support lines as a source of revenue relying on your ignorance to make money from the call.

The target audience is generally Net novices and, as a result, support lines are pretty much jammed all day with queries and connection problems.

Most use premium rate telephone line charges. However, there are a few free ISPs who only charge local or national rates for their telephone helplines.

Reliable Service
Of course all the features in the world won't make a scrap of difference if the ISP is unreliable and you find it impossible to log on. Look out for recommendations from friends and shop around. Interestingly many of the more popular services have become saturated and seem to be in a constant 'upgrading the network' phase.

There is nothing to stop you having more than one free ISP account. Windows will even enable you to run a number of different free ISP connection set-ups on the same PC so you can easily have multiple accounts and just use the best one on the day.

Option A

Bigwig

- 7 POP3 email accounts each with up to 1,000 aliases
- Scans all emails for viruses before they reach you
- 15Mb free Web space
- Access to 25,000 newsgroups
- Technical support at 50p/minute
- Comprehensive online information and easy -to-follow help available

Option B

Arsenal

- 5 POP3 email accounts
- Access to most newsgroups
- 5Mb free Web space
- Technical support at 50p/minute

Option C

ConnectFree

- 5 POP3 email addresses each password-protected
- Full access to newsgroups
- Unlimited Web space
- Free online webpage design service
- Free access to online multi-player games

Option D

Bun

- Unlimited email addresses
- 25Mb Web space
- Online help section
- Free access to CyberPatrol for blocking or restricting access to inappropriate content on the Web

Option E

Free4all

- Unlimited POP3 email accounts
- Email virus protection and junk email filters
- 25Mb of free Web space with option to increase at £1 per Mb per month
- Powerful enough to create quite advanced, functional sites
- Technical support at local call rates

For further details of ISPs try:
www.net4nowt.com
www.ispa.org.uk
www.ispc.org

WRITING　　**7**　Write an article for a newsgroup of your choice. Keep it short and choose a meaningful reference name. Pass it to another student for a reply.

8　If you have access to newsgroups, browse one of the groups dedicated to computing. They have the prefix *comp*. Write a reply to one of the articles posted there. You need not post your reply unless you are confident it will be helpful. Ask your fellow students to read it first.

A Find the answers to these questions in the following text.

1   What purpose does the Internet address have apart from identifying a node?
2   What data-delivery systems are mentioned in the text?
3   What do IP modules need to know about each other to communicate?
4   How many Internet addresses does a gateway have?
5   What does UDP software do?
6   When does the TCP part of TCP/IP come into operation?
7   What processes are performed by TCP software to provide reliable stream service?
8   What standard protocols are mentioned which are used to deal with the data after TCP brings it into the computer?

How TCP/IP Links Dissimilar Machines

At the heart of the Internet Protocol (IP) portion of TCP/IP is a concept called the Internet address. This 32-bit coding system assigns a number to every node on the network. There are
5   various types of addresses designed for networks of different sizes, but you can write every address with a series of numbers that identify the major network and the sub-networks to which a node is attached. Besides identifying a node, the address
10   provides a path that gateways can use to route information from one machine to another.

Although data-delivery systems like Ethernet or X.25 bring their packets to any machine electrically attached to the cable, the IP modules

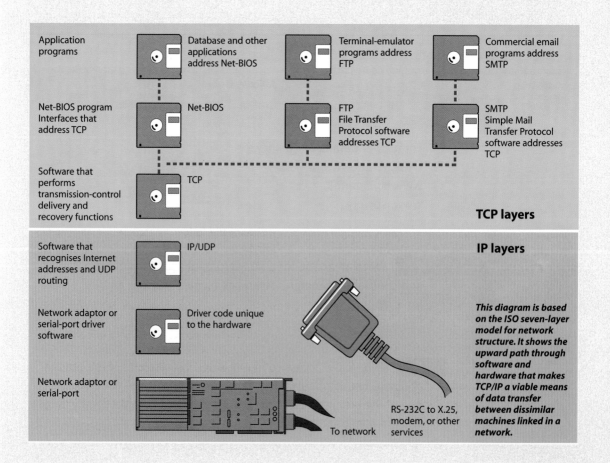

Application programs

Database and other applications address Net-BIOS

Terminal-emulator programs address FTP

Commercial email programs address SMTP

Net-BIOS program Interfaces that address TCP

Net-BIOS

FTP File Transfer Protocol software addresses TCP

SMTP Simple Mail Transfer Protocol software addresses TCP

Software that performs transmission-control delivery and recovery functions

TCP

TCP layers

Software that recognises Internet addresses and UDP routing

IP/UDP

IP layers

Network adaptor or serial-port driver software

Driver code unique to the hardware

Network adaptor or serial-port

To network

RS-232C to X.25, modem, or other services

This diagram is based on the ISO seven-layer model for network structure. It shows the upward path through software and hardware that makes TCP/IP a viable means of data transfer between dissimilar machines linked in a network.

15 must know each other's Internet addresses if they
are to communicate. A machine acting as a
gateway connecting different TCP/IP networks
will have a different Internet address on each
network. Internal look-up tables and software
20 based on another standard – called Resolution
Protocol – are used to route the data through a
gateway between networks.

Another piece of software works with the IP-layer
programs to move information to the right
25 application on the receiving system. This software
follows a standard called the User Datagram
Protocol (UDP). You can think of the UDP
software as creating a data address in the TCP/IP
message that states exactly what application the
30 data block is supposed to contact at the address
the IP software has described. The UDP software
provides the final routing for the data within the
receiving system.

The Transmission Control Protocol (TCP) part of
35 TCP/IP comes into operation once the packet is
delivered to the correct Internet address and
application port. Software packages that follow
the TCP standard run on each machine, establish
a connection to each other, and manage the
40 communication exchanges. A data-delivery
system like Ethernet doesn't promise to deliver a
packet successfully. Neither IP nor UDP knows
anything about recovering packets that aren't
successfully delivered, but TCP structures and
45 buffers the data flow, looks for responses and
takes action to replace missing data blocks. This
concept of data management is called reliable
stream service.

After TCP brings the data packet into a
50 computer, other high-level programs handle it.
Some are enshrined in official US government
standards, like the File Transfer Protocol (FTP)
and the Simple Mail Transfer Protocol (SMTP). If
you use these standard protocols on different
55 kinds of computers, you will at least have ways of
easily transferring files and other kinds of data.

Conceptually, software that supports the TCP
protocol stands alone. It can work with data
received through a serial port, over a packet-
60 switched network, or from a network system like
Ethernet. TCP software doesn't need to use IP or
UDP, it doesn't even have to know they exist. But
in practice TCP is an integral part of the TCP/IP
picture, and it is most frequently used with those
65 two protocols.

[Adapted from 'How TCP/IP Links Dissimilar Machines',
PC Magazine, September 1989]

B Re-read the text to find the answers to
these questions.

**1   Match the terms in Table A with the
statements in Table B.**

Table A

a	Internet address
b	Resolution Protocol
c	Look-up table
d	Gateway
e	User Datagram Protocol
f	Transmission Control Protocol

Table B

i	Standard used for software that routes data through a gateway
ii	Standard used by software that moves information to the correct application on the receiving system of a network
iii	Standard used by software that manages communication exchanges between computers on the Internet
iv	A 32-bit number identifying a node on an IP network
v	Stored information used to route data through a gateway
vi	A device for connecting dissimilar networks

**2   Mark the following statements as True or
False:**

a   Internet addresses are an integral part of the IP protocol.
b   Internet addresses can be written as a series of numbers.
c   UDP software provides the final routing for data within the receiving system.
d   UDP recovers packets that aren't successfully delivered.
e   TCP only works with packet-switched networks.
f   TCP only works when it is combined with IP.

The World Wide Web

1   Study this URL (Uniform Resource Locator).

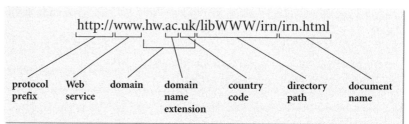

Fig 1
Uniform Resource Locator

Which part of the address tells you:

1   the company is in the UK
2   this is the webpage
3   the type of transmission standard your browser must use to access the data
4   this points to the computer where the webpage is stored
5   this is where the webpage is stored in the computer
6   this is a company
7   this is a Web file

2   Study these approved domain name extensions and their meanings. Then match these suggestions for new extensions to their meanings.

Extension	Meaning
.aero	aviation industry
.biz	businesses
.com (.co in UK)	commercial
.coop	cooperatives
.edu (.ac in UK)	educational and research
.gov	government
.info	general use
.int	international organisation
.mil	military agency
.museum	museums
.name	individuals
.net	gateway or host
.org	non-profit organisation
.pro	professionals

Suggested extension		Meaning	
1	.firm	a	informative
2	.store	b	cultural or entertainment
3	.web	c	personal
4	.arts	d	firm or agency
5	.rec	e	online retail shop
6	.info	f	Web-related
7	.nom	g	recreational

LISTENING   **3**   Study this diagram which illustrates how your browser finds the webpage you want. Label these items:

a   Router
b   Domain Name System (DNS) server
c   Remote Web server
d   Browser PC
e   URL
f   Internet Protocol address

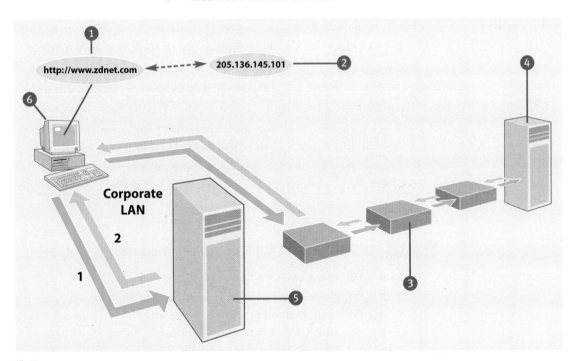

Fig 2
How your browser finds the page you want

4   🎧   Now listen to this recording which explains how the process works and take brief notes on each stage. For example:

Stage 1
Click on a webpage hyperlink or URL.
The browser sends the URL to a DNS server.

LANGUAGE WORK   **Time clauses**

What is the relationship between each of these pairs of actions?

1   a   You click on a URL.
    b   Your browser sends it to a DNS server.
2   a   The packets are passed from router to router.
    b   They reach the Web server.
3   a   The packets may travel by different routes.
    b   They reach the Web server.
4   a   The individual packets reach the Web server.
    b   They are put back together again.

Each pair of actions is linked in time. We can show how actions are linked in time by using time clauses. For example:

We can use *when* to show that one action happens immediately after another action:

1   *When* you click on a URL, your browser sends it to a DNS server.

We can use *once* in place of *when* to emphasise the completion of the first action. It often occurs with the Present perfect. For example:

Once the DNS server has found the IP address, it sends the address back to the browser.

We can use *until* to link an action and the limit of that action:

2   The packets are passed from router to router *until* they reach the Web server.

We can use *before* to show that one action precedes another:

3   The packets may travel by different routes *before* they reach the Web server.

If the subjects are the same in both actions, we can use a participle:

The packets may travel by different routes *before* reaching the Web server.

We can use *as* to link two connected actions happening at the same time:

4   *As* the individual packets reach the Web server, they are put back together again.

---

5   Link each pair of actions using a time clause.

1   a   You use a search engine.
    b   It provides a set of links related to your search.
2   a   With POP3, email is stored on the server.
    b   You check your email account.
3   a   You have clicked on a hyperlink.
    b   You have to wait for the webpage to be copied to your computer.

4 a You listen to the first part of a streamed audio file.

   b The next part is downloading.

5 a The graphics can be displayed gradually.

   b The webpage is downloaded.

6 a You receive an email message.

   b You can forward it to another address.

7 a You click on a hyperlink.

   b The browser checks to see if the linked webpage is stored in the cache.

8 a You can bookmark a webpage to make it easier to find in the future.

   b You find a webpage you like.

9 a You type in a Web address.

   b You should press the Enter key.

10 a You click on the Home button.

   b The browser displays your starting webpage.

6 Fill in the gaps in this description of buffering, a way of ensuring that Web video runs smoothly.

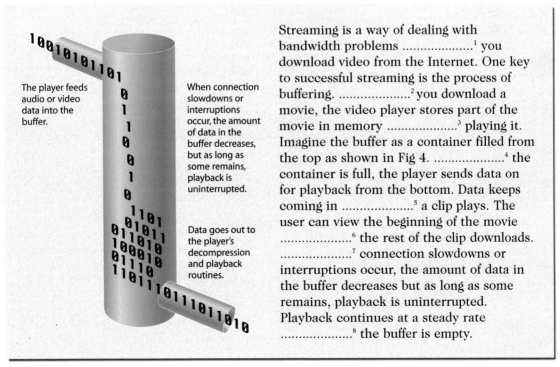

The player feeds audio or video data into the buffer.

When connection slowdowns or interruptions occur, the amount of data in the buffer decreases, but as long as some remains, playback is uninterrupted.

Data goes out to the player's decompression and playback routines.

Streaming is a way of dealing with bandwidth problems ....[1] you download video from the Internet. One key to successful streaming is the process of buffering. ....[2] you download a movie, the video player stores part of the movie in memory ....[3] playing it. Imagine the buffer as a container filled from the top as shown in Fig 4. ....[4] the container is full, the player sends data on for playback from the bottom. Data keeps coming in ....[5] a clip plays. The user can view the beginning of the movie ....[6] the rest of the clip downloads. ....[7] connection slowdowns or interruptions occur, the amount of data in the buffer decreases but as long as some remains, playback is uninterrupted. Playback continues at a steady rate ....[8] the buffer is empty.

Fig 3
Video buffering

PROBLEM-SOLVING   7   **Search engines** Study these tips for conducting searches using AltaVista. Then decide what you would type into the search box to find this data. Compare your answers with others in your group and together decide what would be the best search. Restrict sites to English language.

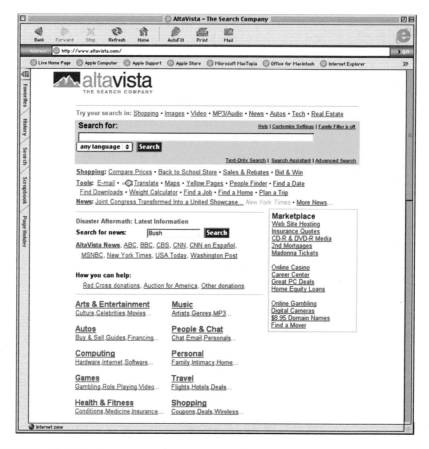

Tip 1
Don't use simple keywords. Typing in the word football is unlikely to help you to find information on your favourite football team. Unless special operators are included, AltaVista assumes the default operator is OR. If, for example, the search query is *American football*, AltaVista will look for documents containing either *American* or *football* although it will list higher those documents which contain both.

Tip 2
AltaVista is specifically case sensitive. If you specify apple as your search term, AltaVista will return matches for apple, Apple and APPLE. However, if you use Apple or apPle, AltaVista will only match Apple and apPle respectively.

Tip 3
AltaVista supports natural language queries. If you really aren't sure where to start looking, try typing a natural language query in the search box. The question Where can I find pages about digital cameras? will find a number of answers but at least it will give you some idea of where to start.

Tip 4 Try using phrase searching. This is where you place quotation marks around your search term, e.g. 'alternative medicine'. This will search for all documents where these two words appear as a phrase.

Tip 5 Attaching a + to a word is a way of narrowing your search. It means that word must be included in your search. For example, if you were looking for information on cancer research, use +cancer +research instead of just cancer.

Tip 6 Attaching a – to a word or using NOT is another way of narrowing your search. This excludes the search item following the word NOT or the – sign. For example, science NOT fiction or science –fiction will exclude sites in which these two words occur together.

Tip 7 Use brackets to group complex searches, for example: (cakes AND recipes) AND (chocolate OR ginger) will find pages including cakes and recipes and either chocolate or ginger or both.

Tip 8 You can refine your search by doing a field search. Put the field, then a colon and then what you are looking for.
For example,
URL:UK +universities will find only British universities.
title: 'English language' will find only sites which contain this phrase in their titles.

Tip 9 AltaVista supports the use of wildcard searches. If you insert a * to the right of a partial word, say hydro*, it will find matches for all words beginning with hydro such as hydrocarbon and hydrofoil. Wildcards can also be used to search for pages containing plurals of the search terms as well as to catch possible spelling variations, for example alumin*m will catch both aluminium (UK) and aluminum (US).

Tip 10 If you are looking for multimedia files then save yourself time by selecting images, audio or video with the radio buttons on AltaVista's search box and then entering your search.

1   a street map of Edinburgh, Scotland
2   train times between London and Paris
3   the exchange rate of your currency against the US dollar
4   a recipe for chocolate chip or hazelnut brownies
5   video clips of the Beatles
6   sumo wrestler competitions in Japan this year
7   the weather in New York city tomorrow
8   heart disease amongst women
9   New Zealand universities which offer courses in computing
10   Sir Isaac Newton's laws of motion

8   Test your answers using AltaVista.

WRITING   9   Write your own description of how your browser finds the page you want. Use Fig 2 to help you. When you have finished, compare your answer with the listening script to Task 4 on page 198.

Email Protocols

A Find the answers to these questions in the following text.

1   Name three different email protocols mentioned in the text.
2   Which email protocol is used to transfer messages between server computers?
3   Why is SMTP unsuitable for delivering messages to desktop PCs?
4   Name two host-based mail systems mentioned in the text.
5   Where are email messages stored in an SMTP system?
6   What happens when you use your Web mail account to access a POP3 mailbox?
7   Give an advantage and a disadvantage of having an option to leave POP3 messages on the server.
8   What are the advantages of using the IMAP4 protocol?

Although the format of a mail message, as transmitted from one machine to another, is rigidly defined, different mail protocols transfer and store messages in slightly different ways. The
5 mail system you're probably used to employs a combination of SMTP and POP3 to send and receive mail respectively. Others may use IMAP4 to retrieve mail, especially where bandwidth is limited or expensive.

10 **Simple Mail Transfer Protocol**
SMTP is used to transfer messages between one mail server and another. It's also used by email programs on PCs to send mail to the server. SMTP is very straightforward, providing only facilities to
15 deliver messages to one or more recipients in batch mode. Once a message has been delivered, it can't be recalled or cancelled. It's also deleted from the sending server once it's been delivered. SMTP uses 'push' operation, meaning that the
20 connection is initiated by the sending server rather than the receiver. This makes it unsuitable for delivering messages to desktop PCs, which aren't guaranteed to be switched on at all times.

Web mail systems use some of the same protocols as client/server mail. Some can access an ISP-based POP3 mailbox, allowing you to read your mail anywhere you can find a browser.

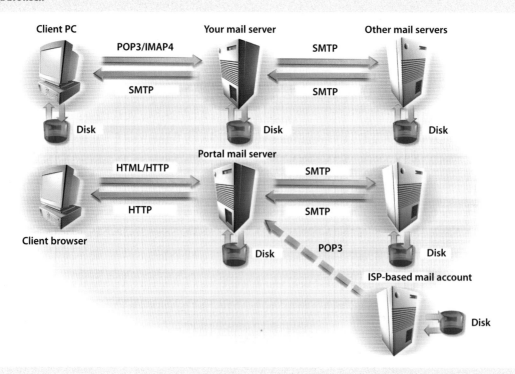

In host-based mail systems, such as Unix and Web
25 mail, SMTP is the only protocol the server uses. Received messages are stored locally and retrieved from the local file system by the mail program. In the case of Web mail, the message is then translated into HTML and transmitted to your
30 browser. SMTP is the only protocol for transferring messages between servers. How they're then stored varies from system to system.

Post Office Protocol

POP is a message-retrieval protocol used by many
35 PC mail clients to get messages from a server, typically your ISP's mail server. It only allows you to download all messages in your mailbox at once. It works in 'pull' mode, the receiving PC initiating the connection. PC-based POP3 mail clients can
40 do this automatically at a preset interval. When you use your Web mail account to access a POP3 mailbox, the mail server opens a connection to the POP3 server just as a PC-based application would. The messages are then copied into your
45 Web mailbox and read via a browser.

Since POP3 downloads all the messages in your mailbox, there's an option to leave messages on the server, so that they can be picked up from different machines without losing any. This does
50 mean that you'll get every message downloaded every time you connect to the server. If you don't clean out your mailbox regularly, this could mean long downloads. When using a Web mail account to retrieve POP3 mail, be careful about leaving
55 messages on the server – if too many build up, each download will take a long time and fill up your inbox. Many Web mail systems won't recognise messages you've already downloaded, so you'll get duplicates of ones you haven't deleted.

60 ### Internet Mail Access Protocol

IMAP is similar in operation to POP, but allows you more choice over what messages you download. Initially, only message headers are retrieved, giving information about the sender and
65 subject. You can then download just those messages you want to read. You can also delete individual messages from the server, and some IMAP4 servers let you organise your mail into folders. This makes download times shorter and
70 there's no danger of losing messages.

[Adapted from 'Using Web-based Email' by Jonathan Bennett, PC Magazine, November 1999]

B Re-read the text to find the answers to these questions.

1 Mark the following statements as True or False:

a Different mail systems transfer emails in different ways.
b IMAP4 requires more bandwidth than the other email protocols.
c SMTP is used for sending emails from a PC to a server.
d SMTP delivers messages one at a time.
e SMTP does not allow a delivered message to be cancelled.
f SMTP is only one of many protocols used to send mail between servers.
g POP protocol allows the user to download one message at a time.

2 Match the terms in Table A with the statements in Table B.

Table A
a SMTP
b 'Push' operation
c POP
d 'Pull' operation
e IMAP

Table B
i An email transfer process in which the connection is initiated by the sending computer rather than the receiving computer.
ii A mail transfer protocol that initially only retrieves the message headers.
iii An email transfer process in which the receiving computer initiates the connection.
iv A simple mail transfer protocol that is used to send messages between servers.
v A message-retrieval protocol that downloads all email messages at the same time.

Websites

STARTER **1** What features make a good website? Make a list of the key features you look for. Then compare your list with others in your group.

2 Study these seven points for evaluating websites. What questions would you ask to evaluate a website on each point?

1 Design
2 Navigation
3 Ease of use
4 Accuracy
5 Up to date
6 Helpful graphics
7 Compatibility

READING **3** **Understanding the writer's purpose** Knowing who the writer is, what their purpose is and who they are writing for can help us to understand a text.

Study these extracts from a text. Decide:

1 What special expertise does the author have in this field?
2 Who are the intended readers?
3 What is the author's purpose?

Title:
Help Web-farers find their way.

Source:
Windows Magazine, E-Business section

Subtitle:
Here are nine ways to make it easy for visitors to navigate your website.

First paragraph:
Your website may be chock full of information about your company and its products, but if visitors to the site can't easily find their way around its pages they may never return. Besides content, the most important aspect of a website is its navigation scheme. Unfortunately, that may also be the most commonly neglected design consideration. These nine site-design pointers will help you build an effective navigation system.

Author information:
Matt Micklewicz offers advice and useful links for Webmasters at his Webmaster Resources site (www.webmaster-resources.com).

4 Work in groups of 3, A, B and C. Summarise the advice in each text you read in one sentence.

Student A Read texts 1 to 3
Student B Read texts 4 to 6
Student C Read texts 7 to 9

1 Trust Text

It's tempting to spice up pages with graphics – but sometimes even a little is too much. If possible your navigation system should be based on text links, rather than image maps or graphical buttons. Studies have shown that visitors will look at and try text links before clicking on graphical buttons.

2 Next Best ALTernative

If you must use a graphical navigation system, include descriptive ALT text captions. The ALT text will make it possible for visitors who use text browsers such as Lynx or who browse with graphics turned off, to find their way around. In addition to the graphical navigation buttons, be sure to include text links at the bottom of every page that provide a clear route to the main areas of your site.

3 Map It

A site map offers a good overview of your site and will provide additional orientation for visitors. It should be in outline form and include all the major sections of your site with key subpages listed beneath those sections. For example, you may group your FAQ, Contact and Troubleshooting pages so they're all accessible from a Support page. It's a good idea to visit a few larger sites to get some ideas on designing an effective site map.

4 Forego Frames

Avoid frames wherever possible. Most veteran browsers dislike them and they can be confusing for visitors who are suddenly presented with multiple scrollbars. If you're committed to using frames on your site, you'd better commit yourself to some extra work too, because you'll have to create a no-frames version of your site for visitors whose browsers don't support frames.

5 Consistency Counts

Don't change the location of your navigation elements, or the color of visited and not-visited links from page to page. And don't get clever with links and buttons that appear and disappear: turning things on and off is usually done as an attempt to let visitors know where they are at a site but more often than not it ends up confusing them.

6 Just a Click Away

Keep content close at hand. Every page on your site should be accessible from every other one within four clicks. You should regularly reexamine your page structure and links, and make necessary adjustments. People come to your site to find information – don't make them dig for it.

7 Shun Search

Most sites have a search function, but try to discourage its use as much as possible. Even the best search engines turn up irrelevant matches, and visitors may not know how to use yours effectively. Logical, clearly placed links are more likely to help visitors find what they want.

8 Passing Lanes

Provide multiple paths through your site so visitors aren't restricted to one style of browsing. For most sites, a pull-down navigation menu is an easy addition that offers an alternative route through your pages, without wasting space.

9 Overwhelming Options

Don't overwhelm visitors by presenting dozens of places that they can go. A large number of choices is not necessarily a good thing.

Finally, if you feel like curling up with a good book, I recommend Jennifer Fleming's *Web Navigation: Designing the User Experience* from O'Reilly & Associates.

5 Now exchange information orally to complete this table summarising the whole text.

Text	Advice		Text	Advice
1			6	
2			7	
3			8	
4			9	
5				

LANGUAGE WORK   **Giving advice**

Study these examples of advice from the texts you read in Task 4.

You can use the modal verb *should*:

1   Your navigation system *should* be based on text links.

You can use an imperative:

2   *Avoid* frames wherever possible.
3   *Don't change* the location of your navigation elements.

Note that *avoid* is followed by the *-ing* form. For example:

4   Avoid *using* frames.

Had better is for advice which is close to a warning. It indicates something unpleasant will happen if the advice is not taken:

5   If you're committed to using frames on your site, *you'd better* commit yourself to some extra work too.

Other ways to give advice are:

6   *I recommend* Jennifer Fleming's *Web Navigation*.
7   *It's a good idea to* visit a few larger sites.

To make advice more persuasive, you can add the reason for your advice. For example:

It's a good idea to visit a few larger sites [advice] to get some ideas on designing an effective site map [reason].

PROBLEM-SOLVING   6   Evaluate any one of these sites using the seven points listed in Task 2 and any of the advice given on website design in this unit.

www.environment-agency.gov.uk
www.compaq.com
www.abcissa.force9.co.uk/birds
news.bbc.co.uk
www.orange.co.uk

7 With the help of the texts summarised in Task 5, give advice on these aspects of navigation design. Use a variety of ways. Add reasons for your advice where possible.

1 text links
2 graphical buttons
3 ALT text captions
4 site map
5 frames
6 position of navigation elements
7 logical links
8 search function
9 number of links on a page

8 With the help of Unit 12, Task 6, give advice on these features of free Internet Service Providers.

1 Sign up software on CD-ROM
2 Local call rates for online time
3 National call rates for online time
4 Initial set-up fee
5 Web-based mail
6 POP3 email
7 Free Web space
8 Access to newsgroups
9 Customer support
10 Reliable service
11 Multiple ISP accounts

SPEAKING **9** Work in pairs, A and B. Complete your website flowchart with the help of your partner. Do not show your section of the flowchart to your partner but do answer any questions your partner asks. Make sure all links are included in your completed chart.

Student A Your section of the flowchart is on page 186.
Student B Your section of the flowchart is on page 192.

WRITING **10** Write an evaluation of one of the websites listed in Task 6 or a website of your choice.

A Find the answers to these questions in the following text.

1 What languages were derived from SGML?
2 What type of language is used to structure and format elements of a document?
3 Name two metalanguages.
4 What elements of data is XML (but not HTML) concerned with?
5 What is meant by the term 'extensible'?
6 What makes XML a more intelligent language than HTML?
7 What does the HTML markup tag <p> indicate?
8 Why are search engines able to do a better job with XML documents?
9 What type of website is particularly likely to benefit from XML?

XML Takes on HTML

Standard Generalized Markup Language (SGML) is the language that spawned both HTML (HyperText Markup Language) and XML (eXtensible Markup Language). SGML is not a true language, it is a
5 metalanguage, which is a language from which you can create other languages. In this case, it is the creation of a markup language (a system of encoded instructions for structuring and formatting electronic document elements).

10 HTML is an application-specific derivation of SGML. It is a set of codes, generally used for webpages, that creates electronic documents according to rules established by SGML. HTML is a language that is all about the presentation of your
15 information, not what the actual data is. You can, therefore, say that HTML is a presentation language.

XML is a subset of SGML, but it is also, like SGML, a metalanguage. XML defines a specific method for
20 creating text formats for data so that files are program independent, platform independent, and support internationalisation (able to read different languages, etc.) In fact, because XML is an extensible language, you don't even have to have a
25 browser to interpret the page. Applications can parse the XML document and read the information without any human intervention.

XML, unlike HTML, is concerned with the identity, meaning and structure of data. XML is extensible
30 because it lets website developers create their own set of customised tags for documents. This ability to define your own tags is the main feature of XML, and it is what gives developers more flexibility.

By defining your own markup tags, you can
35 explicitly define the content in the document. This makes XML a more intelligent markup language than HTML. For example, in HTML, you could have a paragraph tag <p> preceding a paragraph about baseball. Your Web browser sees this tag and
40 knows to present the following text as a paragraph. All your browser knows about the text, however, is that it is text; it doesn't know that it is specifically about baseball. In an XML document, you could define a <BASEBALL> tag to refer specifically to
45 the text in the paragraph in your document. This way, when your XML browser examines the document, the document knows what data it contains, and that makes the content more

XML – INFORMATION ABOUT INFORMATION

How the same information is marked up for HTML and XML web pages. **Source: IBM**

Rendering HTML

```
<p> <b>Mrs. Mary McGoony</b>
<br>
1401 Main Street
<br>
Anytown, NC 34829</p>
```

HTML tags describe how the data will appear on screen.

```
@ BROWSER

Mrs. Mary McGoony
1401 Main Street
Anytown
NC34829
```

Rendering XML

```
<address>
<name>
<title>Mrs.</title>
<first-name>Mary</first-name>
<last-name>McGoony</last-name>
</name>
<street>1401 Main
Street</street>
<city>Anytown</city>
<state>NC</state>
<zipcode>34829</zipcode>
...
</address>
```

XML tags contain information about what the data is.

intelligent. Search engines that make use of XML
50 data can do a better job of finding the pages you
are looking for because of the intelligent nature of
XML content.

XML, by design, does not deal with how the data is
displayed to the end user. Because HTML is a
55 presentation language, XML documents use HTML
tags to help handle the visual formatting of the
document. Also, you can use XML in your HTML
documents to provide metadata, which is data
about data in the document.

60 XML will do to the Web and e-commerce what
HTML originally did to the Internet. XML and its
associated applications have the potential to blow
the roof off the Internet and how we do business.

[Adapted from 'XML Takes On HTML', Smart Computing Guide
Series Volume 8 Issue 1, January 2000. Graphic from 'Web learns
new language', Guardian Online, Thursday November 25 1999]

B Re-read the text to find the answers to these questions.

1 Mark the following statements as True or False:

a HTML is no longer useful for creating webpages.
b SGML is more complex than XML.
c XML files can only be used on Unix systems.
d XML files can only be read by browser programs.
e HTML is a markup language.
f Internet searches will be better with XML files.

2 Match the terms in Table A with the statements in Table B.

Table A	
a	Metadata
b	Metalanguage
c	HTML
d	XML
e	Markup language

Table B	
i	Extensible markup language
ii	A coding system used for structuring and formatting documents
iii	Data about data
iv	An example of a page presentation language
v	A language from which you can create other languages

Webpage Creator

| STARTER | 1 | Match these reviews of websites to their titles. Some words and parts of words have been omitted. Try to replace them. |

1   Babelfish
2   Fish I.D.
3   Strangely Satisfying
4   Sheepnet
5   Download.com

Reviews of website

a

If you want to buy old comics, old toys such as plastic fish for your bath, nodding dogs for your car and many other strange and bizarre items, this site is for you.

b

Everything you ever wanted to know or didn't want to know about *****. Breeds, pictures and fascinating facts including the information that almost all

***** are either white or black. Guaranteed to raise a smile.

c

Trouble identifying *****? This site has pictures, quizzes, a special corner for children and a handy reference on all kinds of aquatic life. It also hosts a discussion area for all concerned with the marine environment.

d

Can't remember the word in English or any other major language? Try ***** for an instant translation. Easy to use. Just type in your text. Choose the

language you want and select 'Search'. You can also translate websites. Only drawback is that you get a literal translation. Don't expect ***** to cope with slang or idioms.

e

Whether it's demos, full freeware or shareware products you are looking for, the chances are you'll be able to find it here. Rather usefully the site also contains all major drivers and development tools – pretty much anything you could ever want to help you get the most out of your PC really. Well worth a visit whatever it is you're looking for.

| 2 | Carry out a survey of websites built by your classmates. Complete this table for at least 4 sites. |

NAME			
SITE NAME			
TOPIC			
SITE ADDRESS			
WHY SPECIAL			
LAST UPDATED			

LISTENING **3** 🎧 John lives in North Dakota. Here he talks about his website.

Listen to the recording and complete this table about his site.

NAME	
SITE NAME	
TOPIC	
SITE ADDRESS	
WHY SPECIAL	
LAST UPDATED	

4 🎧 Listen to the recording again to find the answers to these questions.

1 Why did John choose this topic?
2 What package is Netscape Composer a part of?
3 What previous experience did he have of website creation?
4 What's the price of his 'free' domain name?
5 What does he mean by '*Yahoo! just seems to swallow submissions*'?
6 What do you think Yahoo! Clubs are?
7 List 4 tips he gives for other website builders.
8 List 4 website addresses he mentions.

LANGUAGE WORK *would*

Study this extract from the interview.

I What do you intend to do next with your site?

J I'm going to update the Movie Journal section and *I'd like* to build in new links.

Why doesn't John say, 'and I'm going to build in new links'?

Later John says,

J ... my favorite site *would* have to be the Internet Movie Database.

Why doesn't he say, 'my favorite site has to be the Internet Movie Database'?

We use *would* in conditional sentences.
For example:
If you spilled coffee on the keyboard, you *would* damage it.

Often the condition is implied, not stated.
For example:
(*If I had time*) I'd like to build in new links.
(*If I had to make a choice*) my favorite site would have to be the Internet Movie Database.

What is the implied condition in this extract?
I would look at other sites too for good ideas.

5   Complete the gaps in this dialogue with *will* or *would* or the reduced forms *'ll* and *'d* where appropriate.

A   What ....¹ you do when you finish your diploma?

B   I ....² like to take a course in multimedia.

A   How long ....³ that take?

B   If I choose the certificate, it ....⁴ take 6 months but if I chose the master's, it ....⁵ take a full year.

A   What ....⁶ be the advantage of the master's?

B   I guess I ....⁷ have better job prospects.

A   When ....⁸ you decide?

B   It depends on my finals. If I do well, I ....⁹ go for the master's.

6   Link these statements using an appropriate time clause. Refer to Unit 13, Language Work, if you need help.

1   a   You click the mouse pointer on the file.
    b   It is highlighted.

2   a   You cannot save a file.
    b   You name it.

3   a   The files are transferred.
    b   The transfer is graphically displayed.

4   a   Remove any floppies.
    b   You close down the computer.

5   a   The OK button is clicked.
    b   The copying process begins.

6   a   The percentage of file transferred is displayed.
    b   Your browser downloads from the Internet.

7   a   The virus is not activated.
    b   You open the infected file.

8   a   You repair a PC.
    b   Ensure the machine is disconnected.

9   a   Don't open an email attachment.
    b   You have virus-checked it.

10 a   You add memory.
    b   Change the BIOS settings.

WORD STUDY	7

Definitions and collocations Fill in the gap in these definitions. Check your answers with Unit 11, Task 4.

1   A .... is an interface enabling dissimilar networks to communicate.

2   A .... is a hardware and software combination used to connect the same type of networks.

3   A .... is a network transmission path handling major data traffic.

4   A .... is a special computer directing messages when several networks are linked.

5   A .... is a number of computers and peripherals linked together.

6   A .... is a network connecting computers over a small distance such as within a company.

7   A .... is a powerful computer storing data shared by all the clients in the network.

8   A .... is a network computer used for accessing a service on a server.

9   A .... is a simple computer comprising a processor and memory, display, keyboard, mouse and hard drives only.

10   A .... is an electronic device connecting all the data cabling in a network.

8

Link each word in column A with a word which it often occurs with from column B. In some cases, more than one link is possible.

A		B
1	bulletin	board
2	domain	button
3	file	engine
4	graphical	link
5	mobile	map
6	search	message
7	site	name
8	synchronous	page
9	text	phone
10	web	transmission

SPEAKING   **9**   Work in pairs, A and B. You both have information about some websites. Find out if your partner can suggest a website to help you with your problems. He or she may not have an answer to all your problems.

Student A   Website information and problems are on page 186.
Student B   Website information and problems are on page 192.

10   Visit a website of your choice. Take notes on any special features. You may refer to these seven points for evaluating a site listed in Unit 14, Task 2, if you wish. Then make a short presentation to the class on what makes your chosen site special.

1   Design
2   Navigation
3   Ease of use
4   Accuracy
5   Up to date
6   Helpful graphics
7   Compatibility

WRITING   **11**   Write a brief evaluation of the site you chose in Task 10. If you are unable to access a website, list the good and bad points of this home page.

12 **Planning your website** Study this flowchart for planning a website. Use it as the basis for a short text providing advice on website planning. Your text should have three paragraphs corresponding to the 3 stages in this diagram:

1 Analysis
2 Design and implementation
3 Evaluation

Begin your text like this:
You need to plan your website carefully before you go ahead and create it. There are three stages to the planning process:

KEY QUESTIONS WHEN PLANNING YOUR WEBSITE

Careful planning is essential to maximise the impact of your website. It'll take some effort to achieve, but the results will be worth it.

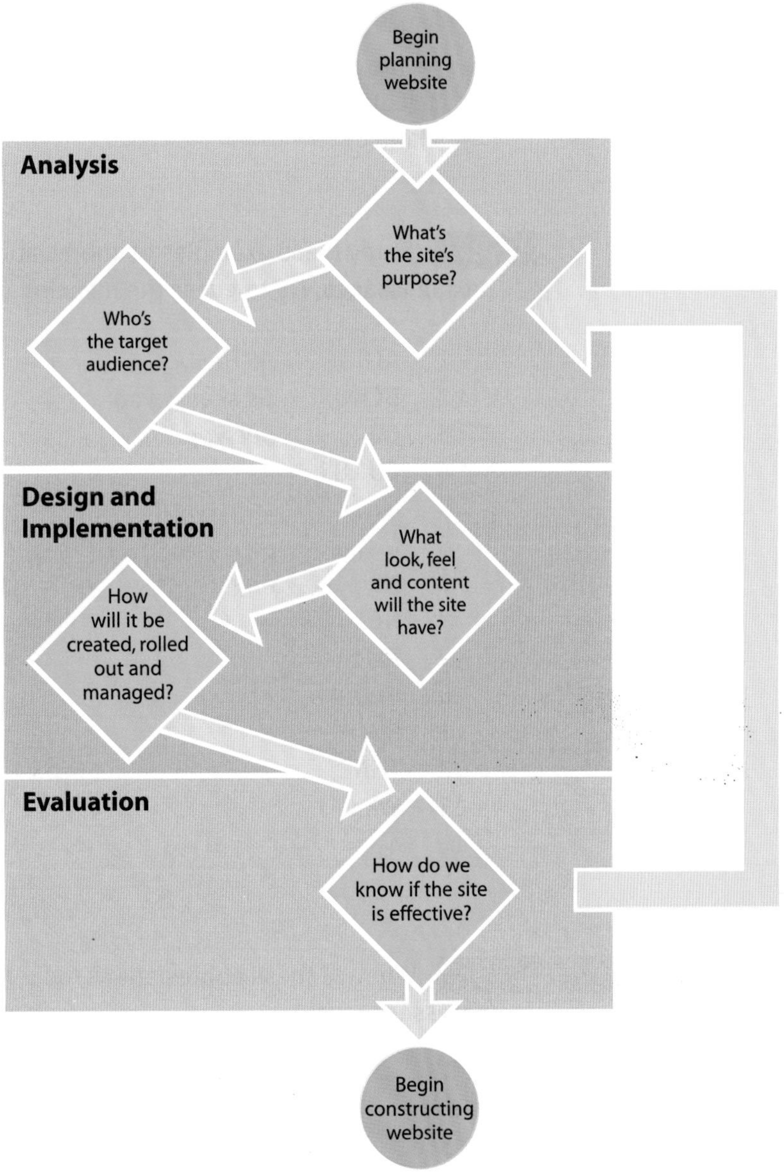

Begin planning website

Analysis

What's the site's purpose?

Who's the target audience?

Design and Implementation

What look, feel and content will the site have?

How will it be created, rolled out and managed?

Evaluation

How do we know if the site is effective?

Begin constructing website

Fig 1
Planning your website

Communications Systems

STARTER | **1** Carry out a survey of mobile phone use amongst your classmates. Find out:

1 How many have mobile phones.
2 What they use them for.
3 What makes they have.
4 How often they use them per day.
5 What additional features their phones have, e.g.
   phone book
   messages
   calls register
   games
   calculator
   alarm call

2 Study these examples of abbreviations used in mobile phone text messages. Try to guess the meaning of the other abbreviations.

1	ATB	*All the best*
2	BCNU	*Be seeing you*
3	CU	*See you*
4	CU L8R	
5	Luv	
6	Msg	
7	NE	*Any*
8	NE1	
9	NO1	
10	PPL	
11	RUOK	
12	THNQ	
13	Wknd	
14	4	

READING | **3** What do these abbreviations mean? Use the Glossary to help if necessary.

GPRS   Wap
HTML   WML
SMS   XML

4   Study this diagram. Find the answers to these questions.

1   What is the predicted Wap phone use by 2005?
2   What developments have made this technology possible?
3   How can you access a favourite website easily?
4   How can one time slot be shared by many users?
5   What peripheral can be attached to some phones?
6   Why cannot Wap phones access all websites?

Fig 1
Wap phone

What is Wap? Wap stands for 'wireless application protocol' which allows users to send emails and access information from the Internet on a mobile phone. This has been made possible by technological advances in 'bandwidths', the amount of data that can be received or sent within a fraction of a second. This means that it can be used for many more purposes than were previously imagined, including video transmission.

Spread Some analysts reckon that Wap phones will overtake PCs as the most common way of surfing the Internet, although PCs will still be used for more complex applications such as spreadsheets and video players.

Lifespan Some industry experts believe that Wap will have a limited lifespan and will quickly be replaced by more sophisticated technology, such as General Packet Radio Service (GPRS) and the Universal Mobile Telecommunications System (UMTS). GPRS increases the bandwith still further and allows you to send up to ten times more information than Wap technology. However, users will still be limited by the size and resolution of the screen on which the data is received. One analyst, Jakob Nielsen, advises companies to forget Wap and plan, instead, for the next generation of phones. He believes that mobile phones are going to become more like palmtop computers.

SMS (Short Message Service) allows the phone to predict likely words from the keystrokes entered with up to 10,000 pre-programmed words which it recognises.

Websites and email addresses have to be keyed in via the numbers, though frequent addresses can be stored in the memory and accessed with a key stroke.

Some phones come with miniature keyboards that slot into the bottom.

HOW DATA IS SENT

Data, cut into packets, is sent in sequence to the receiver, which builds them back together.

One time slot can be shared at the same time by many users.

The user is always on-line but is only charged for the amount of data transmitted.

Language A Wap phone cannot dial into every website. The language of the Web is HTML – hypertext markup language. Wap operates on WML – wireless markup language, so Wap phones can only read pages written in WML. Because the screen on a Wap phone is so small that you are unable to read a normal webpage, WML pages tend to consist of small chunks of information. Soon, however, most webpages will be written in XML – extensible markup language. This can be programmed to ensure that every phone or PC receives transmissions in the language it understands.

Internet Wap allows you to deliver online services to a handheld computer. People are also expected to use Waps to access online news and financial services, sports scores and entertainment information, most of which you should be able to reach by scrolling down a set menu bar. You will also be able to book tickets by Wap.

Email Sending emails is likely to be the application that is used most often, as people will be able to pick up messages at any time from anywhere in the world.

Games Gambling and games, some of which can be downloaded, are also expected to be popular with users. But you can, of course, use the Wap to make regular phone calls.

LANGUAGE WORK | **5** | **Predictions 1: certainty expressions** Rank these predictions according to how certain the speakers are. Put the most certain at the top of your list and the least certain at the bottom. Some predictions can have equal ranking.

a   Wap phones will revolutionise the way we communicate.
b   Wap phones may revolutionise the way we communicate.
c   It's likely Wap phones will revolutionise the way we communicate.
d   It's unlikely Wap phones will revolutionise the way we communicate.
e   It's expected Wap phones will revolutionise the way we communicate.
f   It's probable Wap phones will revolutionise the way we communicate.
g   It's possible Wap phones will revolutionise the way we communicate.
h   Wap phones will certainly revolutionise the way we communicate.

Study this list of certainty expressions:

MORE CERTAIN → LESS	Verbs	Adverbs	Adjectives
	will, will not	certainly	certain
		likely, unlikely	expected
		probably	probable
	could, may, might	possibly	possible

6   🎧   Listen to this expert talking about future developments in computing. Note down his predictions. Then listen again and note the certainty expressions he uses.

7   The recording was made in 2000. Has the situation changed today? Discuss in groups.

8 Make statements about these predictions for the next 5 years. Use the certainty expressions above. For example:

All school children in my country will have mobile phones.
I think it's unlikely that all school children will have mobile phones but it's probable that many of the older pupils will have them.

1 ATM machines will use iris recognition rather than PIN numbers. You will get access to your account by looking at the machine.

2 People will vote in elections online.

3 Taxis will be robot-controlled.

4 TV journalists will be able to transmit what they see by using sensors in their optic nerves.

5 There will be more robots than people in developed countries.

6 Most computers will be voice-controlled.

7 Mobile phones will replace computers as the commonest way to access the Internet.

8 English will no longer be the commonest language for websites.

9 Email will be replaced by a voice-based system.

10 Computers will become more powerful.

PROBLEM-SOLVING **9** Try to write these two text message poems in standard English. Compare your versions with others in your group.

txtin iz messin,
mi headn'me englis,
try2rite essays,
they all come out txtis.
gran not plsed w/letters
shes getn,
swears i wrote better
b4comin2uni.
& she's african.

Hetty Hughes

14: a txt msg pom.

his is r bunsn brnr bl%,
his hair lyk fe filings
w/ac/dc going thru.
I sit by him in kemistry,
it splits my @oms
wen he :-)s @ me.

Julia Bird, Poetry Book Society

SPEAKING **10** **The world of connectivity** Work in pairs, A and B. Complete your diagram classifying computer-mediated communication systems with the help of your partner.

Student A Your diagram is on page 187.
Student B Your diagram is on page 193.

11 Together work out where to add these forms of communication to your diagram.

pagers
MOOs

WRITING **12** **The Global Positioning System** Link each set of sentences to make one sentence. You may omit, change or add words as required. Then form your sentences into two paragraphs to make a description of how the GPS works and its uses.

1 The GPS was developed by the US military.

It was designed to pinpoint locations.

The locations could be anywhere in the world.

2 It consists of 24 earth-orbiting satellites.

The satellites are 17,000 kms. above the earth.

3 Each satellite broadcasts a coded radio signal.

The signal indicates the time and the satellite's exact position.

4 The satellites have atomic clocks.

The clocks are accurate to one second every 70,000 years.

5 A GPS receiver contains a microprocessor.

The microprocessor compares signals.

The signals are from at least three satellites.

The microprocessor calculates the latitude, longitude and altitude of the receiver.

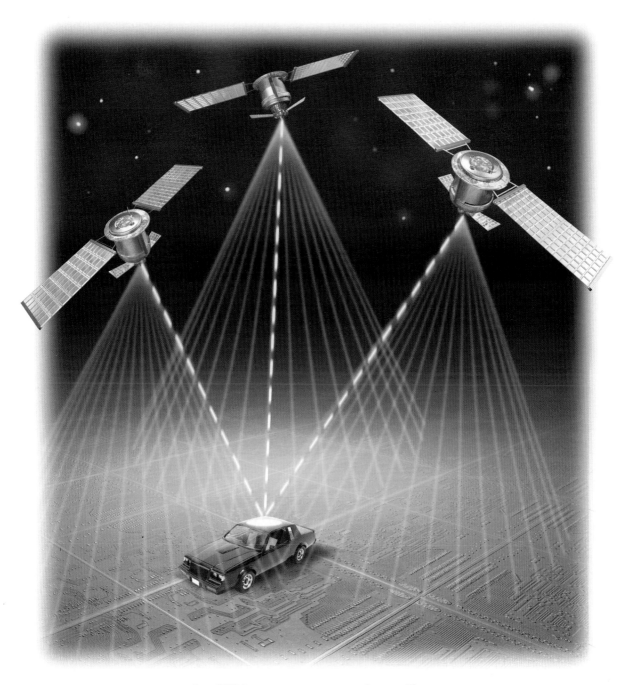

6   GPS has many uses apart from military uses.

GPS can be used for orienting hikers.

GPS can be used for aiding the navigation of ships.

GPS can be used for tracking trucks and buses.

GPS can be used for locating stolen cars.

A Find the answers to these questions in the following text.

1 How many channels does an ISDN system commonly use?
2 What types of wireless systems are named in the text?
3 What do PCs connected to a satellite system use to send data?
4 What types of cables are used in cable network systems?
5 What may need to be upgraded when using a shielded DSL system?
6 Compared to the downstream bandwidth, the upstream bandwidth in an ADSL line is:
   a larger
   b smaller
   c the same
7 Which type of broadband service is the cheapest?

Broadband Communications

Integrated Services Digital Network (ISDN)

ISDN services can be carried over existing telephone network infrastructure to terminal adapters (TAs) in the client machine. A common ISDN interface
5 standard has a digital communications line consisting of three independent channels: two Bearer (B) channels, each at 64Kbit/s, and one Data (D) channel at 16Kbit/s. The D channel is used to carry
10 signalling and supervisory information to the network, while the B channels carry the data and can be linked to provide a 128Kbit/s data channel.

Wireless connections

15 The wireless alternatives come in two forms: satellite and cellular. Satellite systems require the use of a modem to maintain the upload. Downstream bandwidth is provided via a dedicated
20 satellite dish, connector hardware and proprietary software.

Cellular systems use assigned radio frequencies and are based around a network of transmitters that are arranged
25 in a cellular network, much like cellular mobile phone systems.

The cable alternative

Cable companies can also offer affordable broadband services over copper coaxial
30 or fibre infrastructure networks. The

connection is shared by several customers on a branch, so actual connection rates are variable, unlike ISDN and DSL.

Digital Subscriber Line (DSL)

35 DSL technology capitalises on the existing network of copper infrastructure, but allows digital signals to be carried rather than analogue. It allows the full bandwidth of the copper twisted-pair
40 telephone cabling to be utilised.

With splitter-based services, the DSL signal is pulled out from the phone line as it enters your premises and is wired separately to a DSL modem. This
45 involves additional hardware and installation by the service provider at the customer site. The shielded option involves no installation, but the telephone company's equipment and some of your
50 equipment might need upgrading.

With Asymmetric Digital Subscriber Line (ADSL), most of the duplex bandwidth is devoted to the downstream direction, with only a small proportion of
55 bandwidth being available for upstream. Much Internet traffic through the client's connection, such as Web browsing, downloads and video streaming, needs high downstream bandwidth, but user
60 requests and responses are less significant and therefore require less on the upstream. In addition, a small proportion of the downstream bandwidth can be devoted to voice rather than data,
65 allowing you to hold phone conversations without requiring a separate line.

DSL-based services are a very low-cost option when compared to other solutions offering similar bandwidth, so they can
70 be made available to the customer at extremely competitive prices.

[Adapted from 'Infrastructure for Streaming Video', PC Magazine, July 1999]

B Re-read the text to find the answers to these questions.

1 Match the terms in Table A with the statements in Table B.

Table A

a	ISDN
b	TA
c	Data channel
d	Bearer channel
e	DSL
f	Splitter-based services
g	ADSL

Table B

i	DSL system that separates the digital signals from the analogue signals
ii	Digital channel used to carry ISDN signalling and supervisory information to the network
iii	Device installed on a PC to allow it to receive ISDN signals
iv	Integrated Services Digital Network
v	Asymmetric Digital Subscriber Line
vi	Digital channel used to carry ISDN data
vii	Digital Subscriber Line

2 Mark the following statements as True or False:
a ISDN can only operate over a special digital telephone line.
b Two ISDN channels can be combined to give the user double the bandwidth.
c Computers connected to a satellite system do not need a modem.
d Cellular networks work in a similar way to mobile phone systems.
e DSL systems require a special digital telephone line.
f DSL systems use analogue signals.
g You need a separate line to hold normal phone conversations on an ADSL system.

Computing Support

STARTER **1** Find out what the most common computing problems are for your classmates and how they get help with these problems. Use this form to record your results.

Problems	Sources of help
viruses	
monitor problems	
mouse problems	
computer hangs	
printer problems	
computer crashes	
other	

Ask questions like these:

1 Have you ever had a problem with a virus?
2 Have you ever had a software problem?
3 What kind of problem?
4 What did you do about it?
5 How did you get help?

LISTENING **2** Study this form used by computing support staff in a help centre to record problems reported by phone. What questions would you ask to get this information? Compare your questions with your partner.

3 🎧 Now listen to this recording of a computing support officer, David, advising a user. Complete the form to record the main details of the problem.

4 🎧 Listen again to note the questions asked by David. How do they compare with the questions you produced in Task 2?

Help Desk Technician's Name		Date of Call	Time Commenced

Reported By	Address		

Under Warranty	Service Tag No.	Make	Model

Processor	RAM Size	Operation System	Network Type

Problem Description	Diagnosis	

Cleared by Phone	Job Number	

Passed to Supplier	Time	Ref. No.	

Passed to Third Party	Time	Ref. No.	

Requires Visit	Time	Visiting Technician	

Equipment Required	Comments (e.g. case history)	

Fig 1

| LANGUAGE WORK | Diagnosing a fault and giving advice |

Study this extract from the recording:
It sounds as if you may have a driver fault.

David is trying to identify the cause of the problem. He's not completely certain. Compare these versions:
1 It sounds as if you may have a driver fault.
2 It sounds as if you have a driver fault.
3 You probably have a driver fault.
4 You must have a driver fault.

Each statement is more certain than the one before. You can use the expressions studied in Unit 16 to show how certain you are. When you are sure you know the cause of the problem, you can use *must* as in example 4.

Study this further extract:
You could try to reinstall the sound drivers.

Here David is giving advice. Advice usually follows diagnosis.

In Unit 14, you studied these ways to advise someone to do something.

Using an imperative:
1 *Try* to reinstall the sound drivers.

Using the modal verb *should*:
2 You *should* reinstall the sound drivers.

Using *recommend*:
3 *I recommend* reinstalling the sound drivers.

You can also use:
4 *I recommend that* you reinstall the sound drivers.
5 *I advise you to* reinstall the sound drivers.

Or phrases such as:
6 *The best thing to do* is to reinstall the sound drivers.

5   Study these steps to take before you phone for technical support. Rewrite each one using the clue given.

1 Reboot your PC to see if the problem recurs. (should)
2 Use your PC's on-board diagnostic and repair tools. (recommend)
3 Record the details of the problem so you can describe it accurately. (good idea)
4 Note your system's model name and serial number. (advise)
5 Keep a record of hardware and software you've installed along with any changes you've made to settings. (strongly recommend)
6 If you think hardware may be at fault, figure out how to open the case. (should)
7 Visit the vendor's website and check the FAQs. (best thing)
8 Avoid phoning in peak times. (never)
9 Have your system up and running and be near it when you call. (good idea)
10 When you reach a technician, tell him or her if you may have caused the problem. (advise)

6 Diagnose these faults and provide advice on each problem.

1 My laser printer produces very faint copies.
2 When I print, three or four sheets come through the printer at the same time.
3 My spreadsheet does not seem to add up correctly.
4 Everything I type appears in capitals.
5 My PC is switched on but the monitor screen is blank.
6 I tried to print a document but nothing came out of the printer.
7 My monitor picture is too narrow.
8 My monitor screen flickers.
9 My mouse responds erratically.
10 The time display on my computer is one hour slow.
11 When I print out a page, the first two lines are missing.
12 My computer sometimes stops and reboots itself. The lights dim at the same time.

PROBLEM-SOLVING   7 As a class, find out how many had problems with any of these items of hardware in the last twelve months. Calculate the percentages and compare results with these findings from a national survey.

% of users reporting problems in the last 12 months		
	Your class	Other users
Hard disk		17
CD-ROM drive		15
Modem		15
Mouse		13
Monitor		12
Motherboard		11
Sound card		7
Cooling fan		7
Floppy disk drive		7
Battery		7
Keyboard		6
Power supply		6
Memory		5
Graphics/Video		5
CPU		3

SPEAKING   **8**   Work in pairs, A and B. Advise your partner on his/her computing problem. Ask for advice on your computing problem. Complete this form for your partner's problem.

Student A   Your problems and advice are on page 187.
Student B   Your problems and advice are on page 193.

Help Desk Technician's Name		Date of Call	Time Commenced

Reported By		Address	

Under Warranty	Service Tag No.	Make	Model

Processor	RAM Size	Operating System	Network Type

Problem Description	Diagnosis

Cleared by Phone	Job Number

Passed to Supplier	Time	Ref. No.

Passed to Third Party	Time	Ref. No.

Requires Visit	Time	Visiting Technician

Equipment Required	Comments (e.g. case history)

Fig 2

WRITING   **9**   Study this brief report made from the completed form for Task 3. Then write your own report of one of the Task 8 problems using the form you completed for that task. Your report should have these sections:

paragraph 1   user's hardware, software, network connections, etc.
paragraph 2   description of the problem and the possible diagnosis
paragraph 3   action taken

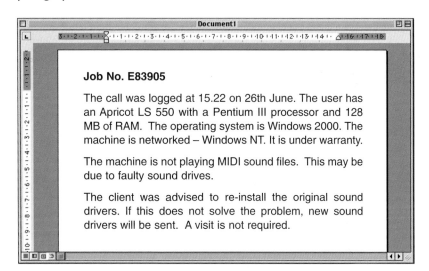

Job No. E83905

The call was logged at 15.22 on 26th June. The user has an Apricot LS 550 with a Pentium III processor and 128 MB of RAM. The operating system is Windows 2000. The machine is networked – Windows NT. It is under warranty.

The machine is not playing MIDI sound files. This may be due to faulty sound drives.

The client was advised to re-install the original sound drivers. If this does not solve the problem, new sound drivers will be sent. A visit is not required.

SPECIALIST READING

A   **Find the answers to these questions in the text and table below.**

1   Give two reasons why server computers often have connected hard drives.

2   Why is RAID 0 particularly suited to imaging and scientific work?

3   What is the advantage of using drive mirroring?

4   To store data, RAID levels higher than 1 require:
   a   At least double the disk space
   b   Up to about a third more disk space
   c   Less than half the disk space

5   Where is the backup data stored in a RAID 5 system?

6   Which levels of RAID can reconstruct data lost in failed drives from the backup data spread across the remaining drives in the array?

7   Which level of RAID is the fastest?

RAIDING HARD DRIVES

Server manufacturers connect hard drives to ensure that data is adequately protected and can be quickly accessed. Computer engineers call such an arrangement a
5 redundant array of inexpensive disks (RAID). By arranging drives in sets, users hope to take advantage of the higher seek times of smaller drives. A special hard disk controller, called a RAID controller, ensures
10 that the RAID array's individual drives are seen by the computer as one large disk drive.

   RAID schemes are numbered, with higher numbers indicating more elaborate
15 methods for ensuring data integrity and fault tolerance (or a computer's ability to recover from hardware errors).

B   **Re-read the text and table to find the answers to these questions.**

1   Match the terms in Table A with the statements in Table B.

Table A
a   RAID
b   RAID controller
c   An array
d   Striping
e   Mirroring
f   Check data

[Raid Technology Primer, PC Advisor, 4 January 1996; Windows Sources, April 1994]

	Raid 0	Raid 1	Raid 2–4	Raid 5
Fault tolerance?	No	Yes	Yes	Yes
What does it do?	Called disk striping, RAID 0 breaks data into blocks that are spread across all drives rather than filling one before writing to the next.	Called disk mirroring, RAID 1 uses two identical drives: data written to the first is duplicated on the second.	RAID 2–4 are rarely used and simply enhance the striping provided by other RAID levels.	Called striping with parity, the popular RAID 5 writes error-correcting, or parity, data across available drives.
What are the advantages?	Improved disk I/O throughput – the fastest of all RAID configurations as it distributes read/write operations across multiple drives. Good for imaging and scientific work where speed is important.	If either drive fails, the other continues to provide uninterrupted access to data.	2 enhances 0 by using additional drives to store parity data. 3 enhances 2 by requiring only one error-checking drive. 4 builds on 3 by using larger block sizes, boosting performance.	If one drive fails, its contents are recovered by analysing the data on the remaining disks and comparing it with the parity data.
What are the disadvantages?	The failure of any single drive means the entire array is lost.	Inefficient use of disk space.	Uses dedicated disks to store the parity data used to reconstruct drive contents. Up to 30% more hard disk space needed than 1.	Not as fast as RAID 0.

Table B

i   Information which is used to restore data if one of the RAID drives fail

ii A process of spreading data across a set of disks

iii Redundant array of inexpensive disks

iv A set

v   A device for controlling a set of hard disks

vi The technique of writing the same information to more than one drive

2   Mark the following statements as True or False:

a   Small disks tend to have lower seek times than large disks.

b   RAID controllers make one large hard disk act like a set of small disks.

c   In RAID systems, one disk is filled with data before the next disk is used.

d   A higher numbered RAID array uses a more elaborate system to protect the integrity of data.

e   RAID 0 provides good data recovery.

f   Small file servers do not usually use RAID level 3.

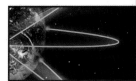

UNIT 18

Data Security 1

STARTER   **1**   What stories do you think followed these headlines? Compare answers within your group.

1   Love bug creates worldwide chaos.
2   Hackers crack Microsoft software codes.
3   Web phone scam.

2   What other types of computer crime are there? Make a list within your group.

READING   **3**   Study this diagram which explains how one type of virus operates. Try to answer these questions.

1   What is the function of the Jump instruction?
2   What are the main parts of the virus code?
3   What is the last act of the virus?

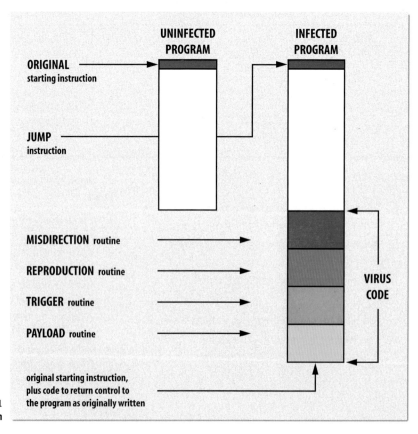

Fig 1
How a virus infects a program

4 Scan this text to check your answers to Task 3. Ignore any parts which do not help you with this task.

THE ANATOMY OF A VIRUS

A biological virus is a very small, simple organism that infects living cells, known as the host, by attaching itself to them and using them to reproduce itself. This often causes harm to the host cells.

Similarly, a computer virus is a very small program routine that infects a computer system and uses its resources to reproduce itself. It often does this by patching the operating system to enable it to detect program files, such as COM or EXE files. It then copies itself into those files. This sometimes causes harm to the host computer system.

When the user runs an infected program, it is loaded into memory carrying the virus. The virus uses a common programming technique to stay resident in memory. It can then use a reproduction routine to infect other programs. This process continues until the computer is switched off.

The virus may also contain a payload that remains dormant until a trigger event activates it, such as the user pressing a particular key. The payload can have a variety of forms. It might do something relatively harmless such as displaying a message on the monitor screen or it might do something more destructive such as deleting files on the hard disk.

When it infects a file, the virus replaces the first instruction in the host program with a command that changes the normal execution sequence. This type of command is known as a JUMP command and causes the virus instructions to be executed before the host program. The virus then returns control to the host program which then continues with its normal sequence of instructions and is executed in the normal way.

To be a virus, a program only needs to have a reproduction routine that enables it to infect other programs. Viruses can, however, have four main parts. A misdirection routine that enables it to hide itself; a reproduction routine that allows it to copy itself to other programs; a trigger that causes the payload to be activated at a particular time or when a particular event takes place; and a payload that may be a fairly harmless joke or may be very destructive. A program that has a payload but does not have a reproduction routine is known as a Trojan.

5 Now read the whole text to find the answers to these questions.

1 How are computer viruses like biological viruses?
2 What is the effect of a virus patching the operating system?
3 Why are some viruses designed to be loaded into memory?
4 What examples of payload does the writer provide?
5 What kind of programs do viruses often attach to?
6 Match each virus routine to its function.

Routine		Function	
1	misdirection	a	does the damage
2	reproduction	b	attaches a copy of itself to another program
3	trigger	c	hides the presence of the code
4	payload	d	decides when and how to activate the payload

7 How does a Trojan differ from a virus?

LANGUAGE WORK   **Cause and effect (1)**

What is the relationship between these actions?

1   A date or event occurs.
2   The trigger routine runs.
3   The payload routine activates.
4   The hard disk is wiped.

These events form part of a cause and effect chain. We can describe the links between each event in a number of ways:

Using *cause + to* V or *make + V*.

1   A date or event occurs which *causes* the trigger routine *to run*.

2   A date or event occurs which *makes* the trigger routine *run*.

Putting the events in sequence and using a causative verb.

3   The trigger routine runs, which *activates* the payload routine.

Using a *when* clause.

4   *When the trigger routine runs*, the payload routine activates.

6   Describe the effects of these viruses and other destructive programs.

1   logic bomb – example
    a   A dismissed employee's name is deleted from the company's payroll.
    b   A logic bomb is activated.
    c   All payroll records are destroyed.

2   *Form* (Boot sector virus)
    a   A certain date occurs.
    b   A trigger routine is activated.
    c   Keys beep when pressed and floppies are corrupted.

3   *Beijing* (Boot sector virus)
    a   The operator starts up the computer for the one hundred and twenty-ninth time.
    b   A trigger routine is activated.
    c   The screen displays, 'Bloody! June 4, 1989'.

4   *AntiEXE*
    a   The infected program is run.
    b   The boot sector is corrupted.
    c   The disk content is overwritten.
    d   Data is lost.

5   *Cascade* (File virus – COM files only)
   a   A particular date occurs.
   b   The payload is triggered.
   c   Characters on a text mode screen slide down to the bottom.

6   macro virus – example
   a   An infected document is opened in the wordprocessor.
   b   The virus macro is executed.
   c   The virus code is attached to the default template.
   d   The user saves another document.
   e   The virus code attaches to the saved document.
   f   The saved document is opened in the wordprocessor.
   g   The virus destroys data, displays a message or plays music.

7   Some verbs beginning or ending with *en* have a causative meaning. Replace the words in italics in these sentences with the appropriate form of *en* verb from this list.

enable	encrypt	ensure
encode	enhance	brighten
encourage	enlarge	widen

1   A MIDI message *makes* sound *into code* as 8-bit bytes of digital information.

2   The teacher is using a new program to *give courage to* children to write stories.

3   The new version of SimCity has been *made better* in many ways.

4   A gateway *makes it possible for* dissimilar networks to communicate.

5   You can *convert* data *to secret code* to make it secure.

6   *Make sure* the machine is disconnected before you remove the case.

7   Designers can offer good ideas for *making* your website *brighter*.

8   Electronic readers allow you to *make* the print size *larger*.

9   Programmers write software which *makes* the computer *able* to carry out particular tasks.

10   You can *make* the picture on your monitor *wider*.

PROBLEM-SOLVING   8   Decide in your group what these kinds of computer crime are. Then match the crimes to the short descriptions which follow.

1   Salami Shaving
2   Denial of Service attack
3   Trojan Horse
4   Trapdoors
5   Mail bombing
6   Software Piracy
7   Piggybacking
8   Spoofing
9   Defacing
10   Hijacking

a   Leaving, within a completed program, an illicit program that allows unauthorised – and unknown – entry.

b   Using another person's identification code or using that person's files before he or she has logged off.

c   Adding concealed instructions to a computer program so that it will still work but will also perform prohibited duties. In other words, it appears to do something useful but actually does something destructive in the background.

d   Tricking a user into revealing confidential information such as an access code or a credit-card number.

e   Inundating an email address with thousands of messages, thereby slowing or even crashing the server.

f   Manipulating programs or data so that small amounts of money are deducted from a large number of transactions or accounts and accumulated elsewhere. The victims are often unaware of the crime because the amount taken from any individual is so small.

g   Unauthorised copying of a program for sale or distributing to other users.

h   Swamping a server with large numbers of requests.

i   Redirecting anyone trying to visit a certain site elsewhere.

j   Changing the information shown on another person's website.

| **SPEAKING** | **9** | Work in pairs, A and B. You both have details of a recent computer crime. Find out from your partner how his/her crime operated and its effects. Take notes of each stage in the process. |

Student A   Your computer crime is on page 187.
Student B   Your computer crime is on page 193.

| **WRITING** | **10** | Using your notes from Task 9, write an explanation of the computer crime described by your partner. When you have finished, compare your explanation with your partner's details on page 187 or 193. |

WHEN YOU HAVE FINISHED THE READING SECTION ON THE FOLLOWING PAGES, COME BACK TO THESE ADDITIONAL EXERCISES

3   Mark each of the following statements with True or False:

a   A message encrypted with a public key can be decrypted by anyone.
b   To send a secure message you must know the recipient's public key.
c   Secure messages are normally encrypted using a private key before they are sent.
d   A message can be reconstructed from its MAC.
e   Two message can often have the same MAC.
f   A digital certificate is sent to a client in an encrypted form.
g   A digital certificate should be signed by a trusted digital-certificate issuer.
h   A MAC is used to check that a message has not been tampered with.

4   Put the following sentences, about sending a secure email, in the correct order:

a   The message is decrypted with the recipient's private key.
b   The message is received by the recipient.
c   The message is encrypted with the recipient's public key.
d   The message is sent by the sender.

Safe Data Transfer

A Find the answers to these questions in the following text.

1 What does data encryption provide?
  a privacy
  b integrity
  c authentication
2 A message encrypted with the recipient's public key can only be decrypted with
  a the sender's private key
  b the sender's public key
  c the recipient's private key
3 What system is commonly used for encryption?
4 What is the opposite of 'encrypt'?
5 A message-digest function is used to:
  a authenticate a user
  b create a MAC
  c encrypt a message
6 What information does a digital certificate give to a client?

Secure transactions across the Internet have three goals. First, the two parties engaging in a transaction (say, an email or a business purchase) don't want a third party to be able to
5 read their transmission. Some form of data encryption is necessary to prevent this. Second, the receiver of the message should be able to detect whether someone has tampered with it in transit. This calls for a message-integrity
10 scheme. Finally, both parties must know that they're communicating with each other, not an impostor. This is done with user authentication.

Today's data encryption methods rely on a technique called public-key cryptography.
15 Everyone using a public-key system has a public key and a private key. Messages are encrypted and decrypted with these keys. A message encrypted with your public key can only be decrypted by a system that knows your private
20 key.

For the system to work, two parties engaging in a secure transaction must know each other's public keys. Private keys, however, are closely guarded secrets known only to their owners.
25 When I want to send you an encrypted message,

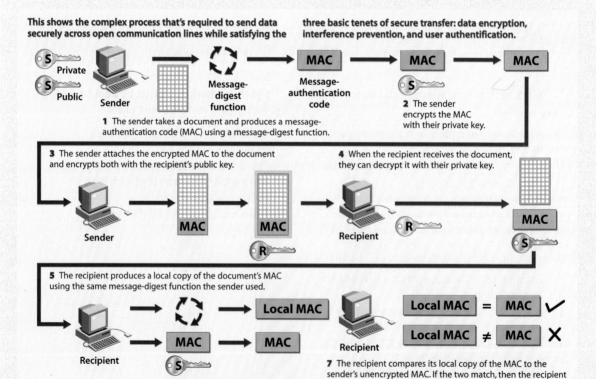

This shows the complex process that's required to send data securely across open communication lines while satisfying the three basic tenets of secure transfer: data encryption, interference prevention, and user authentification.

Private
Public
Sender
Message-digest function
Message-authentication code
MAC   MAC   MAC

1 The sender takes a document and produces a message-authentication code (MAC) using a message-digest function.

2 The sender encrypts the MAC with their private key.

3 The sender attaches the encrypted MAC to the document and encrypts both with the recipient's public key.

Sender
MAC   MAC

4 When the recipient receives the document, they can decrypt it with their private key.

Recipient
MAC

5 The recipient produces a local copy of the document's MAC using the same message-digest function the sender used.

Recipient
Local MAC
MAC   MAC

6 The recipient decrypts the sender's MAC using the sender's public key.

Recipient
Local MAC = MAC ✔
Local MAC ≠ MAC ✗

7 The recipient compares its local copy of the MAC to the sender's unencrypted MAC. If the two match, then the recipient knows the document hasn't been tampered with and that only the sender could have created the original message.

I use your public key to turn my message into
gibberish. I know that only you can turn the
gibberish back into the original message,
because only you know your private key. Public-
30 key cryptography also works in reverse – that is,
only your public key can decipher your private
key's encryption.

To make a message tamper-proof (providing
message integrity), the sender runs each
35 message through a message-digest function. This
function within an application produces a
number called a message-authentication code
(MAC). The system works because it's almost
impossible for an altered message to have the
40 same MAC as another message. Also, you can't
take a MAC and turn it back into the original
message.

The software being used for a given exchange
produces a MAC for a message before it's
45 encrypted. Next, it encrypts the MAC with the
sender's private key. It then encrypts both the
message and the encrypted MAC with the
recipient's public key and sends the message.

When the recipient gets the message and
50 decrypts it, they also get an encrypted MAC. The
software takes the message and runs it through
the same message-digest function that the
sender used and creates its own MAC. Then it
decrypts the sender's MAC. If the two are the
55 same, then the message hasn't been tampered
with.

The dynamics of the Web dictate that a user-
authentication system must exist. This can be
done using digital certificates.

60 A server authenticates itself to a client by
sending an unencrypted ASCII-based digital
certificate. A digital certificate contains
information about the company operating the
server, including the server's public key. The
65 digital certificate is 'signed' by a trusted digital-
certificate issuer, which means that the issuer
has investigated the company operating the
server and believes it to be legitimate. If the
client trusts the issuer, then it can trust the
70 server. The issuer 'signs' the certificate by
generating a MAC for it, then encrypts the MAC
with the issuer's private key. If the client trusts
the issuer, then it already knows the issuer's
public key.

75 The dynamics and standards of secure
transactions will change, but the three basic
tenets of secure transactions will remain the
same. If you understand the basics, then you're
already three steps ahead of everyone else.

[Jeff Downey, Power User Tutor, PC Magazine, August 1998]

B Re-read the text to find the answers to these questions.

1 Match the functions in Table 1 with the keys in Table 2.

Table 1
a   to encrypt a message for sending
b   to decrypt a received message
c   to encrypt the MAC of a message
d   to encrypt the MAC of a digital signature

Table 2
i   sender's private key
ii   trusted issuer's private key
iii the recipient's private key
iv   the recipient's public key

2 Match the terms in Table A with the statements in Table B.

Table A
a   Gibberish
b   Impostor
c   Decipher
d   MAC
e   Tenets
f   Tamper

Table B
i   Message-authentication code
ii   Principal features
iii Meaningless data
iv   Person pretending to be someone else
v   Make unauthorised changes
vi   Convert to meaningful data

▶ Additional exercises on page 129

Data Security 2

STARTER **1** Consider these examples of computer disasters. How could you prevent them or limit their effects? Compare answers within your group.

1 You open an email attachment which contains a very destructive virus.
2 Someone guesses your password (the type of car you drive plus the day and month of your birth) and copies sensitive data.
3 Your hard disk crashes and much of your data is lost permanently.
4 Someone walks into your computer lab and steals the memory chips from all the PCs.
5 Your backup tapes fail to restore properly.

READING **2** Study this table of security measures to protect hardware and software. Which measures would prevent or limit the effects of the disasters in Task 1?

Control Access to Hardware and Software

* Lock physical locations and equipment.
* Install a physical security system.
* Monitor access 24 hours a day.

Implement Network Controls

* Install firewalls to protect networks from external and internal attacks.
* Password-protect programs and data with passwords which cannot easily be cracked.
* Monitor username and password use – require changes to passwords regularly.
* Encrypt data.
* Install a callback system.
* Use signature verification or biometric security devices to ensure user authorization.

Protect against Natural Disasters

* Install uninterruptible power supplies and surge protectors.

3 Find words or phrases in the table which mean:

1 copies of changes to files made to reduce the risk of loss of data
2 software available for a short time on a free trial basis; if adopted a fee is payable to the author
3 cannot be disrupted or cut
4 put at risk
5 deciphered, worked out
6 protect data by putting it in a form only authorised users can understand
7 a combination of hardware and software to protect networks from unauthorised users
8 observe and record systematically
9 measuring physical characteristics such as distance between the eyes
10 at regular intervals

Backup Data and Programs

* Make incremental backups, which are copies of just changes to files, at frequent intervals.
* Make full backups, which copy all files, periodically.
* To protect files from natural disasters such as fire and flood, as well as from crimes and errors, keep backups in separate locations, in fireproof containers, under lock and key.

Separate and Rotate Functions

* If functions are separate, then two or more employees would need to conspire to commit a crime.
* If functions are rotated, employees would have less time to develop methods to compromise a program or system.
* Perform periodic audits.

Protect against Viruses

* Use virus protection programs.
* Use only vendor-supplied software or public domain or shareware products that are supplied by services that guarantee they are virus-free.

LANGUAGE WORK	**Cause and effect (2) links using *allow* and *prevent***

What is the relationship between these events?	What is the relationship between these events?
1 The scanner finds a match for your fingerprint.	4 The scanner does not find a match for your fingerprint.
2 The keyboard is unlocked.	5 The keyboard remains locked.
3 You can use the PC.	6 You cannot use the PC.
1 and 2 are cause and effect. We can link them using the methods studied in Unit 18. In addition we can use an *if*-sentence. Note that the tenses for both cause and effect are the same. For example:	**We can show that 4 and 5 are cause and effect using the methods studied in Unit 18. We can also use *therefore*.**
If the scanner finds a match for your fingerprint, the keyboard is unlocked.	The scanner does not find a match for your fingerprint, *therefore* the keyboard remains locked.
2 allows 3 to happen. We can link 2 and 3 using *allow* or *permit*.	**5 prevents 6 from happening. We can link 5 and 6 using *prevent* or *stop*.**
The keyboard is unlocked, *allowing/permitting* you *to use* the PC.	The keyboard remains locked, *preventing* you *(from) using* the PC.
	The keyboard remains locked, *stopping* you *(from) using* the PC.

4   Put the verbs in brackets in the correct form in this description of how smart cards work.

Smart cards prevent unauthorised users ....[1] (access) systems and permit authorised users ....[2] (have) access to a wide range of facilities. Some computers have smart card readers ....[3] (allow) you ....[4] (buy) things on the Web easily and safely with digital cash. A smart card can also send data to a reader via an antenna ....[5] (coil) inside the card. When the card comes within range, the reader's radio signal ....[6] (create) a slight current in the antenna ....[7] (cause) the card ....[8] (broadcast) information to the reader which ....[9] (allow) the user, for example, ...[10] (withdraw) money from an ATM or ....[11] (get) access to a system.

5   Decide on the relationship between these events. Then link them using structures from this and earlier units.

1   Anti-virus program
   a   A user runs anti-virus software.
   b   The software checks files for virus coding.
   c   Coding is matched to a known virus in a virus database.
   d   A message is displayed to the user that a virus has been found.
   e   The user removes the virus or deletes the infected file.
   f   The virus cannot spread or cause further damage.

2   Face recognition
   a   You approach a high-security network.
   b   Key features of your face are scanned.
   c   The system matches your features to a database record of authorised staff.
   d   Your identity is verified.
   e   You can log on.
   f   Your identity is not verified.
   g   You cannot use the system.

3   Voice recognition
   a   Computers without keyboards will become more common.
   b   These computers are voice-activated.
   c   The user wants to log on.
   d   She speaks to the computer.
   e   It matches her voice to a database of voice patterns.
   f   The user has a cold or sore throat.
   g   She can use the system.
   h   Stress and intonation patterns remain the same.

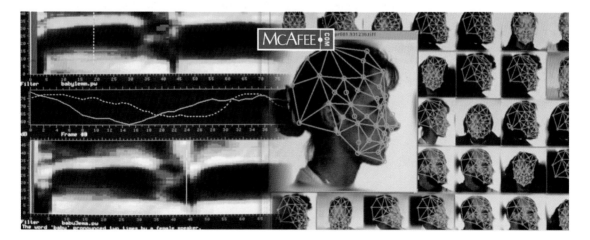

PROBLEM-SOLVING **6** Study these illustrations for two forms of security scanning. Write your own captions for each of the numbered points.

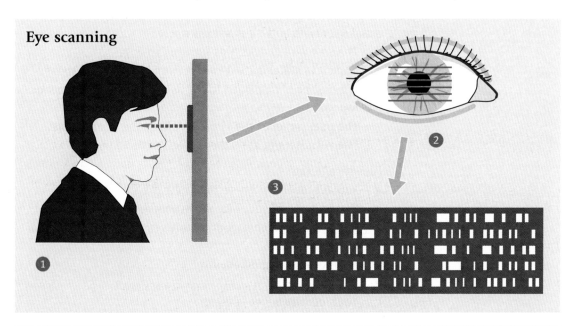

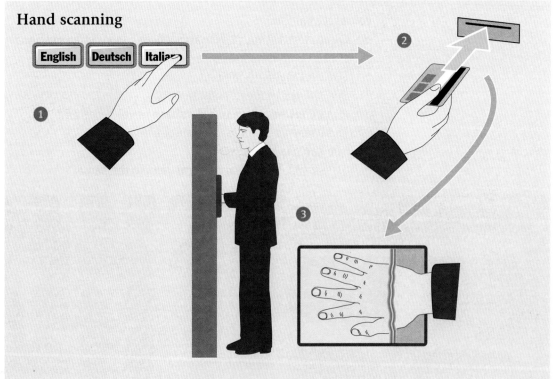

Fig 1
Scanning technology

SPEAKING **7** **Backups** Work in pairs, A and B. You each have details of one form of backup. Explain to your partner how your form of backup works. Make sure you understand the form of backup your partner has. Ask for clarification if anything is unclear.

Student A Your information is on page 180.
Student B Your information is on page 194.

WRITING **8** **Firewalls** Study this diagram of a firewalled network system. Write a description of how it operates. You may need to do some research on firewalls to supplement the diagram. Your description should answer these questions:

1 What is its function?
2 What does it consist of?
3 How are the firewalls managed?
4 How does it control outgoing communications?
5 How does it prevent external attack?

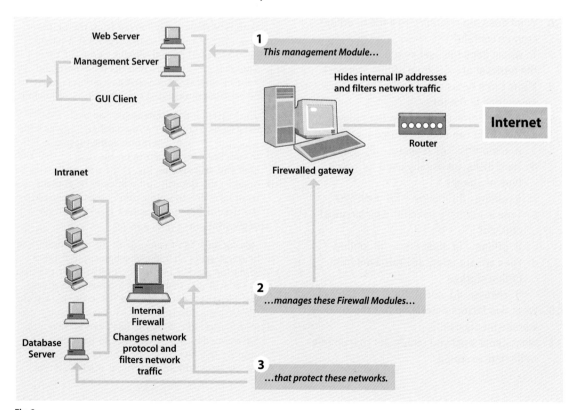

Fig 2
How a firewall works

Backup HSM and Media Choice

A Find the answers to these questions in the following text.

1 What factor determines which type of storage is used to store a file in an HSM system?

2 Complete the following table using information from the text.

Storage Type	Media	Speed
		very fast with quickest access speed
	optical	
offline		

3 What happens to data that is not accessed for a long time?

4 How does the system record that a file is in near-line storage?

5 What happens when a user tries to access a file in near-line storage?

6 What does the reference to a file in offline storage contain?

7 To whom does the user send a request for the retrieval of a file from offline storage?

8 Name three types of magnetic tape mentioned in the text.

9 Select the correct answers in the following:
   a How long can data be stored on tape?
      i) 6 months   ii) 2 years   iii) 10 years
   b Hard disks are usually used for which type of storage?
      i) offline   ii) online   iii) near-line
   c Tape is normally used for which type of storage?
      i) offline   ii) near-line   iii) online
   d Files are automatically retrieved from offline storage
      i) always   ii) sometimes   iii) never

10 What two factors determine the choice of storage media used?

11 What items must you remember to maintain while data is stored?

Near-line and offline storage (often called Hierarchical Storage Management) is the modern way of dealing with current storage needs. Hard disks are becoming cheaper, but data storage
5 requirements are higher, so its better to plan for HSM than assume disks can continually be added to systems.

HSM is essentially the automatic movement of data between media, the media type used
10 depending on when it was last accessed. Many software and hardware vendors have HSM solutions, and all are based on the same basic techniques.

The most common HSM setup is where there's
15 online storage (the hard disk), near-line storage (some sort of fast media from where a file can be quickly retrieved), and offline storage (slower media that might take some time for files to be recovered, but it is cheaper for a long-term
20 storage). This arrangement is the major thrust of today's systems. Most of the time these systems will comprise optical media for near-line and tape media for offline storage.

Data is automatically moved from the online
25 disk to the near-line optical media if it hasn't been accessed for a definable period of time. This is typically three months (depending on your business). This near-line system is likely to be erasable optical disks in some form of jukebox.

30 The system has to operate on the basis that a user won't know that a file has been moved into near-line storage. Therefore some marker is left in the directory structure on the disk so that the user can still see the file. If the user then tries to
35 open it, the file will automatically be copied from near-line to online storage, and opened for the user. All the user notices is a slight time delay while the file is opened.

Moving data from near-line to offline storage can
40 be done using a similar mechanism, but more often the marker left in the directory for the user to see will just contain a reference. This gives the user the facility to request the file back from the systems administrator, and could have
45 information like 'This file has been archived to offline media' and a reference to the tape number that the file is on. This is then sent to the systems administrator and the file can be recovered from tape in the usual way.

50 Some modern systems have the ability to keep multiple tapes in a tape changer or jukebox

system, so retrieval from offline to online storage can be automatic. However, it is more likely that when a file goes into offline storage it
55 will never be recovered, as it has probably been untouched for several months (again depending on the business). Therefore the requirement to recover from offline to online is reasonably infrequent.

60 The choice of storage media type is a crucial aspect of HSM. The cheapest is undoubtedly tape (be it digital, analogue or digital linear), so this tends to be used for offline storage. However, tape has no guarantee of data integrity beyond
65 one or two years, whereas optical systems, such as CDs, WORMs and MO disks, have much better data integrity over a longer period of time. Depending on the precise application, archiving systems are usually based on the media type
70 that has the best integrity. The major suppliers within the HSM market are totally open about the media that can be used with their software. Current HSM systems support most hardware devices, so you can mix and match media to suit
75 requirements. Given the fact that media choice depends on the length of time you want your data to remain intact, and also the speed at which you want to recover it, the choice for many system managers is as follows.

80 Tape is used for backup systems where large amounts of data need to be backed up on a regular basis. Tape is cheap, integrity is good over the short to medium term, and retrieval from a backup can be made acceptable with good
85 tape storage practices.

Near-line storage should be based on erasable optical disks. This is because access is random, so the access speed to find and retrieve a particular file needs to be fast, and data integrity
90 is also good.

Archiving systems should probably be CD- or WORM-based, as again access speeds are good, media costs are reasonably cheap and, importantly, the integrity of the media over the
95 medium to long term is good.

One important thing to remember with archiving systems is the stored data's format. The data might be held perfectly for 10 or 15 years, but when you need to get it back, it's essential that
100 you maintain appropriate hardware and software to enable you to read it.

[Adapted from 'Backup HSM and media choice' by Phil Crewe, Tape Backup, PC Magazine, May 1996]

B Re-read the text to find the answers to these questions.

1 Mark each of the following statements with True or False:

a Hard disks are still very expensive.
b Near-line storage needs to have a quick access speed.
c Near-line storage is usually some form of jukebox.
d Offline storage needs to have a fast access speed.
e Users are aware that their files have been moved to near-line storage.
f The movement of files between near-line and online storage is automatic.
g The user sometimes has to request files from the systems administrator.
h Files are frequently recovered from offline storage.
I Tape has much better data integrity than optical media.
j It is usually possible to use whatever media you want in an HSM system.

The ex-hacker

STARTER   **1**   Find the answers to these questions as quickly as you can.

1   Which group hacked into Hotmail?
2   Who was 'The Analyser' and what did he do?
3   Which hacker was sent to jail for fraud?
4   What was the effect of the 1996 raid on Scotland Yard?
5   Which of the cases reported here involved teenagers?
6   What did hackers do to the Yahoo! website?
7   What crime was Raphael Gray accused of?

Kevin Mitnick is the hackers' hero. His latest spell in jail was a 46-month sentence for fraud relating to breaking into the systems of several multinational corporations. He was released on condition that he did not have any contact with a computer.

Hotmail, Microsoft's free email service, was hacked into last September, exposing the correspondence of more than 40m users. A group calling itself Hackers Unite posted a Web address with details of how to access any Hotmail account. The service was shut down for five hours.

In March 2000, a Welsh teenager allegedly stole information from more than 26,000 credit card accounts across Britain, the US, Japan, Canada and Thailand, and published the details on the Internet. FBI agents and British police raided the home of Raphael Gray,18, and arrested him and his friend. He has been charged with 10 counts of downloading unauthorised information.

The UK Department of Trade and Industry has twice been prey to hackers, once in 1996 and again in 2000 when a DTI computer was programmed to reroute email. The Home Office investigated nine cases of hacking last year, one of which was the leaking of a report on a murder. In August 1996 hackers ran up a £1m phone bill for Scotland Yard but did not access files.

In 1998 Washington revealed that an Israeli hacker called 'The Analyser' was responsible for 'the most organised attempt to penetrate the Pentagon's computer systems'. He turned out to be Ehud Tenenbaum, 18, who had planted a list of his own passwords in the Pentagon system and passed them to other hackers.

In 1997 hackers got into the Yahoo! website, replacing the homepage with a ransom note demanding the release of their hero, Kevin Mitnick. Unless the demand was met, the note said, a virus would be released in all Yahoo!'s computers. The company dismissed the threat as a hoax, but the 'Free Kevin' slogan continued to appear on other hijacked sites.

In 1997 the son of a fraud squad detective walked free from a court in London after charges of breaching the security of the US air force were dropped. Three years earlier Mathew Bevan, then 19, and a friend, Richard Pryce, 16, used the Internet to gain access to several US military bases. Pryce was fined £1,200 after admitting several other offences.

LISTENING **2** Think about these questions before you listen.

1 How could you hack into a system?
2 How could you stop people hacking into a system?

3 🎧 Now listen to Part 1 of the recording to check your answers to Task 2 and to find the answers to these questions:

1 What was Ralph arrested for?
2 What does he do now?
3 Why does he say people are too trusting?
4 What passwords does he suggest for trying to get into a system?
5 What does a firewall do?
6 What is the advantage of a callback system?
7 To prevent hacking, what sort of passwords should you avoid?
8 What do event logs show?

4 🎧 Now listen to Part 2 of the recording and find the answers to these questions:

1 How did Ralph start thinking about computer security?
2 How did he find the most senior ID in the American company's system?
3 According to Ralph, why do people hack?
4 Why did he and his friend hack?
5 How did the police find him?
6 Why does he say companies should use his services?
7 Do hackers know each other?
8 What's the difference between Hollywood hackers and the real world?
9 How risky is credit card use on the Internet?
10 What advice does he give for people intending to use credit cards over the Internet?

5 🎧 Now listen to both parts again to find the answers to these questions:

1 What evidence did Ralph and his friend leave to show that they had hacked into the American company's system?
2 What is a 'white hat' hacker?
3 What two ways does Ralph give for hacking into a system?
4 What terms does Ralph use to describe someone obsessed by computers?
5 How does he maintain contact with the policeman who arrested him?
6 How does he describe his lack of enthusiasm for the Hollywood hacker?
7 What does he mean by 'It's the retailers who get done'?
8 What's the problem with using smart cards for Internet purchases?

LANGUAGE WORK	Phrasal verbs

A phrasal verb is a verb + preposition combination. For example, *look up, take down, turn over*. Phrasal verbs are common in informal, spoken English. Sometimes they have a more formal one word equivalent, for example, *work out* = determine. Often phrasal verbs have two meanings.	One we can work out from the meaning of the two words separately: She *looked up* at the roof. A special meaning which does not easily relate to the separate meanings of the words: She *looked up* a word in the dictionary.

---

6 Study these phrasal verbs from the Task 1 texts and the recording:

break into	grow up	throw away
get into	phone up	log on
hack into	run up	find out
go about	keep at	track down
set about	shut down	hand over
keep ahead		

Now complete each blank with the appropriate phrasal verb in the correct form. In some cases, more than one answer is possible.

1   Hackers try to .... passwords so they can penetrate a system.
2   Don't .... your password to anyone who asks for it.
3   The police .... Ralph .... by talking to his friends and acquaintances.
4   Some hackers .... systems to get commercially valuable information.
5   When you .... to a network, you have to provide an ID.
6   How do you .... hacking into a system?
7   Hackers may .... , pretending to be from your company, and ask for your password.
8   Never .... your credit card receipts where someone can find them.
9   Ralph was a hacker as a teenager but he's .... now and become more responsible.
10 .... a system is strictly illegal nowadays.
11 It's a constant race to .... of the hackers.

7   Replace the verb in italics with a phrasal verb of similar meaning. All the phrasal verbs required have been used in this book.

1   Don't *discard* your credit card receipts; they could help fraudsters.

2   Trying to *penetrate* computer systems is against the law.

3   The typical hacker is a young person who has not *matured* yet.

4   The best way to *begin* hacking into a system is to try to get hold of a password.

5   If someone *telephones* you and asks for your password, don't *provide* it.

6   Hackers *closed* Hotmail for five hours.

7   Hackers *accumulated* a telephone bill of £1m for Scotland Yard.

8   The difficult thing was to *determine* how the website would look.

9   So you won't forget, *record* the ID number the support technician gives you.

10 *Examine* the manufacturers' websites before you phone for help.

A	**B**	**C**	**D**	**E**
Viruses and other destructive programs	Data protection	Communication systems	Internet	World Wide Web

WORD STUDY | **8**   **Semantic groups** Group these terms into the five headings, A to E, below.

anti-virus software   FTP   passwords
backups   GPS   router
bandwidth   IRC   trigger routine
browser   ISP   Trojan
domain name   hyperlink   URL
encryption   logic bomb Usenet
firewalls   pagers   XML

SPEAKING | **9**   **Role play** Work in pairs. Together make up your own questions on these prompts. Then play the parts of the interviewer and Ralph.

1   first interested in hacking
2   reason for being arrested
3   present job
4   ways to avoid hackers
5   views on Hollywood hackers
6   safe ways of paying for Internet shopping

WRITING | **10**   Write a news item like the short newspaper texts given in Task 1 about Ralph or about any other hacking case known to you.

11 Study this extract from a virus information database. Then make a flowchart to show each step in the method of infection for this virus. Steps 1 and 2 are done for you.

Step 1   An infected .EXE file arrives as an email attachment.
Step 2   The infected .EXE file is opened.

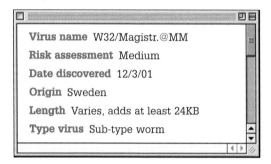

Virus name W32/Magistr.@MM
Risk assessment Medium
Date discovered 12/3/01
Origin Sweden
Length Varies, adds at least 24KB
Type virus Sub-type worm

Method of infection

This is a combination of a files infector virus and an email worm.

The virus arrives as an .EXE file with varying filenames. When you execute the attachment, your machine is infected and in turn is used to spread the virus.

When first run, the virus may copy one .EXE file in the Windows or Windows System directory using the same name but with the final character of the filename decreased by a factor of 1. For example, EHGEDI57.EXE will become EHGEDI56.EXE, TCONTRACT.EXE will become TCONTRACS.EXE.

This copy is then infected and a WIN.INI entry, or registry run key value may be created, to execute the infected file when the system starts up.

This copied executable infects other 32 bit .EXE files in the Windows directory and subdirectories, when run.

Five minutes after the file is opened, the email worm attempts a mailing routine. It creates a .DAT file hidden somewhere on the hard disk. This contains strings of the files used to grab email addresses from address books and mailboxes. The .DAT file name will be named after the machine name in a coded fashion. For example, y becomes a, x becomes b. Numbers are not changed. The worm uses mass mailing techniques to send itself to these addresses. The subject headings, text and attachments will vary. The text is taken from other files on the victim's computer.

This worm may also alter the REPLY-TO email address when mailing itself to others. One letter of the address will be changed. This makes it difficult to warn the victim that their machine is infecting others as the message will be returned to sender.

Software Engineering

STARTER **1** Put these five stages of programming in the correct sequence.

a Design a solution
b Code the program
c Document and maintain the program
d Clarify the problem
e Test the program

2 To which stage do each of these steps belong?

1 Clarify objectives and users
2 Debug the program
3 Write programmer documentation
4 Do a structured walkthrough
5 Select the appropriate programming language

LISTENING **3** You are going to hear an interview between a systems analyst and a hotel owner who wants to introduce a better computer system. What questions do you think the analyst will ask? Make a list; then compare your list with others in your group.

4 🎧 Listen to the recording to compare your list of questions with those asked by the analyst.

5 🎧 Listen again to find the answers to these questions:

1 What system does the hotelier have at present?
2 What problem is there with the existing system?
3 What form of output does the hotelier want?
4 Who will use the new system?
5 Which members of staff will require the most training?
6 What concerns has the hotelier about the new system?
7 What kind of hardware will be required?
8 What is the next step?

Revision: *If X, then Y*

In this section, we will revise structures commonly used in programming. You have met these structures in earlier units but in different contexts.

Study this decision table. It shows the rules that apply when certain conditions occur and what actions to take. Using it, we can make rules like this:

1   *If* a guest stays 3 nights in January and *if* one night is Sunday, *then* charge 2 nights at full price and 1 night at half-price.
2   *If* a guest stays 3 nights and one night is not Sunday and it is not January, *then* charge 3 nights at full price.

CONDITIONS	DECISION RULES	
	1	2
guest stays 3 nights	Y	Y
1 night is Sunday	Y	N
month is January	Y	N
Actions		
charge 3 nights at full price	N	Y
charge 2 nights at full price	Y	N
charge 1 night at half-price	Y	N

6   Now make similar statements about this decision table.

Conditions	Decision Rules					
	1	2	3	4	5	6
guest books bed and breakfast	Y	Y	Y	N	N	N
guest books half-board	N	N	N	Y	Y	N
guest books full-board	N	N	N	N	N	Y
and guest has lunch	N	Y	N	N	Y	–
and guest has dinner	N	N	Y	–	–	–
Actions						
charge rate A	Y	Y	Y	N	N	N
charge rate B	N	N	N	Y	Y	N
charge rate C	N	N	N	N	N	Y
charge menu price less 20%	N	Y	Y	N	Y	N

LANGUAGE WORK   **Do until, do while**

Study these extracts from a program flowchart.
They show iteration or loop structures in which a process
is repeated as long as certain conditions remain true.

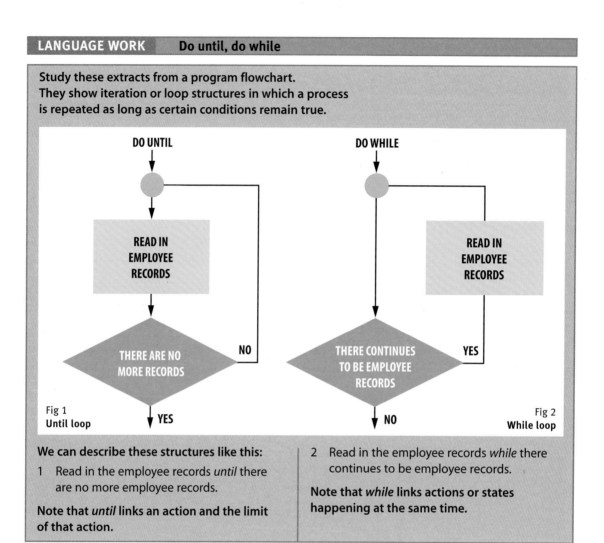

DO UNTIL

READ IN
EMPLOYEE
RECORDS

THERE ARE NO
MORE RECORDS

NO

Fig 1
Until loop

YES

DO WHILE

READ IN
EMPLOYEE
RECORDS

THERE CONTINUES
TO BE EMPLOYEE
RECORDS

YES

NO

Fig 2
While loop

We can describe these structures like this:

1   Read in the employee records *until* there
are no more employee records.

Note that *until* links an action and the limit
of that action.

2   Read in the employee records *while* there
continues to be employee records.

Note that *while* links actions or states
happening at the same time.

7   Link these statements with *while* or *until*, whichever is most
appropriate.

1   Calculate all sales. There are no more sales.
2   Search for records containing the term. There are still records
containing the term.
3   Total extra items. Extra items remain.
4   Search member records. There are no more records.
5   Print all addresses. There are still addresses available.
6   Display client names. There are no names remaining.
7   List all guests. There are no guests left.
8   Total monthly sales. There are no more sales for the current year.

8 Flowcharts are sometimes used for designing parts of programs. Describe this extract from a program flowchart using the structures revised in this unit and the sequence expressions listed in Unit 2, Task 11.

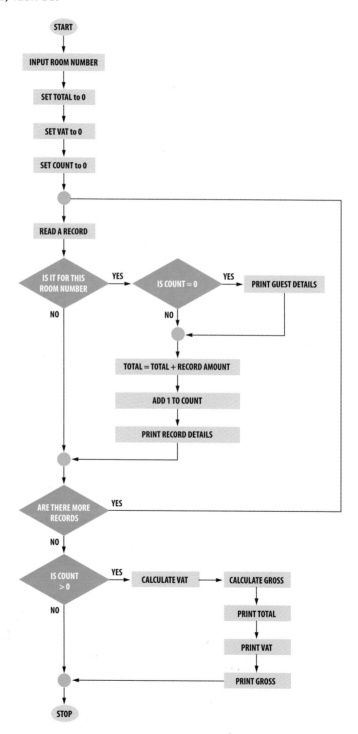

Fig 3
Hotel accommodation invoicing flowchart

SPEAKING **9** Work in pairs, A and B. You each have information about some programming languages. Together decide what would be the most appropriate language to use for each of these situations.

1 A schoolteacher wants his young pupils to learn some basic mathematics by controlling a simple robot.

2 The owner of a small business wants to create a simple database program to keep track of his stock.

3 An engineer wants to develop a program for calculating the stresses in a mechanical device.

4 A student wants to create webpages for a personal website.

5 A systems programmer wants to add some new modules to an operating system.

6 A programmer working for the US army wants to create a program for controlling a new type of weapon.

7 A finance company needs to process data from its branch offices on its mainframe computer.

8 A website designer wants to enable the data on his website to be easily processed by a number of different programs.

9 A student studying artificial intelligence wants to write some programs for a course project.

10 A college lecturer wants his students to learn the principles of programming.

11 A professional programmer wants to create and sell a program for use in language learning.

12 A website designer wants to password-protect a section of a website.

Student A   Your languages are on page 188.
Student B   Your languages are on page 194.

WRITING   **10**   **Converting to a new system** Write a paragraph describing each of these strategies for converting to a new computer system. Explain what its advantages and disadvantages are. The first strategy is described for you as an example.

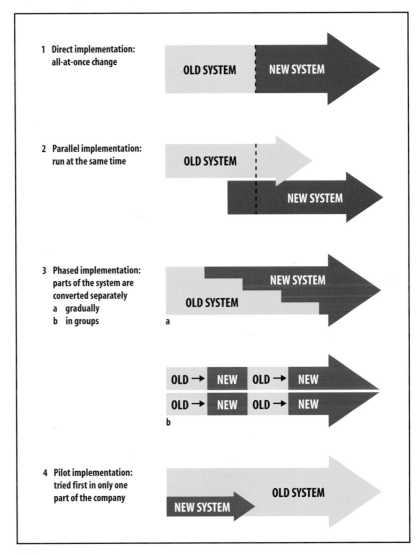

Fig 4
Strategies for converting to a new computer system

1   *Direct implementation:*
    Direct implementation means that the user simply stops using the old system and starts using the new one. The advantage is that you do not have to run two systems at the same time. The disadvantage of this approach is that if the new system does not operate properly, there is nothing to fall back on.

A Find the answers to these questions in the following text.

1   What advantages of using object-oriented programming are mentioned in the text?
2   What are the three key features of OOP?
3   What multimedia data types are referred to in the text?
4   List the different types of triangle mentioned in the text.
5   What feature avoids the problem of deciding how each separate type of data is integrated and synchronized into a working whole?
6   What specific type of rectangle is named in the text?
7   What common properties of a rectangle are mentioned in the text?
8   What features are made quicker by code reusability?

OBJECT-ORIENTED PROGRAMMING

One of the principal motivations for using OOP is to handle multimedia applications in which such diverse data types as sound and video can be packaged together into executable modules.
5 Another is writing program code that's more intuitive and reusable; in other words, code that shortens program-development time.

Perhaps the key feature of OOP is encapsulation – bundling data and program instructions into
10 modules called 'objects'. Here's an example of how objects work. An icon on a display screen might be called 'Triangles'. When the user selects the Triangles icon – which is an object composed of the properties of triangles (see fig. below) and
15 other data and instructions – a menu might appear on the screen offering several choices. The choices may be (1) create a new triangle and (2) fetch a triangle already in storage. The menu, too, is an object, as are the choices on it. Each
20 time a user selects an object, instructions inside the object are executed with whatever properties or data the object holds, to get to the next step. For instance, when the user wants to create a

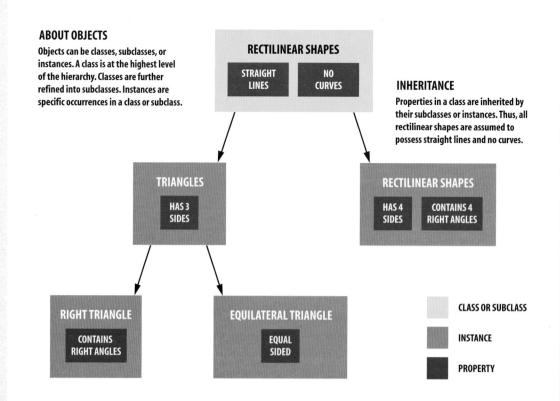

ABOUT OBJECTS

Objects can be classes, subclasses, or instances. A class is at the highest level of the hierarchy. Classes are further refined into subclasses. Instances are specific occurrences in a class or subclass.

RECTILINEAR SHAPES

| STRAIGHT LINES | NO CURVES |

INHERITANCE

Properties in a class are inherited by their subclasses or instances. Thus, all rectilinear shapes are assumed to possess straight lines and no curves.

TRIANGLES

HAS 3 SIDES

RECTILINEAR SHAPES

| HAS 4 SIDES | CONTAINS 4 RIGHT ANGLES |

RIGHT TRIANGLE

CONTAINS RIGHT ANGLES

EQUILATERAL TRIANGLE

EQUAL SIDED

CLASS OR SUBCLASS

INSTANCE

PROPERTY

triangle, the application might execute a set of
25 instructions that displays several types of
triangles – right, equilateral, isosceles, and so on.

Many industry observers feel that the
encapsulation feature of OOP is the natural tool
for complex applications in which speech and
30 moving images are integrated with text and
graphics. With moving images and voice built
into the objects themselves, program developers
avoid the sticky problem of deciding how each
separate type of data is to be integrated and
35 synchronized into a working whole.

A second key feature of OOP is inheritance. This
allows OOP developers to define one class of
objects, say 'Rectangles', and a specific instance
of this class, say 'Squares' (a rectangle with equal
40 sides). Thus, all properties of rectangles – 'Has 4
sides' and 'Contains 4 right angles' are the two
shown here – are automatically inherited by
Squares. Inheritance is a useful property in
rapidly processing business data. For instance,
45 consider a business that has a class called
'Employees at the Dearborn Plant' and a specific
instance of this class, 'Welders'. If employees at
the Dearborn plant are eligible for a specific
benefits package, welders automatically qualify
50 for the package. If a welder named John Smith is
later relocated from Dearborn to Birmingham,
Alabama, where a different benefits package is
available, revision is simple. An icon
representing John Smith – such as John Smith's
55 face – can be selected on the screen and dragged
with a mouse to an icon representing the
Birmingham plant. He then automatically
'inherits' the Birmingham benefit package.

A third principle behind OOP is polymorphism.
60 This means that different objects can receive the
same instructions but deal with them in different
ways. For instance, consider again the triangles
example. If the user right clicks the mouse on
'Right triangle', a voice clip might explain the
65 properties of right triangles. However, if the
mouse is right clicked on 'Equilateral triangle'
the voice instead explains properties of
equilateral triangles.

The combination of encapsulation, inheritance
70 and polymorphism leads to code reusability.
'Reusable code' means that new programs can
easily be copied and pasted together from old
programs. All one has to do is access a library of
objects and stitch them into a working whole.
75 This eliminates the need to write code from
scratch and then debug it. Code reusability
makes both program development and program
maintenance faster.

[Adapted from Understanding Computers Today and Tomorrow,
1998 edition, Charles S. Parker, The Dryden Press]

B Re-read the text to find the answers to
these questions.

1 **Match the terms in Table A with the
statements in Table B.**

Table A
a OOP
b Encapsulation
c Object
d Menu
e Square
f Polymorphism
g Library

Table B
i An OOP property that allows data and program instructions to be bundled into an object
ii A list of choices
iii An OOP property that enables different objects to deal with the same instruction in different ways
iv A reusable collection of objects
v A module containing data and program instructions
vi Object-Oriented Programming
vii A rectangle with equal sides

2 **Complete the following text using words
from the reading text:**

Encapsulation, ... and polymorphism are
key features of .... programming.
Encapsulation allows data and program
instructions to be bundled together in ....
called objects. Inheritance means that specific
.... of a class of objects .... the
properties of the class of objects. Polymorphism
means that instructions are treated differently by
different .... The combination of these
.... features of OOP means that program
code is reusable. This speeds up .... and
.... of programs.

People in Computing

STARTER	**1**

What do the following people in computing do? Compare answers with your partner.

1 Webmaster
2 Help-desk troubleshooter
3 Applications programmer
4 Security specialist
5 Systems programmer

READING	**2**

Work in groups of three: A, B and C. Read your text and complete this table. You may not find information for each section of your table.

	A	B	C
1 job title			
2 nature of work			
3 formal qualifications			
4 personal qualities			
5 technical skills			
6 how to get started			
7 how to make progress			

Text A

How to become a programming expert

The primary requirements for being a good programmer are nothing more than a good memory, an attention to detail, a logical mind and the ability to work through a problem in a methodical manner breaking tasks down into smaller, more manageable pieces.

However, it's not enough just to turn up for a job interview with a logical mind as your sole qualification. An employer will want to see some sort of formal qualification and a proven track record. But if you can show someone an impressive piece of software with your name on it, it will count for a lot more than a string of academic qualifications.

So what specific skills are employers looking for? The Windows market is booming and there's a demand for good C, C++, Delphi, Java and Visual Basic developers. Avoid older languages such as FORTRAN and COBOL unless you want to work as a contract programmer.

For someone starting out, my best advice would be to subscribe to the programming magazines such as Microsoft Systems Journal. Get one or two of the low-cost 'student' editions of C++, Visual Basic and Delphi. Get a decent book on Windows programming. If you decide programming is really for you, spend more money on a training course.

How to become a Computer Consultant

The first key point to realise is that you can't know everything. However you mustn't become an expert in too narrow a field. The second key point is that you must be interested in your subject. The third key point is to differentiate between contract work and consultancy. Good contractors move from job to job every few months. A consultant is different. A consultant often works on very small timescales – a few days here, a week there, but often for a core collection of companies that keep coming back again and again.

There's a lot of work out there for people who know Visual Basic, C++, and so on. And there are lots of people who know it too, so you have to be better than them. Qualifications are important. Microsoft has a raft of exams you can take, as does Novell, and in my experience these are very useful pieces of paper. University degrees are useless. They merely prove you can think, and

will hopefully get you into a job where you can learn something useful. Exams like Microsoft Certified Systems Engineer are well worth doing. The same goes for NetWare Certification. However, this won't guarantee an understanding of the product, its positioning in the market, how it relates to other products and so on. That's where the all-important experience comes in.

Here's the road map. After leaving university you get a technical role in a company and spend your evenings and weekends learning the tools of your trade – and getting your current employer to pay for your exams. You don't stay in one company for more than two years. After a couple of hops like that, you may be in a good position to move into a junior consultancy position in one of the larger consultancy companies. By the age of 30, you've run big projects, rolled out major solutions and are well known. Maybe then it's time to make the leap and run your own life.

How to become an IT Manager

IT managers manage projects, technology and people. Any large organisation will have at least one IT manager responsible for ensuring that everyone who actually needs a PC has one and that it works properly. This means taking responsibility for the maintenance of servers and the installation of new software, and for staffing a help-desk and a support group.

Medium to large companies are also likely to have an IT systems manager. They are responsible for developing and implementing computer software that supports the operations of the business. They're responsible for multiple development projects and oversee the implementation and support of the systems. Companies will have two or three major systems that are probably bought off the shelf and then tailored by an in-house development team.

Apart from basic hardware and software expertise, an IT manager will typically have over five years'

experience in the industry. Most are between 30 and 45. Since IT managers have to take responsibility for budgets and for staff, employers look for both of these factors in any potential recruit.

Nearly all IT managers have at least a first degree if not a second one as well. Interestingly, many of them don't have degrees in computing science. In any case, the best qualification for becoming a manager is experience. If your personality is such that you're unlikely to be asked to take responsibility for a small team or a project, then you can forget being an IT manager. You need to be bright, communicative and be able to earn the trust of your teams. Most of this can't be taught, so if you don't have these skills then divert your career elsewhere.

3 Now share information orally about your text with others in your group to complete the table for each of the occupations described.

4 For which of the careers described are these statements true? More than one career may match each statement.

1   You may work for only a few days or a week for a company.
2   It's a good idea to buy books on languages such as C++.
3   You are responsible for developing and implementing the software a company needs to run its operations.
4   You need to be able to break down a problem into a number of smaller tasks.
5   It's worth paying for a training course if you get serious about this career.
6   Microsoft Certified Systems Engineer is a useful qualification for your career.
7   Your objective is to become self-employed.
8   It's important you have the right personality to lead a team.

LANGUAGE WORK   Requirements: *need to, have to, must, be + essential, critical*

Note how we describe requirements for particular jobs:

1   You *need to* be able to empathise with the person at the other end of the phone.
2   IT managers *have to* take responsibility for budgets.
3   You *must* be interested in your subject.
4   You *must have* worked for at least two years in systems analysis.
5   Experience with mainframes *is essential/critical*.

We can describe things which are not requirements like this:

6   You *don't need to* have a degree in computing science.

We can also treat *need* **as a modal verb and use the negative form** *needn't*:

7   You *needn't* have a degree in computing science.

Have to **is an ordinary verb. Its negative form is made in the usual way:**

8   You *don't have to* be an expert in everything.

Mustn't **has a quite different meaning. It means it is important** *not* **to do something. It is used for warnings, rules and strong advice. For example:**

9   You *mustn't* make unauthorised copies of software.

5   Fill in the blanks with the appropriate form of the verbs, *need to*, *have to* and *must*, to make sensible statements. More than one answer is possible in some examples.

1   Technical qualifications .... to be renewed at intervals to ensure they do not go out of date.
2   You .... become an expert in too narrow a field.
3   You .... to have good communication skills to become an IT Manager.
4   You .... be an expert in hardware to become a programmer.
5   You .... have worked with IBM mainframes for at least two years.
6   You .... be able to show leadership.
7   You .... have a degree but it .... be in computing science.
8   You .... to have experience in JavaScript.
9   You .... be able to use C++.
10   These days you .... study BASIC.

6   Study these requirements for different jobs in computing advertised on the Internet. Then describe the requirements using the methods studied in this unit.

1 Systems Manager/Programmer	2 Support Analyst: IBM Mainframe MVS	3 Programmer
• technical specialist • min. 2 yrs work in systems programming • plus exp. of Netview/automation design & support	• IBM MVS support technician • 1 yr exp. of VTAM, NCP, SSP, NPM, IBM 3745-900 hardware • authorised to work in the EU	• 3 yrs exp. SAP Basic Technical Environment • team player with strong analytical and problem-solving skills • ability to communicate issues and solutions and manage time effectively
4 Webmaster	**5 Cisco Technician**	**6 IS Manager**
• strong Unix experience • able to use HTML, DHTML and JavaScript • knowledge of Shell Scripts	• CCNA qualified • excellent skills in the surrounding technologies • min. 2 yrs work in support	• knowledge of NT and Netware • experience of ERP systems implementation • very strong managerial skills

PROBLEM-SOLVING   7   Work in pairs. Study these job requirements. Then try to match the requirements to the list of jobs which follows.

1	2	3
• at least 5 years (2 at senior level) in: Unix, SYBASE or ORACLE, NT or Windows 2000, Terminal Server, TCP/IP, Internet. • strong project management (2 years) • willingness to travel abroad	• able to manage, lead and develop a team • knowledge of C, C++, Delphi • experience of object-oriented design within a commercial environment • ability to deliver software projects against agreed schedules and within agreed estimates	• proven track record in the delivery of e-solutions in banking environment • knowledge of Unix, NT and Oracle • willingness to travel internationally

4	5	6
• minimum 4 years lifecycle development experience • demonstrable skills using VB, SQL, RDBMS • able to develop core s/w • excellent communication skills	• minimum of 18 months commercial experience of Web development • knowledge of HTML, Java, ASP • full portfolio of URLs as examples	• experience of NT, Exchange, SQL Server, Monitoring Software, Verta, TCP/IP • solid grasp of networking • 2 to 5 years experience in a network environment

a Visual Basic Developer
b IT Engineer (Network & Database)
c Web Developer
d Network Support
e E-commerce Consultant
f Team Leader

SPEAKING   8   Work in pairs, A and B. Choose one of the computing careers from the list provided. Your partner must find out what your job is by asking only Yes/No questions. Your partner cannot ask 'Are you a programmer, etc?'

Student A   Your careers are on page 189.
Student B   Your careers are on page 195.

WRITING **9** Study the c.v. of Paul who was interviewed in Unit 5. Then write your own c.v. in the same way. For the purpose of this task, you can invent experience and assume you have passed all your examinations!

CURRICULUM VITAE
Paul W Cair

Personal details

Date of birth 30/5/79

Address 7 Linden Crescent, Stonebridge EH21 3TZ

email p.w.cair@btinternet.com

Education

1991–1995 Standard grades in Maths, English, Spanish, Computer Studies, Geography, Science, James High School

1996–1997 HNC in Computing Maxwell College

1997–1999 HND in Computing Support Maxwell College

Other qualifications

Jan 2000 CTEC

Work experience

1999–present IT support consultant Novasystems

Novasystems is an IT company that provides a complete range of computing services for its corporate clients.

My experience includes:
- advising clients on IT issues and strategies
- 1st line customer telephone support
- database design
- configuration and installation of hardware and software to clients' specifications
- network administration and implementation
- PC assembly

I have knowledge of these areas:
- Windows 2000 Server/Professional
- Office 97, 2000
- Sage Line 50 & 100
- Windows 95/98
- TCP/IP Networking
- Windows NT4 Server/Workstation
- Exchange Server 5.5
- Veritas Backup Exec for NT

Hobbies and interests

volleyball

Referees

1 Academic Dr L. Thin, IT Department, Maxwell College

2 Work Ms Y. Leith, Personnel Officer, Novasystems

A Find the answers to these questions in the following text.

1   What advice is given for someone who is stuck in a computing support job?
2   What questions should you ask yourself if you are thinking of getting extra training?
3   What computer program is mentioned in the text?
4   Name two ways of studying that are mentioned in the text.
5   What two factors will be affected by your level of experience?
6   Why is it important to become used to answering exam questions?
7   What factors help you decide whether the course will be suitable or cost effective?
8   What happens if you don't upgrade your certification?

Becoming Certified

Suppose you're a support engineer. You're stuck in a job you don't like and you want to make a change. One way of making that change is to improve your marketability to potential employers
5   by upgrading your skill-set. If you're going to train yourself up however, whose training should you undertake? If you need certificates, whose certificates should they be? Even if you get those certificates, how certain can you be that your
10   salary will rise as a result? One solution is the range of certifications on offer from Microsoft.

Microsoft offers a large array of certification programmes aimed at anyone from the user of a single program such as Microsoft Word, to
15   someone who wants to become a certified support engineer. There are a myriad of certificates to study for too. If you're the proud holder of any of those qualifications, then you're entitled to call yourself a Microsoft Certified
20   Professional (MCP).

Once you've decided which track you want to take, you should consider just how qualified you already are in terms of experience and knowledge. Will you need to go and take some
25   courses with a training company, or are you the type who can make good use of self-study materials? How much time do you genuinely have to devote towards this? Will your employer pay for your course? Will it grant you leave to go and
30   do the course – assuming you can find one – on either a full-time or part-time basis?

The key question here is experience. This will not only influence the amount of work you'll have to do to get up to speed for the exams, it could also
35   mean the difference between passing or failing the exam.

While you're busy learning all you need to know for your certification, the practice exams are an absolute godsend. They show you the type of
40   questions you'll encounter, and they familiarise

you with the structure of the exam. This is
essential if you want to pass: the exams have time
limits, and you need to get used to answering the
requisite number of questions within the allotted
45 time. It's as simple as that.

If you decide a training course will help you out,
don't let the title of a course alone convince you
that it will be suitable or cost effective. Find out
exactly what the course offers and whether there
50 are pre-requisites for attendants. You should also
find out what the training company is prepared to
do if attendants don't have the minimum
knowledge necessary to be on the course.

As exams are replaced by 'updated' ones, you
55 need to upgrade your certification to stay current.
Ultimately it's your responsibility to make sure you
stay up to date. If you don't, you lose your
certification until you take an update.

As a support engineer, you get the satisfaction of
60 knowing that you passed a tough test, and the
happy knowledge that your network manager is
sweating a bit over the fact that you could be
head-hunted at any time.

QUALIFICATIONS

65 • **Microsoft Certified Systems Engineer
(MCSE)**

MCSEs design, install, support and troubleshoot
information systems. MCSEs are network gurus,
support technicians and operating system
70 experts.

• **Microsoft Certified Solution Developer
(MCSD)**

MCSDs use development tools and platforms to
create business solutions.

75 • **Microsoft Certified Product Specialist
(MCPS)**

MCPSes know all about at least one Microsoft
operating system. Some also specialise in other
Microsoft products, development tools or
80 desktop applications.

• **Microsoft Certified Trainer (MCT)**

MCTs teach others about Microsoft products
using the Microsoft Official Curriculum at
Microsoft Authorised Technical Education
85 Centres.

B Re-read the text to find the answers to
these questions.

**1 Which qualification would be most useful if
you wanted to do each of the following:**

a be an operating system expert
b troubleshoot systems
c teach computing
d design business solutions

**2 Mark the following statements as True or
False:**

a Microsoft offers a large range of certification
programmes to study.
b You must get an advanced certificate before
you can call yourself a Microsoft Certified
Professional.
c All Microsoft training courses involve a
period of full-time study.
d Practice exams allow you to become familiar
with the structure of the exams.
e You can decide on the suitability of a course
by its title.
f It is your responsibility to make sure that
your certification is kept up to date.
g Gaining a certificate is likely to make you
more attractive to other employers.

[Adapted from Becoming Certified by David Moss, Network Pro
Section of PC Pro Magazine, November 1997]

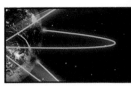

Recent Developments in IT

1 Study these predictions of developments in Information Technology from 1997. Which, if any, have come true? How likely are the others to come true? Give reasons for your decisions and compare answers with your partner.

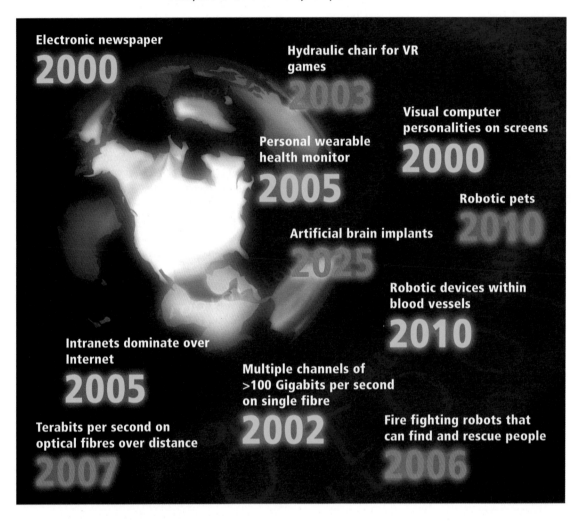

Electronic newspaper
2000

Hydraulic chair for VR games
2003

Visual computer personalities on screens
2000

Personal wearable health monitor
2005

Robotic pets
2010

Artificial brain implants
2025

Robotic devices within blood vessels
2010

Intranets dominate over Internet
2005

Multiple channels of >100 Gigabits per second on single fibre
2002

Terabits per second on optical fibres over distance
2007

Fire fighting robots that can find and rescue people
2006

2 Study the texts on recent developments in one area of Information Technology, A, B or C, as your teacher directs and make brief notes on the main points in each of the two texts.

A Domestic appliances
B Avatars
C Robotics

A1

Licence to chill

Barcodes in the packaging of groceries will soon be replaced with radio-frequency tags that can be read at a distance and with greater reliability. As well as indicating what the product is, the data in the tags will include additional information such as the 'best before' date and even nutritional data. Now, imagine that a fridge could read these tags and keep track of the items placed there.

If an item is about to exceed its 'use by' date, the fridge tells you, and you can either use it or throw it out. Fancy something different for dinner? No problem, ask the fridge to suggest some menus based on the ingredients it knows you have in stock. Or tell the fridge the menu you require and it will provide you with a shopping list of the items you don't have or order the items via email. This is the Screenfridge from Electrolux.

But why 'Screenfridge'? On the door is a touch-sensitive panel or screen that provides a means of communicating with the users. For many households, life revolves around the kitchen. This is the assumption Electrolux made in designing the Screenfridge. The same screen is a messaging centre. Since the fridge is equipped with a microphone, speaker and video-camera, you're not limited to textual information. The fridge is connected to the Internet, so it can be used to send and receive email or you could surf the Web to find a new recipe.

Many people have a TV in the kitchen, but if you already have a screen on the fridge, why clutter up the work surface with a TV? Call the Screenfridge's TV mode and watch your favourite programme on the fridge. The Screenfridge can be interfaced to a surveillance camera to check out visitors or to keep an eye on the children. Finally, the Screenfridge can perform some of the household management tasks normally associated with a PC. For example, it has a diary, address pad and a notepad.

A2

Talking to the washing

A washing machine that can communicate with the Internet using its own built-in mobile phone has been launched by Ariston.

The margherita2000.com washing machine will be able to send breakdown reports for repair and download new washing cycles from its own website. And the householder will be able to control the washing cycle remotely using a mobile phone or by logging on to the machine's own website.

But the importance of the machine is that it is the first of a line-up of Web-connected domestic appliances that will be able to talk to each other using a new open communication system called WRAP – Web-Ready Appliances Protocol.

Ariston will be launching a dishwasher, fridge and oven using WRAP early next year according to Francesco Caio, head of Ariston's parent company Merloni Elettrodomestici. Eventually it will be joined by Leon@rdo, a touch-screen kitchen computer. All the machines will communicate through the house's ring main, and to the Web through the washing machine's mobile phone.

Mr Caio believes he can sell 30 to 50,000 washing machines each year in Europe. But he must leap some big hurdles before the system can become widely accepted. WRAP is a proprietary Merloni standard, and people are unlikely to buy if locked in to Ariston for other networked appliances. Caio claims the standard is open to other manufacturers to adopt but so far none have signed up, whereas the huge Japanese manufacturers are adopting rival systems. The main obstacle is the cost – the margherita2000.com will cost much more than a traditional washing machine.

B1

Dawn of the cyberbabes

Stratumsoft are developing the first electronic virtual assistant, or EVA. If EVAs live up to the developers' claims, they could provide the illusion of personal service without the cost. Call centres, online advertisers and Internet service providers are among the initial targets. Eighty per cent of call centre requests could, Stratumsoft argues, be dealt with by an EVA. E-commerce is another application. 'The best experience you can have as a shopper is personal contact, and EVA is designed to give that', says Stratumsoft's director of marketing.

The technology behind EVA combines two global trends in website design. One, developed out of the computer animation and gaming industry, is the ability to give Web images the impression of three dimensions. The other is the use of dynamic database skills and artificial intelligence-style searching to retrieve information from data banks.

Each EVA can be programmed with information such as a product catalogue, answers to frequently asked questions or an online encyclopaedia. It is also equipped with a search engine to interpret customer requests made in colloquial language. Queries are typed in and answered via on-screen text boxes.

If the EVA does not have an answer, it will interrogate the questioner, record the response, and add the answer to its database for future enquiries. EVAs are not fully animated to imitate human features but they can be programmed to gesture and imitate different moods. An EVA is run via a Java applet – a small, self-contained program coded to download on to any type of personal computer rather than being transmitted over the Internet.

B2

Ananova

Ananova is the world's first digital newsreader. She was created to front an Internet 24 hours a day news service by Digital Animations Group, a Scottish 3D digital entertainment company and PA New Media.

Mark Hird, Director of PA New Media said, 'We have given her a full range of human characteristics after researching the personality most people want to read news and other information. Ananova has been programmed to deliver breaking news 24 hours a day via the Internet, and later on mobile phones, televisions and other digital devices.'

The Ananova character fronts a computer system which is constantly updated with news, sport, share prices, weather and other information. This is converted into speech while another program simultaneously creates real-time animated graphics. This ensures that the virtual newscaster can be on top of the news as it breaks, with very little delay at all. People using the service can also tailor their own news bulletins by using search words to hear the latest information on their chosen subjects.

Mr Hird believes the invention will dramatically change the role of the traditional newscaster, 'In 20 years time we could be seeing that type of job being replaced by computer-generated images.' But not everyone agrees. Professor Bill Scott said that people prefer people to teach them things and in a world where information was increasingly important, an established face was important in terms of public trust. 'You don't get that confidence with computer characters.'

C1

The rise of the robots

Japan produced the first commercially available robotic pet, called Aibo, a small electronic dog that several owners on Aibonet.com describe as part of the family. Aibo is not alone, Dr Thomas Consi of MIT has produced the 'robolobster' which is capable of imitating lobsters' abilities to sense chemicals in the water surrounding them. Researchers at Edinburgh's Mobile Robot Group have made the world's first cyber-cricket.

These machines are important because they demonstrate that simple processes can result in complex behaviours. The robots use 'neural nets', connected processors that have an input level associated with each processor. When an input signal exceeds a certain value, the processor 'fires' a signal to other processors as output. Because neural nets can recognise patterns in data, they can be 'trained' with samples of data which are then revised to improve the response.

The most important crossover, however, is not between animal and robot but between man and machine. Quadriplegics and paraplegics have been testing computer connections for some time to bypass injured nerves, but Professor Kevin Warwick, head of the Department of Cybernetics at the University of Reading, is currently conducting experiments which could lead to more of us becoming cyborgs.

Professor Warwick has previously had a chip fitted into his arm which could activate sensors in doors and computers as he approached. He will soon have another transponder surgically implanted in his arm to record electrical signals controlling his movements, which can be played back so that he is then controlled by a prerecorded self. He predicts that such a technology could, one day, enable us to interact with machines in a completely different way. For example, we could soon be driving cars without steering wheels.

C2

Sporting robots

Each year teams take part in an international football competition. The teams are organised into five leagues and the prize is a cup. Not just any cup, but the Robocup, for the players are all robots. They don't play on turf but the objective is the same, to hit a ball into a goal. The aim behind the Robocup is to promote the development of robots which can work together. Football is a good test of co-operation for any team and the robots are no exception. Although robot footballers are poor competition for a human team, each year their performance gets better and each year the standards expected are raised so that competitors must constantly develop better hardware and software.

The top league is the Sony legged robot division. They use modified versions of the well-known Sony robodog AIBO. A humanoid league will start as soon as there are sufficient two-legged players. The organiser of the Robocup is confident in the future of robotics, 'By mid-21st century, a team of fully autonomous humanoid soccer players will win a soccer game, complying with the official rules of FIFA, against the winner of the most recent World Cup.'

Other sporting events for robots exist. For example, The British Association for the Advancement of Science organises a two-a-side event called Robot Volley Ball. The players' task is simply to return a ball within 60 seconds of its being served. The objective again, is to promote the development of robots which can work co-operatively. The advantages of having robots which can tackle a range of tasks together rather than constructing single expensive robots designed for one task only are obvious.

3 Work in groups of 3, A, B and C. Play these roles in rotation: *Speaker*, *Reporter* and *Judge*.

The *Speaker* explains the main points of one text using only their notes.
The *Reporter* listens carefully and reports back to the Speaker a summary of the main points.
The *Judge* listens carefully to both Speaker and Reporter and points out any mistakes, main points omitted or additions the Reporter has made.
Repeat this activity until you have played all three roles and all of your texts have been covered.

4 List the predictions, if any, in the articles you have read. Have any of them already taken place since the article was written? How likely are the others to happen in the near future? Discuss your answers with others who have read the same texts.

Text	Predictions

LANGUAGE WORK   **Ability:** *can, could, be able to*

Study these ways to describe ability:

1   Swarming robots *can* work together to perform searches.
2   Washing machines *will be able to* report any breakdowns for repair.
3   Imagine *being able to* send music files to your MP3 player without a wire connection.
4   Professor Warwick had a chip fitted into his arm which *could* activate sensors in doors and computers as he approached.
5   Marconi *was able to* send a radio signal from Britain to Newfoundland.

We use *can* and *be able to* to describe ability in the present but *can* is more common. We use *could* for general abilities in the past but *was/were able to* describe an ability on a specific occasion. This table summarises their uses:

Ability		
present	can	be able to
future	X	will be able to
present perfect	X	has/have been able to
-ing form	X	being able to
past (specific action)	X	was/were able to
past (general and with verbs of sensation)	could	X

For past negatives and questions both verbs are possible. For example:

Early computers *could not/were not able to* operate at high speeds.
Could they/were they able to store much data?

5   Complete the blanks in this text using the correct form of *can* or *be able to*. In some cases there is more than one possible answer.

Imagine ....[1] open doors and switch on computers as you approach them. Professor Warwick ....[2] because he had an electronic chip fitted into his arm for a month. He ....[3] demonstrate to the press how computers would greet him with, 'Good morning, Professor Warwick' as he walked past. Next he wants to record the signals from his brain to his arm to see if he ....[4] program a computer to operate his arm. In the long term, this may help people who ....[5] use their limbs. His wife too will have a chip implanted. They hope ....[6] feed messages into each other's brains. According to the Professor, one day we ....[7] communicate directly with machines. If he is right, we ....[8] drive a car from the passenger seat and we ....[9] operate a computer without using a mouse or keyboard. However, there is also the alarming prospect that someone ....[10] hack into your brain.

6 Use an appropriate certainty expression from the list studied in Unit 16 to complete these predictions from the Task 2 texts. More than one answer is possible in some cases.

1 Barcodes .... soon be replaced with radio-frequency tags.

2 People are .... to buy if locked in to Ariston for other networked appliances.

3 If EVAs live up to the developers' claims, they .... provide the illusion of personal service without the cost.

4 Mr Hird believes the invention will dramatically change the role of the traditional newscaster, 'In 20 years' time we .... be seeing that type of job being replaced by computer-generated images.'

5 We .... soon be driving cars without steering wheels.

6 Professor Warwick is currently conducting experiments which .... lead to more of us becoming cyborgs.

7 By mid-21st century, a team of fully autonomous humanoid soccer players .... win a soccer game against the winner of the most recent World Cup.

8 A virtual world populated by virtual humans .... become a very tangible reality.

PROBLEM-SOLVING **7** In groups, choose a domestic appliance and decide what functions an in-built computer would allow it to perform in addition to its basic function. Consider also how it could be marketed. Present your ideas to the rest of the class.

SPEAKING **8** Search for the latest developments in the area of Information Technology you read about in Task 2. Make a summary of your findings to report to the rest of the class. In addition to journals, magazines and newspapers, you can try these websites:

Domestic appliances
www.electrolux.co.uk
www.merloni.com
www.margherita.com
www.aristonchannel.com
www.zanussi.co.uk
www.sony.co.uk

Avatars
www.pulse3d.com
www.kiwilogic.com
www.softimage.com
www.ananova.com
www.biovirtual.com
www.i-dtv.com
www.bt.com/talkzone
www.digimask.com
www.channel5.co.uk

Robotics
www.aibo-europe.com
www.honda.co.jp/english/technology/robot
www.robotbooks.com/Mitsubishi-robots.htm

WRITING **9** Convert your notes for Task 8 into a written report. Your report should have these sections:

1 Area of IT – definition
2 Technology involved – hardware and software
3 Applications
4 Possible future developments

A Find the answers to these questions in the following text.

1 What frustrating problem does Bluetooth solve?

2 Who first developed Bluetooth?

3 In what ways is Bluetooth particularly suited to portable systems?

4 What do Bluetooth devices share with microwave ovens?

5 List some devices that are suitable for use with Bluetooth.

6 Why is Bluetooth suitable for use on aeroplanes?

7 What factors provide security for Bluetooth communications?

8 How is the output power level of the transmitter set?

9 Why is there no collision detection in the Bluetooth specification?

10 Why are all devices on a piconet synchronized and controlled by a master device?

11 What are the consequences of Bluetooth having the following characteristics?

   a It is good at avoiding conflicting signals from other sources.

   b The transmitter output level is kept as low as possible.

   c It uses power-saving modes when devices aren't transmitting.

Bluetooth

As portable computing devices get smarter and more capable, connectivity frustrations increase.

This is where Bluetooth comes in. The brainchild of Ericsson, IBM, Intel, Nokia and Toshiba,
5 Bluetooth is a microwave high-speed wireless link system that's designed to work with portable equipment. To that end, it's low power, very small and very low cost. It uses the same frequencies as existing radio LANs (and, incidentally, microwave
10 ovens) to create a secure 1 Mbit/s link between devices within 10m of each other. These devices can be laptops, PDAs, cellphones, wired telephone access points, even wristwatch devices, headphones, digital cameras and so on. With
15 them, your notebook PC will be able to access your cellular phone – and thus the Internet – without your having to take the phone out of your pocket. Files can be exchanged and communications set up for voice and data
20 between just about any device capable of handling the information.

Bluetooth operates in the unlicensed SM (Industrial, Scientific and Medical) band at 2.45GHz, which is globally available for products.
25 There's 89MHz of bandwidth allocated here, and since Bluetooth is very low power, it actually radiates less than most national and international standards allow non-transmitting devices to leak as part of their normal operation. This is key, as it
30 allows the technology to operate without restriction on aircraft.

As befits their status as radio frequency experts, Ericsson and Nokia developed the RF side of Bluetooth. The link works in a similar way to the
35 IEEE 802.11 wireless networking system, with a packet-switching protocol based on fast-frequency hopping direct sequence spread spectrum. In other words, it constantly switches channel to avoid interference. It changes frequency 1,600
40 times a second through 79 frequency bands. It's expected that this will be so good at avoiding conflicting signals from other sources that the transmission power can be kept very low.

Security is taken care of through the frequency
45 hopping and 40-bit encryption. As the system uses
radio, it can work through some barriers –
briefcases, shirt pockets and desktops, for
example – but it won't carry through office
buildings. The power level of the transmitter can
50 be varied, with feedback from the remote side of
the link used to set the output to the lowest level
commensurate with error-free operation. This
saves power and increases the usable density of
devices. The device can operate at up to 1mW (an
55 optional power amplifier can increase this to
100mW) and the whole lot consumes between
8mA and 30mA at 2.7V. Various power-saving
modes can be used when a device isn't
transmitting, trading off speed of response for
60 battery life. These work with current levels
between 300pA and 60pA.

Within the 10m radius of a unit, up to 10
independent full-speed piconets can operate, with
bandwidth reduced proportionately if more than
65 this are in use. Each can handle up to eight
devices, and can be further subdivided into
separate services: 432Kbit/s full-duplex data,
721/56Kbit/s asymmetric duplex, or 384Kbit/s
third-generation GSM. Each channel can also
70 support three 64Kbit/s full-duplex voice
channels. An optional variation in modulation
technique would double the basic data rate to
2Mbit/s.

Power consumption and cost were very significant
75 factors in Bluetooth's design, and it was decided
not to make the system a fully-fledged LAN. As a
result, there's no collision detection. All devices
on a piconet are synchronized to a master device
and are controlled by it to prevent simultaneous
80 operation on the same frequency. Any device can
be a master, and is elected dynamically when the
link starts up.

The standard is open and royalty-free to members
of the Bluetooth special interest group.

[Adapted from Fast Forward by Rupert Goodwins, PC Magazine,
August 1998]

B Re-read the text to find the answers to these questions.

1 Match the terms in Table A with the statements in Table B.

Table A
a Bluetooth
b SM band
c RF
d IEEE 802.11
e Frequency hopping
f Usable density
g piconet

Table B
i Radio frequency
ii The number of devices that can be used in the same area
iii A microwave high-speed wireless link system designed to work with portable equipment
iv Very low power network links between Bluetooth devices
v An unlicensed frequency range at 2.45GHz
vi A standard for networking systems with a packet-switching protocol
vii Constantly switching channels

2 Mark the following as True or False:

a Bluetooth is an expensive system.
b Bluetooth devices can communicate at a distance of up to 20m.
c The SM band is available throughout the world.
d Bluetooth has a very low radiation level.
e Each Bluetooth connection operates at one fixed frequency.
f Bluetooth signals will pass through walls of buildings.
g The master Bluetooth device is determined when a link is first established.

The Future of IT

1 How do you think developments in IT will affect these areas of life in the next ten years?

1 commerce
2 work
3 the relationship between humans and computers

2 Compare your predictions with others in your group. Try to agree on a ranking from *most likely* to *least likely*.

3 Read the three opening paragraphs of the text below and answer these questions:

1 How does the author justify his claim that we are 'in the midst of convergence'?
2 What will be the difference between computers and humans after 2015?
3 What does he mean by a 'positive feedback loop' in computer development?
4 Why will knowledge of a major language be the only IT skill needed?
5 Which of the author's predictions do you accept?

The future of Information Technology

We are in the midst of convergence. At the hardware layer, computers, phones and consumer electronics are converging. At the applications layer, we see convergence of information, entertainment, communications, shopping, commerce, and education.

Computers have come from nowhere 50 years ago and are rapidly catching up in capability with the human brain. We can expect human:machine equivalence by about 2015. But after this, computers will continue to get smarter. There is a noticeable positive feedback loop in technology development, with each generation of improved computers giving us more assistance in the design and development of the next. Ultimately, they will design their offspring with little or no human involvement. This technology development will push every field of knowledge forwards, not just computing. It will be almost as though extraterrestrials had landed in 2020 and given us all their advanced technology overnight.

But we will never get far unless we can solve the interface problem. In the near future we may have electronic pets, with video camera eyes and microphone ears, linked by radio to the family computer. With voice and language recognition we will have easy access to all that the Internet can provide. We can tell the pet what we want and it will sort it out for us. It will be impossible to be technophobic about such an interface, and the only IT skill needed will be to speak any major language.

4 Now work in groups of three, A, B and C. Read your text extract and complete parts 1 and 2 of this table.

1 Area of IT	
2 Predictions	
3 Comments	

Text A

Telecoms applications will soon be bundled together in much the same way as office application suites are today. A major example is the electronic marketplace, which will bring customers and suppliers together in smart databases and virtual environments, with ID verification, encryption and translation. It will then implement the billing, taxation and electronic funds transfer, while automatically producing accounts and auditing. The whole suite of services will be based on voice processing, allowing a natural voice interface to talk to the computer, all the AI to carry out the request, and voice synthesis and visualisation technology to get the answer out.

Electronic money will be very secure but much more versatile than physical alternatives. E-cash can be completely global and could be used as a de facto standard. It does not have to be linked to any national currency, so can be independent of local currency fluctuations. Its growing use on the Net will lead to its acceptance on the street and we may hold a large proportion of our total funds in this global electronic cash. People will increasingly buy direct from customised manufacturers. Shops will be places where people try on clothes, not buy them. Their exact measurements can be sent instantly to the manufacturer as soon as they have chosen an outfit. The shops may be paid by the manufacturer instead.

Text B

Employment patterns will change, as many jobs are automated and new jobs come into existence to serve new technologies. Some organisations will follow the virtual company model, where a small core of key employees is supported by contractors on a project by project basis, bringing together the right people regardless of where they live. The desks they will use will have multiple flat screens, voice interfaces, computer programs with human-like faces and personalities, full-screen videoconferencing and 3D sound positioning. All this will be without any communication cables since the whole system uses high capacity infrared links. The many short-term contractors may not have enough space in their homes for an office and may go instead to a new breed of local telework centre.

Of course, workers can be fully mobile, and we could see some people abandon offices completely, roaming the world and staying in touch via satellite systems. Even in trains and planes there may be infrared distribution to each seat to guarantee high bandwidth communication. One tool they may have in a few years is effectively a communicator badge. This will give them a voice link to computers across the network, perhaps on their office desk. Using this voice link, they can access their files and email and carry out most computer-based work. Their earphones will allow voice synthesisers to read out their mail, and glasses with a projection system built into the arms and reflectors on the lenses will allow a head-up display of visual information. Perhaps by 2010, these glasses could be replaced by an active contact lens that writes pictures directly onto the retina using tiny lasers.

Finally and frivolously to the very long term. By around 2030, we may have the technology to directly link our brain to the ultra-smart computers that will be around then, giving us so much extra brainpower that we deserve a new name, Homo Cyberneticus. In much the same time frame, geneticists may have created the first biologically optimised humans, Homo Optimus. It would make sense to combine this expertise with information technology wizardry to make something like the Borg, Homo Hybridus, with the body of an Olympic athlete and a brain literally the size of the planet, the whole global superhighway and every machine connected to it. Over time, this new form may converge with the machine world, as more and more of his thoughts occur in cyberspace. With a complete backup on the network, Homo Hybridus would be completely immortal. Ordinary biological humans would eventually accept the transition and plain old Homo Sapiens could become voluntarily extinct, perhaps as early as 2200.

5   Now exchange information with others in your group to list all the predictions made in the text. Discuss with your group the predictions made and add your own comments on the predictions in the last section of the table.

LANGUAGE WORK   Predictions (2): Future perfect and *It* in subject position

We use the Future perfect to predict actions which will be completed before a particular time in the future. It is often used with time expressions such as *by 2020, before the end of the century*. For example:

1   By 2010 scientists *will have developed* active contact lenses.

We can vary the strength of our predictions using the certainty verbs studied in Unit 16 instead of *will*. For example:

2   By 2030 geneticists *may/might/could* have created the first biologically optimised humans.

We can also make predictions using *It* in subject position when the true subject of the prediction is a *that* clause. For example,

1   It's likely that computers will be used to develop other faster computers.
2   It's possible that we'll work from telework centres in future.

---

6   Make predictions for 2020 for each of the following using the methods studied here. You may wish to use these verbs:

develop   disappear   increase   replace   take over

1   computing power
2   interfaces
3   monitors
4   teleworking
5   money
6   shops
7   machine intelligence compared to human intelligence
8   the Internet
9   keyboards
10   speech recognition

7 Write sentences similar in meaning to each of these predictions with *It* in subject position. For example:

I don't think we'll use cable connections in future.   (unlikely)
It's unlikely that we'll use cable connections in future.

1 I'm sure we won't use magnetic tape.   (certain)
2 We may well have electronic chips in our bodies.   (probable)
3 Computers could easily be used to develop other computers. (likely)
4 I don't think we'll replace teachers with robots.   (unlikely)
5 There's a chance we'll develop alternatives to silicon. (possible)
6 I really don't think we'll have replaced the motor car before 2020.   (very unlikely)
7 I'm almost sure we'll replace the CRT monitor in the next few years.   (highly probable)
8 I'm definite we'll have more virtual personalities on the Web. (certain)
9 We might adopt Bluetooth as a standard for wireless applications.   (possible)
10 Doctors may be able to operate on patients at a distance. (quite likely)

SPEAKING   **8** Think of arguments for and against this statement.

Computers will catch up with the power and speed of the human brain by 2050. Some time after that they will start outstripping us and taking over from us.

9   🎧 Choose one side only – for or against the statement. Now listen to the recording and note down any points in support of your side.

10 Using your notes and your own ideas, try to persuade the rest of your group to accept your views on the statement in Task 8.

WRITING   **11** Summarise the views of Pearson and of the experts you heard on the recording on the Future of Information Technology. Give your own comments on their views. Write about 250 words.

A **Find the answers to these questions in the text below.**

1 Of what is Professor Cochrane completely convinced?

2 What is stored in the professor's signet ring?

3 What will change dramatically when we start using rings like these?

4 What is the BT lab developing with artificial intelligence?

5 What effect are the professor's AI experiments having on evolution?

6 What does the professor see as the negative side of the electronic revolution?

7 What was the result of combining the Internet with TV?

8 What developments does the professor suggest in the field of biotechnology?

9 According to the professor, what will happen by the year 2015?

FUTURES

Talking to Professor Cochrane is probably as close as you can get to time travelling without leaving the current dimension, as his vision stretches far into the 21st century and beyond.

5 His seemingly unshakeable conviction is that anything is possible if you really put your mind to it. In fact, BT (British Telecom) is already sitting on a host of innovations poised to blow your mind during this century.

10 Designed for the 21st century, Peter Cochrane's signet ring is built around a chip that holds all the details of his passport, bank account, medical records and driving licence. According to Cochrane, it's set to revolutionise shopping.

15 The ring is already a fully operational prototype, but it will be some time before you'll be trading your credit card in for the ultimate fashion accessory.

It's not just jewellery that's set to get smarter.

20 One of the biggest projects down at the Lab is looking at artificial intelligence as a way of creating software programs, networks, telephones and machines with a degree of intelligence built in. By sensing their

25 environment, they should be able to develop new capacities as demands change. 'I have software that is breeding, which is interchanging genes and creating adaptable behaviour. This means you'll see the network come alive – it

30 will watch what you do and it will adapt.'

It doesn't stop there, though, as BT has taken artificial intelligence one step further and created machines that are solving their own problems. 'We've created solutions that a

35 human being could never have dreamed of. We have solutions, and although we don't understand how they work, they do work. We're effectively increasing the speed of evolution', says Cochrane.

40 It's already good to talk, but with artificially intelligent phones on the way it will be even better. Cochrane is at present working on smart phones that can translate English into German, Japanese and French in real-time. 'Some of it's

45 rocket science, but a lot of it's extremely simple. What we've built is a kernel of understanding inside a machine that extracts meaning from the sentence itself – at the moment we can do simple things such as phrase books,' he says.

50 The system uses a non-linear approach that sends the English to the understanding kernel in the machine and then fans it out to all the other languages simultaneously.

There's no doubt that Cochrane is putting a lot
55 of faith in intelligent machines, particularly when it comes to cutting through the deluge of information that he says is the downside of the electronic revolution. BT's solution is the development of intelligent agents that watch,
60 learn and start communicating.

It's not all work down at the Lab, though. BT's also involved in an on-going trial that it claims will revolutionise our leisure time, in particular the way we watch TV. 'We put people on the
65 Internet and broadcast TV at the same time, so that the people at home could actually influence what was happening on their TV sets. As a result, it became interactive and therefore more active.'

70 BT has its fingers in multiple pies and has made biotechnology another core focus of R&D. 'Personally, I think hospitals are very dangerous places to be. There are lots of viable alternatives. For a start, we can stop bunging up
75 hospital wards by putting people online.' BT has already developed a pack for heart attack victims that monitors their progress and uploads information via a radio link back to the hospital.

So what will the 21st century hold for us if Peter
80 Cochrane and his futurologists have their way? Well, by the year 2015, it's likely that we will be eclipsed by a supercomputer more powerful than the human brain. And if that's got visions of Terminator dancing in your head, don't worry
85 – Cochrane's got it covered. 'I'd really hate one morning to find myself considered an infestation of this planet. Our inclination is to nurture life and not to destroy it. Before we let loose a bunch of artificial intelligence, we ought to be
90 thinking through the necessity of building in a number of rules that hold your life as a human being sacrosanct.'

[Adapted from Futures, Celebrity Squares, Professor Peter Cochrane, PC Pro Magazine, February 1998]

B Re-read the text to find the answers to these questions.

1 Match the terms in Table A with the statements in Table B.

Table A
a BT
b Smart phone
c Intelligent agent
d Rocket science
e R&D
f Upload
g Supercomputer

Table B
i A computer program that watches, learns and communicates with the user
ii Most powerful type of computer
iii Research and development
iv Transfer data from a client device to a server computer
v A telephone that can translate English into various languages in real-time
vi British Telecom
vii Very advanced study

2 Mark the following statements as True or False:

a BT has a lot of new ideas that will astound people.

b Jewellery that can store large amounts of personal data has started to replace credit cards.

c BT's smart phone can only translate English into one other language at a time.

d Intelligent agents can help users deal with an overload of information.

e Watching TV will be a more active pastime in the future.

f The professor thinks that humanity will be destroyed by very powerful computers in the future.

Electronic Publishing

STARTER **1** Which of these should be published in electronic form and which in traditional paper versions? Compare answers with others in your group. Give reasons for your decisions.

1 a national newspaper
2 a textbook on information technology
3 a laser printer manual
4 Shakespeare's plays
5 a detective story
6 a traveller's guide to India
7 schoolbooks
8 an encyclopaedia

LISTENING **2** What opinions do you think these people will have about e-publishing?

1 a telecommunications engineer
2 an author
3 an electronic publisher
4 the developer of an ebook reader
5 a keen reader

3 ⌒ Now listen to the recording. Note the points made by each of the speakers for or against e-publishing. Compare your list with your predictions from Task 2.

Speaker	Points for	Points against
telecommunications engineer		
author		
electronic publisher		
developer of an ebook reader		
keen reader		

LANGUAGE WORK   Emphasising: cleft sentences

Compare these sentences:

1   We need an electronic version available anywhere and updated regularly.
2   What we need is *an electronic version available anywhere and updated regularly.*

In (2) the object of the sentence is made more important. We can use *What ... be* in this way to emphasise the subject or object of a sentence.

Now compare these:

3   Babbage invented the world's first mechanical computer.
4   It was *Babbage* that invented the world's first mechanical computer.
5   It was *the world's first mechanical computer* that Babbage invented.

We can use *It is/was ... that* to emphasise almost any part of a sentence.

4   Rewrite these sentences to emphasise the words in italics.

1   I like *the fact that my books are available everywhere.*
2   Bill Gates introduced the Windows NT operating system *in 1993.*
3   *Bill Gates* introduced the Windows NT operating system in 1993.
4   Bill Gates introduced *the Windows NT operating system* in 1993.
5   I need *information* quickly.
6   Ebooks will replace *all the throwaway books we read.*
7   *Ebooks* will replace all the throwaway books we read.
8   It's not *cheap.*
9   I like *the look and the feel of books.*
10 I don't like *reading off a computer screen.*

5   With the help of these facts about the history of PCs, correct the statements which follow using any of the structures studied in this Unit.

1968	Engelbart demonstrated first mouse.		**1982**	Acorn produced the BBC Micro.
1971	Intel designed first microprocessor.		**1984**	Apple Macintosh
1975	MITS Altair 8800 - home construction kit personal computer		**1990**	Windows 3.0
1975	Gates and Allen founded Microsoft in Albuquerque, New Mexico.		**1993**	Intel Pentium, Microsoft Windows NT
1980	Sinclair ZX80		**2001**	Apple launched OS X operating system. Microsoft launched Windows XP.
1981	IBM Personal Computer with Microsoft MS-DOS operating system			

1   Gates and Bush founded Microsoft in 1975.

2   Sinclair launched the ZX81 in 1980.

3   Windows 3 was introduced in 1993.

4   IBM designed the first microprocessor.

5   The first Apple-IBM appeared in 1984.

6   Apple launched their new XP operating system in 2001.

7   Acorn produced the Archimedes computer in 1982.

8   The Intel Pentium was launched in 1983.

9   In 1981 IBM introduced a personal computer with a Unix operating system.

10   Microsoft was founded in Mexico in 1975.

6   Fill in the blanks with the correct forms of these verbs: *need, have to, must, can, could, be able to*. In some cases, more than one answer is possible.

1   After the success of Windows 95, Microsoft .... outsell any competitor.

2   Computer consultants .... specialise in too narrow a field.

3   Programmers .... to know a range of up-to-date languages.

4   To be a successful consultant, you .... be better than the competition.

5   Before IBM set the standard for PCs, software houses .... write different versions of their programs for every make of computer.

6   When he was a schoolboy, Bill Gates .... write programs in BASIC.

7   Support engineers must .... empathise with users.

8   The Altair 8800 was one of the first computers you .... assemble at home.

9   Most website designers .... use HTML and XML.

10   You .... learn COBOL unless you want to work with business software.

WORD STUDY	Prefixes, *-ise* verbs

These prefixes are common in IT terminology.

Quantity

prefix	meaning	examples
bi	two	bi-directional
uni	one	uni-directional
tera	10^{12}	terabyte*
giga	10^9	gigahertz
mega	10^6	megahertz
kilo	10^3	kilohm
milli	10^3	millisecond
macro	large	macroinstruction
micro	small	microcomputer
multi	many	multimedia

Prepositions

prefix	meaning	examples
anti	against	anti-virus software
infra	below	infrared
intra	within	intranet
inter	between	Internet
hyper	above, beyond	hyperlink
tele	distant, far	telecommunications

Others

prefix	meaning	examples
auto	by itself	automated
cyber	machine control	cyberspace
super	higher in quantity or degree	superhighway

(* approximate decimal value)

7   Find an IT term for each of these definitions. Each term includes one of the prefixes listed above. All of the terms are used in this book.

1   working at a distance
2   a system of numbers with 2 as its base
3   a way of communicating between a user and a computer
4   1048576 bytes of information
5   describes a program which allows two way communication between user and computer
6   set of computer instructions operating as one unit
7   having many different modes of input
8   a computer higher in scale than any other
9   a machine which provides cash to bank customers without requiring a human operator: an A ... Teller Machine
10   a very small but powerful processor
11   a system used by many people
12   a wordprocessing feature which corrects by itself

8 Verbs ending in *-ise* (US *-ize*) often have a causative meaning. For example:

New phones will *revolutionise* the way we communicate.
= New phones will *make a revolution in* the way we communicate.

Replace the words in italics in each sentence with the appropriate form of an *-ise* verb. All the verbs have been used in this book.

1 Players let you group songs into playlists and *make* the selection *random*.

2 If you adopt differential backup, this *reduces to a minimum* the size of your backup set.

3 Most hotels use systems *which have been converted for computers*.

4 Software developers can produce solutions *which are tailored to the customer*.

5 Some software houses produce *specially written* applications.

6 Utilities can be *put into categories* as editors, filters or communications programs.

7 You can protect data by putting it in a form only users *with authority* can understand.

8 It is an offence to make copies of software *which are done without authority*.

SPEAKING **9** What features should an electronic book reader have? In your group decide on the best specifications. Compare your list with the reader described on the recording and, if possible, with the specifications for the readers described at these websites:

www.franklin.com
www.ebook-gemstar.com
www.bookstore.glassbook.com

10 Now present your specifications to the rest of the class. Each member of your group should present some of the specifications with reasons for their choice.

Pairwork: Student A

UNIT 2

- Workgroup server
- Dual Pentium IV 1.4GHz processor
- 133MHz system bus
- 256MB ECC SDRAM (upgradeable to 2GB)

- Hot plug 60GB 7200rpm LVD SCSI hard drive upgradeable to 180GB of internal storage
- Dell 19" (17.9" VIS) SVGA colour monitor
- 24/52X EIDE CD-ROM drive and 3.5" 1.44MB floppy disk drive

Options
- APC 1400 SmartUPS
- High performance RAID adapter with 128MB cache
- Hot-plug redundant power supplies
- 3 Year Next-business-day on-site service

UNIT 3

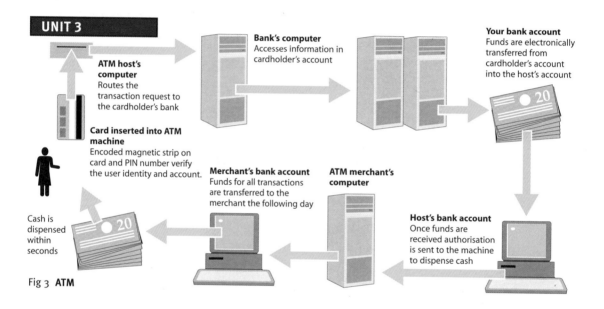

Bank's computer Accesses information in cardholder's account

Your bank account Funds are electronically transferred from cardholder's account into the host's account

ATM host's computer Routes the transaction request to the cardholder's bank

Card inserted into ATM machine Encoded magnetic strip on card and PIN number verify the user identity and account.

Merchant's bank account Funds for all transactions are transferred to the merchant the following day

ATM merchant's computer

Cash is dispensed within seconds

Host's bank account Once funds are received authorisation is sent to the machine to dispense cash

Fig 3 **ATM**

UNIT 6

Mac OS The graphically-oriented operating system used on Apple Macintosh microcomputers.

MS-DOS The most widely used operating system ever on PC-compatible microcomputers; MS-DOS has been technologically surpassed in recent years and is no longer being revised.

MVS, VM, OS/390 Operating systems used on IBM mainframes.

NetWare A widely used operating system on local area networks (LANs).

OS/2 The operating system designed for high-end PC-compatible microcomputers; was available in both desktop version and a version for network administration.

Penpoint An operating system designed for pen-based computers.

Windows NT Microsoft Windows operating system built from ideas developed in VMS and used for servers and workstations. More secure and stable than Windows 9X systems.

UNIT 8

Tomb Raider 4: The Last Revelation

Sega Dreamcast | Core Design/Eidos | ★★★

Although this is essentially the same game that recently appeared on the PlayStation, some fancy enhancements push this up to accelerated PC level. In fact, The Last Revelation is probably the best-looking version so far.

The Dreamcast remains unstretched but the visuals capture the Egyptian mood perfectly. The plot sees Lara returning to what she does best – raiding tombs in her usual physics-defying manner – but this time she stays in Egypt rather than globe-trotting.

So, what is The Last Revelation? The chances are only a few will ever find out because this is a very tricky game. You will need to prepare for periods of intense frustration and annoyance, punctuated by some superb sequences.

If only Lara would move in the direction you point. If only she jumped when you press 'jump' rather than run those fatal final steps. If only the puzzles were less obscure.

So why bother? Well, the characterisation and the storyline are of sufficient quality to encourage perseverance. Also, solving a stubborn puzzle or back-flipping over a chasm is undeniably good fun. This is the best version yet and will do for now, but a radical overhaul is needed before Lara returns again.

Greg Howson

UNIT 9

Explain to your partner with the help of these notes what DVD disks are, how DVD disks store such large quantities of information and how that information is read.

DVD = Digital Versatile Disk
- can hold complete movie
- like CD in size and thickness
- but CD drives use red laser light, DVD drives use blue
- blue laser has shorter wavelength therefore data can be denser

DVDs can be double-sided
- each side can have two layers
- top layer 4.7GB, bottom layer 3.8GB, total capacity = 17GB
- data transfer rate twice rate of CD-ROM

UNIT 11

Asynchronous transmission

This method, used with most microcomputers, is also called start-stop transmission. In asynchronous transmission, data is sent one byte (or character) at a time. Each string of bits making up the byte is bracketed, or marked off, with special control bits. That is, a 'start' bit represents the beginning of a character, and a 'stop' bit represents its end. As a means of checking that the whole character has been transmitted, an error check bit is generated immediately after each character.

Transmitting only one byte at a time makes this a relatively slow method. As a result, asynchronous transmission is not used when great amounts of data must be sent rapidly. Its advantage is that the data can be transmitted whenever it is convenient for the sender.

UNIT 14

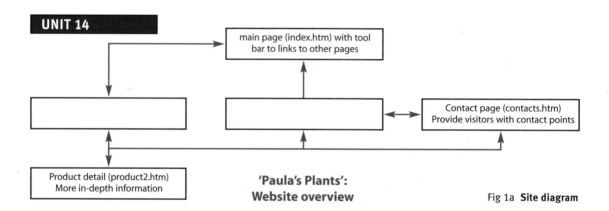

'Paula's Plants':
Website overview

Fig 1a **Site diagram**

UNIT 15

Problems

1 You want to brighten up your website.
2 You would like to reserve seats on the London to Edinburgh train.
3 You want some help with a project on computer security.
4 You're feeling a bit flabby and would like to take up marathon running. How can you prepare for this?

Weather Reports

Several weather-related sites can give you up-to-the-minute weather reports and precipitation radar for your city or local region or for an area in which you'll be travelling. You'll also find extended forecasts. Some weather sites provide safety tips for dealing with severe weather.
www.weather.com

Comic Strips

Everyone needs a laugh from time to time, and few things can put a smile on your face more quickly than a classic comic strip. You can check out dozens of your favourite comics and, in some cases, even send a comic strip to a friend.
www.unitedmedia.com
www.uexpress.com

Maps

Websites can give you detailed street maps for major cities, or they can give you a map of Interstate highways. Some sites can help you find a particular address or suggest the best method of travel to your destination. You can also print maps at many websites.
www.mapblast.com

UNIT 16

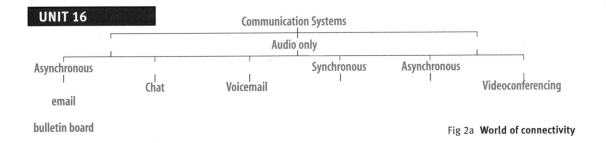

Fig 2a **World of connectivity**

UNIT 17

Problem A
Monitor power light flashing but display screen is completely blank.

SYSTEM	SOLUTION	
Make and model Dell, GS205X **Service Number** X3457 **Processor** Pentium IV **Memory** 256MB **O.S.** Windows XP **Configuration** standalone	**INSTRUCTIONS**	**RESULT**
	Check to see if the computer system unit power light comes on when the computer is switched on.	Computer power seems to be O.K.
	Check that the monitor data cable is connected correctly to the VGA port at the rear of the computer.	Data cable is plugged in O.K.
	Check that the graphics expansion card is installed properly by: • Switching off the computer. • Disconnecting the power cable. • Opening the computer case by removing the four securing screws. • Inspecting the graphics card to see if it is seated properly in the expansion slot.	Graphics card is loose.
	Correct the fault and check the system by: • Pushing the graphics card fully into the expansion slot. • Replacing the casing. • Reconnecting the power supply. • Switching on the computer and checking that the monitor is functioning correctly.	Monitor functioning O.K.

UNIT 18

Getting the bug

How the simple yet clever virus was able to spread so quickly

Bugged email arrives in in-tray labelled ILOVEYOU

Email contains an attachment called LOVE-LETTER-FOR-YOU.TXT This is where the virus is found. At this point the virus is still inactive.

Opening the attachment launches a Visual Basic script, a program which Love Bug uses to do three tasks ...

Copies itself by overwriting files ending with vbs, vbe, js, jse, css, wsh, sct, hta, jpg, jpeg, mp2 and mp3

Sends a copy of itself to all names in the computer's Microsoft Outlook address book.

Attempts to download password – stealing Trojan Horse program from the web.

Facts of Love

- Lovebug spread twice as fast as the Melissa virus which affected 300,000 US computers in March 1999.

- Experts believe the worst is still to come with 21 new variants of the original virus detected so far.

Fig 2 **The spread of the love bug**

UNIT 19

Incremental backup

An incremental backup includes only files with their archive bit on. The archive bit indicates whether a file has been backed up since it was last changed. Whenever you back up a file in Windows, the operating system automatically sets the archive bit to 0 (off). 1 (on) indicates a file has not been backed up since it was last worked on. This way, as you append a series of incrementals to your full backup, each contains only those files that are new or have changed since your last backup. This keeps your backup set up to date using a minimum of time and tape. The disadvantage is that it may need many tapes to fully restore the hard disk.

UNIT 21

Java Developed by Sun Microsystems in the mid-1990s, Java is widely used for developing interactive applications for the Internet.

Ada Named after Countess Ada Lovelace (one of the first programmers); it is a superset of Pascal. Ada is a structured language developed and used by the US Department of Defense.

Logo Logo is an easy-to-use language that is primarily used to teach children how to program.

LISP Stands for LISt Processor; LISP is designed to process non-numeric data – that is, symbols such as characters or words. It is used to develop applications in the field of artificial intelligence.

FORTRAN Stands for FORmula TRANslator; FORTRAN was designed by scientists in 1954 and is oriented toward manipulating formulas for scientific, mathematical, and engineering problem-solving applications.

HTML Stands for HyperText Markup Language; HTML is a page-description language used to prepare a text for display in a browser program.

Perl Its name comes from Practical Report and Extraction Language. It first appeared in 1987 as a Unix-based tool for producing reports but is now widely used for creating interactive webpages.

Prolog Stands for PROgramming LOGic; Prolog is used to develop applications in the field of artificial intelligence. It is a popular tool for natural-language programming.

UNIT 22

1 Systems Analyst

Studies methods of working within an organisation to decide how tasks can be done efficiently by computers. Makes a detailed analysis of the employer's requirements and work patterns to prepare a report on different options for using information technology. This may involve consideration of hardware as well as software. Either uses standard computer packages or writes a specification for programmers to adapt existing software or to prepare new software. May oversee the implementation and testing of a system and acts as a link between the user and the programmer.

2 Software Engineer/Designer

Produces the programs which control the internal operations of computers. Converts the system analyst's specification to a logical series of steps. Translates these into the appropriate computer language. Often compiles programs from libraries or sub-programs, combining these to make up a complete systems program. Designs, tests and improves programs for computer-aided design and manufacture, business applications, computer networks and games.

3 Computer Services Engineering Technician

Can be responsible for installation, maintenance or repair of computers and associated equipment. Installs hardware, ranging from personal computers to mainframe machines, and tests by running special software. Some technicians carry out routine servicing of large mainframe systems, aiming to avoid breakdowns. Others are called in to identify and repair faults as quickly as possible usually by replacing faulty parts. Work can also involve upgrading machines usually on customers' premises.

4 Network Support Person or Computer Engineer: Network Support

Maintains the link between PCs and workstations connected in a network. Use telecommunications, software and electronic skills and knowledge of the networking software to locate and correct faults. This may involve work with the controlling software, on the wiring, printed circuit boards, software or microchips on a file server, or on cables either within or outside the building.

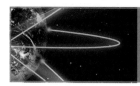

Pairwork: Student B

UNIT 2

- Portable
- Mobile Pentium III Processor 850MHz
- 100 MHz system bus
- 20GB EIDE Hard Disk
- 128MB SDRAM
- Modular 16/40X DVD Drive and 3.5" Floppy Drive

- High Performance 256-bit 32MB Graphics
- 15" SXGA (1400 x 1050) High Resolution TFT Display
- Microsoft Windows 2000

Options
- Upgrade to 256MB RAM
- 56Kbps PCMCIA Modem
- 3 Year International Next-business-day on-site service
- Spare lithium ion battery
- 10/100 Ethernet Port Replicator

UNIT 3

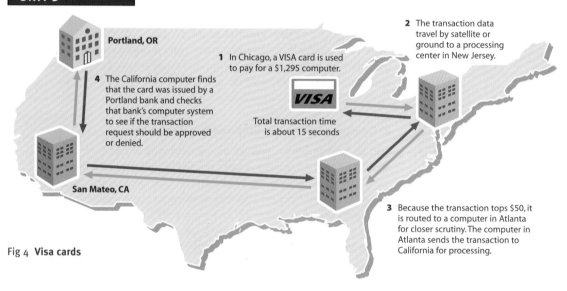

Portland, OR

1 In Chicago, a VISA card is used to pay for a $1,295 computer.

2 The transaction data travel by satellite or ground to a processing center in New Jersey.

4 The California computer finds that the card was issued by a Portland bank and checks that bank's computer system to see if the transaction request should be approved or denied.

Total transaction time is about 15 seconds

San Mateo, CA

3 Because the transaction tops $50, it is routed to a computer in Atlanta for closer scrutiny. The computer in Atlanta sends the transaction to California for processing.

Fig 4 **Visa cards**

UNIT 6

PC–DOS An operating system similar to MS-DOS that has been widely used on IBM microcomputers.

Unix An operating system used on all sizes of computers, but mostly large ones; available in many versions, such as Linux, HP-UX, Xenix, Venix, Ultrix, A/UX, AIX, Solaris, and PowerOpen.

VAX/VMS An operating system used by DEC VAX minicomputers.

Windows 3.x* Refers to the Windows 3.0 and Windows 3.1 operating environments, and to variants such as Windows for Workgroups 3.11; each of these is a graphically-oriented shell program for Microsoft's MS-DOS operating system.

Windows 9X The operating system that replaced MS-DOS and Windows 3.1, combining the functionality of both programs and much more into a single package; two versions were produced, Windows 95 and Windows 98, although various editions were made available.

Windows 2000 An operating system targeted primarily to corporate client-server applications; available in both a desktop version and a version for network administration.

*Not a full operating system

UNIT 8

Sim City 3000: World edition

PC | Maxis/Electronic Arts | ★★★★

The basic game is the same as it was when it first appeared on the Commodore 64: zone land, build roads, set taxes and let simulated citizens build the city of your dreams or nightmares. A huge amount of detail has been added since then, and the World edition integrates hundreds of new buildings, a building editor, a terrain editor, and a scenario editor.

You no longer have to build American cities, and you can quickly flip them into a European (German) or Asian (Korean/Japanese) style. You can add landmarks such as the Brandenburg Gate and the Eiffel Tower.

The amount of detail in the 3D buildings, cars and pedestrians is stunning. A new website is introduced also (www.simcity.com). There you can download even more buildings and swap files, buildings, city photos and scenarios with fellow fans.

If you gave up on SC2000, this will restore your faith; and if you haven't played Sim City before, this is a good place to start.

Jack Schofield

UNIT 9

Explain to your partner with the help of these notes what MPEG Video is and how it operates.

MPEG = method of compressing/decompressing video signals to reduce size by up to 95%
- video sequences stored in series of frames
- intraframe (I-frame) every 1/3rd second has most important picture information
- between I-frames are predicted frames (P-frames) and bidirectional frames (B-frames)
- P- and B-frames store changes only
- P- and B-frames preserve video quality between I-frames
- Human eye can't detect information discarded

UNIT 11

Synchronous transmission

Synchronous transmission sends data in blocks of characters. Start and stop bit patterns, called synch bytes, are transmitted at the beginning and end of the blocks. These start and end bit patterns synchronize internal clocks in the sending and receiving devices so that they are in time with each other. Error check bytes are included immediately after each block of characters to ensure that the whole sequence of characters has been correctly transmitted.

This method is rarely used with microcomputers because it is more complicated and expensive than asynchronous transmission. It also requires careful timing between sending and receiving equipment. It is appropriate for computer systems that need to transmit great quantities of data quickly.

UNIT 14

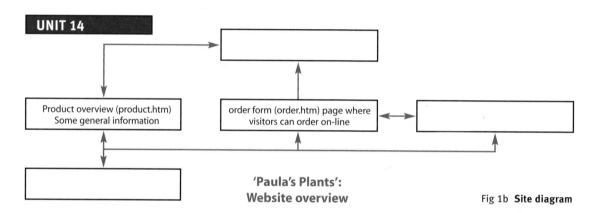

Product overview (product.htm)
Some general information

order form (order.htm) page where
visitors can order on-line

'Paula's Plants':
Website overview

Fig 1b **Site diagram**

UNIT 15

Problems

1 You would like to cheer up a friend.
2 You're going to rent a car in the USA and travel from Miami to New Orleans. You would like to plan a route.
3 You're going walking in the mountains this weekend. You would like to know what the chances are of rain.
4 You want to forward a video email attachment you've received to a friend and it won't go.

Travel Research

Whether you're looking for the best airline and hotel fares or researching the best travel destinations, the Web can help. Several websites also offer tips for travelling by airplane or with small children. Some allow you to book train tickets.
www.expedia.com
www.concierge.com
www.thetrainline.co.uk

Neon City

If you have a webpage that's looking a little dull, you might want to add some neon signs, words or tubes. Neon City produces a variety of cool neon clipart that you are free to use on your personal webpage so long as you link to the page you got the design from.
www.neoncity.co.uk

Exercise information

If your current exercise program doesn't seem to be working, consult the Web. While Web surfing doesn't qualify as exercise, you can use the Web to find information on an exercise program you'll enjoy. Some websites also help to track your progress.
www.fitnesslink.com
www.runnersworld.com

UNIT 16

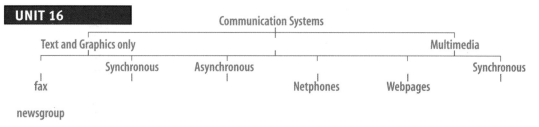

Fig 2b **World of connectivity**

UNIT 17

Problem B
The monitor display screen is flickering.

SYSTEM	SOLUTION	
Make and model Compaq, CV602	**INSTRUCTIONS**	**RESULT**
Service Number 8JD3	Change the monitor refresh rate setting by: • Right clicking with the mouse on the desktop • Selecting 'Properties-Settings' • Clicking on the Advanced button • Choosing the 'Monitor' tab. • Making sure that the 'Hide modes that this monitor cannot display' checkbox is ticked. • Selecting a higher refresh rate (i.e. 75Hz or more). • Rebooting the computer. • Checking that the monitor is functioning properly.	Monitor no longer flickering.
Processor Pentium III		
Memory 128MB		
O.S. Windows 2000		
Configuration Windows 2000 network		

UNIT 18

Stealing by stealth
How a Trojan may have penetrated Microsoft's defences

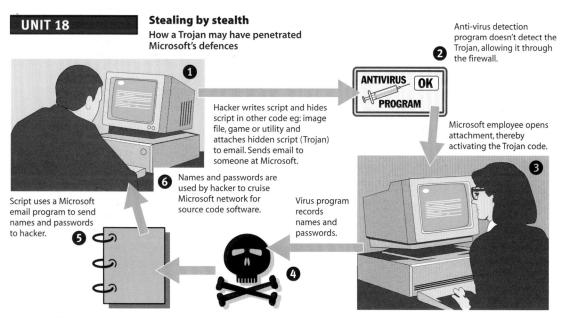

Fig 3 **Stealing by stealth**

UNIT 19

Differential backup

A differential backup doesn't set the archive bit to the off position after backing up the file. In a full backup in Windows, the operating system automatically sets the archive bit to 0 (off). 1 (on) indicates a file has not been backed up since it was last worked on. Thus, if you do a series of differentials, each backs up all the files created or modified since the last full backup, not just those that have changed. Normally, you keep only the most recent differential backup on hand. This minimizes the size of your backup set, since it will never contain more than two copies of any file – one in the full set and one in the differential. This method is mostly used when you're backing up to disks. The downside is that it won't back up files that were created and deleted before the differential backup.

UNIT 21

XML Stands for eXtensible Markup Language; XML is a metalanguage for creating webpages with meaningful data that can be used by a variety of programs.

C++ C++ is an object-oriented superset of C which combines the best features of a structured high-level language and an assembly language – that is, it's relatively easy to code and uses computer resources efficiently. C was originally designed to write systems software but is now considered a general-purpose language.

Visual Basic BASIC stands for Beginners' All-purpose Symbolic Instruction Code; Visual Basic is a simple-to-use language that has a graphical interface. It makes it particularly easy for an inexperienced programmer to create database programs.

Pascal Pascal, named after the mathematician Blaise Pascal, was created primarily to fill the need for a teaching vehicle that would encourage structured programming. It is often used in college computing courses.

COBOL Stands for COmmon Business-Oriented Language; it has been around for a long number of years but is still an important transaction-processing language used to process the records of large organisations on mainframe computers.

UNIT 22

1 Computer Salesperson

Advises potential customers about available hardware and sells equipment to suit individual requirements. Discusses computing needs with the client to ensure that a suitable system can be supplied. Organises the sale and delivery and, if necessary, installation and testing. May arrange support or training, maintenance and consultation. Must have sufficient technical knowledge.

2 Applications Programmer

Writes the programs which enable a computer to carry out particular tasks. May write new programs or adapt existing programs, perhaps altering computer packages to meet the needs of an individual company. When writing a new program, follows a specification provided by a systems analyst. Devises a series of logical steps and converts these to the appropriate computer language. Checks programs for faults and does extensive testing.

3 Systems Support Person

Systems support people are analyst programmers who are responsible for maintaining, updating and modifying the software used by a company. Some specialise in software which handles the basic operation of the computers. This involves use of machine codes and specialised low-level computer languages. Most handle applications software. May sort out problems encountered by users. Solving problems may involve amending an area of code in the software, retrieving files and data lost when a system crashes and a basic knowledge of hardware.

4 Hardware Engineer

Researches, designs and develops computers, or parts of computers and the computerised element of appliances, machines and vehicles. Also involved in their manufacture, installation and testing. May specialise in different areas: research and development, design, manufacturing. Has to be aware of cost, efficiency, safety and environmental factors as well as engineering aspects.

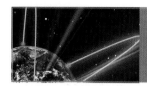

Listening Script

UNIT 1

Computer Users

primary school teacher We've got a new program with 3D graphics to encourage young children to tell stories. We tried it out last term and now we use it regularly. There's a mat in front of the monitor, like a carpet. There are pressure pads under the mat. When the children stand on them, they can move about inside the pictures on the screen. If they stand on the right, they, er, can move to the right, and so on. The good thing is that it works better if there are more children on the mat. This encourages them to work together.

What I like about this program is that if you ask the children what they've been doing, they don't say, 'We've been working with the computer', they say 'We've been telling stories'. The computer doesn't get in the way of learning, it's just a tool. We don't get that reaction when we sit them down at a keyboard.

Open University student I've had a computer for about, oh, three years now. I'm an OU student doing a degree in mathematics. I work full time so I study at home in the evenings and at weekends. Some Saturdays there are tutorials I can attend in town but mostly I work alone. I use the computer to write my assignments. I also use the Internet to email my tutor if I have any problems with the course work. There's a help group too on the Web made up of other students doing my course ... not just here in the UK but around the world. We can chat about assignments and help each other out if we're in difficulty.

Louise, aged 6 Well, I make cards for my friends. I made one for Mary's birthday last week. I use Word and you go into clipart. Then these things come up on the screen. And you can click on any one like animals and two people with a heart, and a star and a hat. I've got CD-ROMS. I like Splat the Cat and Pets 3. You click on Go to the Adoption Centre, then you go to Pick a Pet and you can choose what you want, a cat or a dog. And you can give it a name and feed it. The one I'm going to adopt is a cat. ... And you've got to give your cat a name. But first I'll take its picture, then I'll save it.

artist I paint mainly figures in imaginary interiors. Erm, they represent myths. I work in acrylics although I also make woodcuts. Erm, I keep photographs of most of what I've done apart from the work I've destroyed ... the ones I didn't like. I've scanned in about a third of these photographs, around 100 paintings, to make a CD. I've organised the paintings into themes and added a sound track so that each group of paintings is accompanied by music. Erm, I'll send the CD to dealers. In the past it would have been slides. I'm also going to start my own website to try to sell directly. The difficult thing is trying to get people to visit your site.

UNIT 4

Peripherals

PART 1

A What's the difference between an ordinary camera ... a conventional camera, and a digital camera?

B At the most basic level, a digital camera isn't much different from a conventional camera. There's a lens, a viewfinder and it takes pictures. The only fundamental change is that a charge coupled device – a CCD – is used in place of the film.

A What's a CCD?

B It's an assembly ... a set of thousands of photo-transistors – one for each pixel in the image. You know what a pixel is?

A Yes, it's a kind of dot ... it makes up a picture, an image on a screen.

B It's short for picture element. Well, each pixel in the CCD consists of three photo-transistors, one covered by a red filter, one by a blue one and one by a green. Three images – one for each of these colours – are built up. When they're combined, you get a full-colour photograph.

A What are the advantages, the plus points, of a digital camera?

B You never have to buy another film, there's no film, there's no chemical processing involved. There's no delay waiting for the film to be developed. Instead of being held on film, the images are written to solid state memory. Most cameras have an LCD on the back. You can see straight away what your last shot looks like. If you don't like it, you can delete it and take another. You can download the images to a PC for retouching, manipulating, or printing out.

A Do you need any special software?

B Yes, but it comes with the camera. It's not difficult to install. You can also use your TV to give slide shows and you can email copies to your friends.

PART 2

A Any disadvantages? What's the down side?

B Well, they're still pricey but they're getting cheaper. And the quality isn't as sharp as a good 35 mm. People forget too that if you want prints, you have to invest in a photo-quality colour printer. That can be expensive and printing costs can also be high – the paper, the ink and so on.

A Anything else?

B Batteries. You get through them. Digitals are power-hungry especially if you use the LCD a lot for playback.

A If I wanted to buy one, what should I look for?

B First of all, the resolution. It's like buying a monitor. The higher the resolution, the more details you'll be able to get in the picture. Don't buy anything less than two million pixels.

A second major specification, and it's tied up with image quality, is the number of pictures you can store before the camera is full and you need to download to your PC. A 1280 by 960 image takes over a megabyte of memory. That doesn't leave much room for many shots on a typical 16 megabyte Flash card. Fortunately you can compress the data and squeeze a lot more lower resolution shots onto one card.

It's worth considering too the type of battery used. Get one with rechargeable cells.

UNIT 5

Interview: Former Student

PART 1

Interviewer What was your course called?

Paul The first one was a Higher National Certificate in Computing. That was mainly programming.

I Uhum.

P And the second one was a Higher National Diploma in Computing Support.

I Ah, that's quite a change. Did you

originally think of being a programmer?

P Yeh, but when I finished the course there weren't a lot of jobs in programming and there seemed to be more in support. So support seemed a better career move.

I Erm, what were the main subjects in your diploma course?

P Hardware, Planning, Design, Software development, Applications, Communication. We did some programming too.

I Communication, anything to do with Telecommunications?

P No, it's, er, language skills. How to get your point over. How to make a presentation. We also had Maths. I've always liked Maths.

I Was there a practical component in the course?

P Yes, we had to assemble computers.

I And how small were the components you started with? Was it down to the level of the motherboard, for example?

P Yes, we had to link the motherboard and the CPU and all the other components of a computer and make it run.

PART 2

I How up to date did you feel the course was?

P I always felt it was a bit behind current developments.

I That question really relates to my next one. Is there anything that you would add to or take away from the course?

P Erm, I would change the programming component. We did Pascal. That's one reason I didn't want to continue with programming because you never saw any jobs which asked for Pascal. We did COBOL also but that was quite old too and even the banks were stopping using it. A more up to date language like C++ would've been better. And I would add work experience. I always felt they should have given some sort of work experience. I know some colleges do.

I Erm, that would be a great thing because most students have paper qualifications and no practical experience.

P I think that even if it was just summer work it would be really useful. Employers are looking for qualifications and experience.

I Which of the subjects you studied have you found most useful in your work?

P Erm, Learning Access. I've had to do

database designs for a couple of customers. Systems Building as well. I've had to go in and replace components for customers and we've had to build computers from scratch. Last Christmas I had to assemble fifty in a four week period.

I Hm! What about Communication? I'm sure a lot of students would see Communication and say that's really the least important thing in the course.

P Oh, I've found it very useful. I have to go to customers I've never met before and put my points across. It's been helpful too in going for job interviews. Just getting confidence in presenting yourself.

I Did they give you any practice in explaining things to non-specialists? In simple, non-technical ways to users?

P Erm, what you had to do in front of a video camera, was to choose a subject and, erm, break it down so that everyone could understand it. Even though your classmates were all technically-minded, you had to make it so that the teacher could understand it. The teacher who was marking it had to understand. If she didn't, she wouldn't pass you.

PART 3

I Now that the course is over, how do you keep up?

P That's the difficult thing. You get a lot from work when you're thrown into situations you don't know much about. You have to learn fast.

I Uhum.

P I've noticed a few times when I've gone to customers who want something fixed that I don't know about that I learn really fast.

I So you're teaching yourself.

P Yes. You have to do this from books and manuals and by reading the PC magazines.

P Did the college give you any advice on the best magazines to read?

P No.

I So how did you get that information? How did you know where to look for help?

P There was one lecturer. He used to work for a chip company. Even the college technical staff used to ask him for advice. He gave us some advice on where to look. The magazines themselves often recommend books to buy. The Internet's good. You go to the Microsoft websites and the manufacturers' websites also help.

I That's not something the college gave you. They didn't say, er, 'Here are a useful set of Web addresses'?

P No. There was a set book on support which was useful but it was full of mistakes so you had to check it against other books to make sure what was right.

I OK. One last question. Would you ever go back to college?

P Yes, I'd like to do my degree some time but it's getting the time and the money to do this.

UNIT 10

Interview: Computing Support Officer

PART 1

Clive Erm, I've got a whole lot of files in a folder which I call 'Contract' which has just grown over the years so, er, if I go into it and let you see it ... these are all Word files. Each time a new contract has come along, I've simply added it there and it's got the label sometimes of the client, sometimes it's got a country label. It's got so enormous that I'm, er, it's now taking time to find things. What I want to do is to create subfolders for certain countries where we have a lot of clients.

Barbara OK

C Starting with Japan, for example, so I want to have Contract as the main heading, if you like, and I want to be able to have subfolders ...

B Underneath there ...

C ... underneath, certainly for Japan, Italy, Finland and Hungary, and there may be others.

PART 2

B OK. So the way I'll do it is to go through Windows Explorer.

C So, OK, so how do I get into Windows Explorer?

B So let's click on Start on your status bar. The Start button and ...

C Er, sorry, where are we?

B If you bring your cursor down to the very bottom. You see that little status bar that comes up.

C Oh, right. OK

B And there should be a Windows Explorer option ... And you don't have one!

C Erm, how odd.

B OK. Not a problem though. Instead of

clicking on Programs, you can click on Run on your Start menu and just type in the word Explorer and hit …

C In this box? Just Explore.

B Explorer. And hit OK. And that should launch it.

C Oh, yeh.

B OK. This is Windows Explorer and if you'll notice next to where it says Windows in your C drive there's a little minus sign.

C Right …

B If you click on that, that'll just compact your C drive.

C Single click?

B Yes. And that just gets it out of the way so now we can see all of our drives.

C Right …

B And you store everything on DIRDATA? Is that right?

C Yes.

B So, right next to your T drive there's a little plus sign. If you click on that.

C What … ? OK …

B That opens up and shows you all your folders.

C Why are … Does the plus indicate that there are other folders?

B Yes. If there were no other folders in there you wouldn't have a little box there. You'd just have the one folder name whatever it was.

C And what's the minus? Is that just open and close?

B Yes, basically. So expand and contract.

C OK …

B And you're storing them in Word, are you?

C Yes.

B So click on the little plus sign next to the Word folder. And that shows you all your folders in Word.

C Right

B And now you want your Contract folder. So we can click once on Contract and you'll notice on the right hand side it shows us all the files we have within that folder.

C Right …

B So what we can do now is … in our Explorer window click on File on the menu bar and click on the word New on the top.

C Uhuh, right …

B And that will bring us another little box up … And click on Folder. And that's going to create a subfolder in Contract because we had Contract highlighted.

C Ah, OK …

B And now we can give it a new name. It gives a default name of New Folder and we want to type in what we want to actually call it.

C So within … where it says New Folder, I remove that and I put in whatever the

name of the new folder is.

B Yes, you can delete that.

C So let's put in the new name 'Japan' and …

B You can either hit Enter or just click outside the box. OK and is that the only folder you want to create?

C No, I'm going to create Italy, Finland and Hungary.

B OK, so we want to make sure that we have Contract highlighted. Right now Japan remains highlighted and if you clicked File, New and Folder now it would create a folder in Japan.

C Ah, so it would create a sub-sub-folder?

B Right …

C OK …

B So you just need to click on Contract to make sure it's highlighted and go File and there you are.

C So it's the same again. File, New, Folder.

PART 3

C OK. Now if I want to start moving into that sub-folder some of these files how do I do that?

B Well how I would do it is … You'll notice on the left hand … on the left hand side where it's showing you all your folders … that Contract now has a little plus sign next to it …

C Right …

B … because we've created sub-folders within Contract.

C Uhuh …

B So if you click on the little plus sign next to your Contract folder …

C Right …

B … it shows you your two sub-folders in there.

C Oh, yeh. OK. So Hungary and Japan.

B And on your right hand side you're still looking at all of your files that are within Contract.

C Right …

B So now you can actually click on one of those files, hold your mouse button down, and drag it over to the sub-folder …

C OK …

B … and that will drop it into the sub-folder.

C This is one?

B Yeh. Bring it over and it'll highlight the sub-folders.

C Just over the top of Japan?

B Yes, because Japan is highlighted now that's telling you that's where it's going to go.

C So just like that. As soon as it's highlighted that's it?

B Yeh. So if you click on to the Japan folder on the left you'll notice on the

right it shows you your file there.

C Oh, right. How do I go back?

B Click on Contract again on the left.

C OK. And that's it.

B Yeh. And if you actually drag anything over there and you realise you've dragged it to the wrong place, and you're not sure if you dragged it to the right place, there is an Undo. Under Edit on the menu bar.

C Right …

B So that's a handy tool. Sometimes you drag something and then your hand twitches and you never know …

C Right. I think I can do it.

B OK.

UNIT 13

The World Wide Web

To find the webpage you want, you have to click on a webpage hyperlink or enter a URL, a Uniform Resource Locator into a browser. The URL is the address of the page. When you do that, the browser sends the URL to a DNS server.

The DNS server is the Domain Name Server. It uses a look-up table to find the IP address of the Web server referred to in the URL. The IP address is a unique, 32-bit, set of numbers. Erm, every computer on the Web has its own IP address.

Once the DNS server has found the IP address, it sends it back to the browser.

The browser then uses this IP address to send a request to the Web server. The request is sent as a series of separate data packets which include both the IP address of the Web server and the IP address of the browser computer. These data packets are first sent to a router computer, which uses the IP address of the Web server to determine the best available route for each packet.

The packets are passed from router to router until they reach the Web server. They may travel by different routes before reaching the server.

As the individual packets reach the Web server, they're put back together again.

The Web server now services the request by sending the requested webpage back to the browser computer. Again it travels as a series of separate data packets from router to router. This time the router uses the IP address of the browser computer to work out the best available path for each packet.

As the packets arrive at the browser computer they're combined to form the webpage you requested and are displayed in your browser.

UNIT 15

Interview: Wepage Creator

Interviewer How long has your site been up?

John Just a couple of months. It's brand new.

I What's your site all about?

J It's called The Movie Shrine, www.the movieshrine.com, and it's just a site with movie reviews, strange things I've noticed about certain films, and lots of links to other movie sites.

I Why dedicate your site to this subject?

J I decided to make a site about movies because I've been a huge movie fan for a long time. Right now, films are my biggest hobby.

I What makes your site special?

J I guess my site is just a little less formal than most of the film sites on the Internet. I've tried to make the layout unique and include material for movie fans of all types. It's for people who like movies of all kinds. There are plenty of sites for fans of particular actors or genres of movies like sci-fi, horror, films noirs and so on.

I How did you create your site?

J I created the site pretty easily using Netscape Composer, which is a program contained in Netscape Communicator. The actual address is www.geocities.com/orangecow, but I got a free domain name which redirects it to the site.

I What was the most difficult part?

J Oh, the design. Just working out how the site would look and how the pages would link up. I'd tried to put up a couple of websites before but after constructing the main page, I'd lost interest.

I How did you get your domain name?

J I got a free domain name from www.domainzero.com. The price of a 'free' domain is that all kinds of advertising is sent to your email, but that's a small price to pay.

I Have you registered your site on a search engine?

J No, I haven't gotten around to registering on a search engine yet. I'm told you have to really persevere to get listed. Yahoo! just seems to swallow submissions.

I Have you included links to other sites?

J I include many links to other sites. That may be the best thing about my site, the huge number of links. I'm also in a lot of Yahoo! Clubs and I've linked to them too.

I Has anyone linked to you?

J Since my site hasn't been around for very long at all, I don't think anybody has linked to me yet except for a couple of Yahoo! Clubs.

I How long do you spend updating your site?

J As often as possible but it's difficult during the week. My studies don't leave me a lot of time and I've got other interests. And I need to watch movies sometimes! Generally one update will take from forty-five minutes to an hour.

I What sort of feedback do you get from visitors?

J I haven't really gotten much feedback so far except from people I know and they like it, or say they do! I'm hoping that after more people discover the site I'll start to get more reactions via email.

I Do you have any tips for others creating a homepage?

J Pick a topic you're really interested in. Get a good domain name. Keep your site updated – nobody likes a static site. I would look at lots of other sites too for good ideas.

I What do you intend to do next with your site?

J I'm going to update the Movie Journal section and I'd like to build in new links.

I What's your favourite site?

J It would ... my favourite site would have to be the Internet Movie Database www.imdb.com. That's not a very original answer but that site just has such a wealth of information about every kind of movie that it's probably my favourite.

UNIT 16

Communications Systems

In the short term, computers are certainly going to become more powerful and they'll also get cheaper. Erm, that means they'll become much more commonly available. It's likely they'll be integrated with other devices, erm, and may even become specialised ... specialised devices you throw away when they go wrong. Monitors are going to change from cathode ray tube monitors to flat screen panels because they take up less space and use less power. Erm, there's likely to be devices used for security, biometric devices, for scanning your eye or taking your fingerprints. They'll be used instead of passwords. Printing ... printers ... colour printers, colour laser printers are becoming cheaper so more printing will be done in colour. Er, you'll print your holiday snaps straight from a laser. The shape and design of computers are likely to change and become much more varied because we can now construct the motherboards in flexible form. Er, on the software side, companies are trying hard to improve voice control so you'll be able to talk to your computer to control it without using a keyboard.

Erm, yeh, another development which I expect to become more common in the near future is video. You'll be able to use your computer as a video-recorder and edit video on your computer. I expect the way that software is sold will change too. Erm, instead of buying individual packages people may rent or hire the components they need – wordprocessor or whatever – and connect to them over the Internet. Service providers will make different components available and you'll be charged a fee for the ones you use.

In the longer term they won't be able to make computers any more powerful using electronics so other methods may come in for the data signals in the computer. Perhaps laser light or even quantum methods will be used. Computers will probably be integrated more with TV systems and with telephony and become much more communication devices. It's likely much smaller devices will be made ... probably built into clothing so that you can walk about wearing a computer which will allow you to communicate wherever you go. At home our fridges, cookers and other devices almost certainly will be computer controlled. In the longer term there may even be devices implanted into our bodies to help people with disabilities. Computers might be implanted into the human brain. We might not call them computers in the future but they'll be everywhere.

UNIT 17

Computing Support

David Hello, this is Apricot Computers Service Division. My name's David, how can I help you?

Jennifer Hello, my name is Jennifer and we're having a problem with one of our Apricot computers.

D Now can you tell me what model of

computer you have?

J Yeh, it's an Apricot LS 550.

D An Apricot LS 550. OK, is the computer still under warranty?

J Yes, we only got it a month ago. So it should still be covered.

D Can you give me the service tag number?

J Yes, let me have a look. It's AM 964 ... 70.

D That's AM96470. Wait a moment and I'll just look it up in my database. ... Is that University of Edinburgh, 21 Hill Place?

J Yes, that's us.

D So can you describe what the problem is.

J Well it doesn't seem to be playing MIDI sound files from the Internet.

D Erm, MIDI sound files. Does it play other types of sound files?

J Yeh.

D And is it only when you're in the browser on the Internet that you're having this problem?

J No, we're getting the same fault when we use other programs like ... erm ... Microsoft Encarta.

D Right. What operating system are you using?

J Microsoft Windows.

D Which version of Windows?

J It's Windows 2000.

D And what type of processor do you have in the computer?

J It's got a Pentium 3.

D And how much RAM is installed?

J Let's see ... 128 Megabytes.

D Is the computer connected to any kind of network?

J Yes, we have a LAN.

D What type of network?

J It's a Windows NT network.

D OK. Right. It sounds as if you may have a driver fault. Do you still have the original driver disk you got with the machine?

J Yes, we've only had it a month so it's all there.

D Well, you could try to reinstall the sound drivers and see if that cures the problem. If that doesn't cure the problem, can you contact us again and we'll send you out some new drivers to try.

J OK, I'll give that a try and get back to you if we have a problem.

D Er, if you're going to contact us again with this problem, can you quote this job number. It's E83095.

J Er, just a moment. I need to get a pen. Can you repeat that?

D OK, E ... 83095.

J E83095.

D That's correct.

J Can I take down your name?

D Yes, my name's David, David Lister.

J OK, thank you, David and ... er ... we'll be in touch if there's any further problems.

D OK.

J Bye.

D Bye.

UNIT 20

Interview: The ex-hacker

PART 1

Interviewer Ralph was one of two 18-year-olds arrested in the 1990s for hacking into a large American company. They got into the CEO's personal files and left a very rude message. Well, he's grown up a bit and has been putting his knowledge to very good use. He's now a computer security expert, a 'white hat' hacker who uses his skills to make cyberspace safer. Ralph, what exactly is hacking and how do you go about hacking into a system?

Ralph Hacking simply means getting into computer systems ... you don't have permission to get into. Erm, there are various ways of doing it. You can get in by trying to guess somebody's password. Or you find a bug in a computer system that will allow people with certain passwords to get in where they shouldn't.

I So you're sitting in front of your computer ... somewhere, how do you set about getting into someone else's system?

R Sometimes it's very simple. People who hack into systems for a living – because they're employed by companies to test their systems – would say the first thing you do is to phone up someone who uses the system and you say 'Hello, I'm from your company. We want to test a new system. ... We need your password, please, so that we can include you in the trial.' People are too trusting. They normally hand it over.

That's the easy way. If that doesn't work, then you find out by trying to connect to it over the Internet. And normally that's not desperately difficult.

Once you connect to the computer it will ... ask you to ... log on and type an ID and password. You might at the simplest level try typing in 'guest' or 'demo' or 'help' and see what it gives you.

I How can you avoid being hacked into?

R There's a lot you can do but you have to keep at it to keep ahead of the hackers. Erm, you can install firewalls to restrict access to a network. You can have a callback system to make sure remote clients are who they say they are. Having really secure passwords helps. Don't use a common name or a dictionary word or anything short. Check the system regularly using event logs to find failed access attempts.

PART 2

I How did you get into this business in the first place? Were you a computer geek at school?

R I was a computer geek, a young anorak. I got into computers at school. I discovered that what the computers in the lab would let me see depended on what password I typed in and that's really where I started thinking about security.

I And how did you manage to get into the American company's files?

R I guessed some passwords and so on and because of various very silly mistakes the operators of the system made I managed to get right into the system at the highest level.

I And managed to get into the CEO's personal files.

R Yes, what happened there was I got into part of the system that said 'Please enter your ID' and then underneath that on the same screen told you what the ID was. It was the most senior ID on the system so I typed it in. It said 'You're logged on as systems manager what would you like to do?' And I said, I'll have some passwords please. And because I was logged on at the highest level it said 'Whose do you want?' And I said 'The CEO' because there was an account on the system in his name. And it gave it to me.

I Did you feel terribly excited?

R Yes, absolutely. People sometimes hack for money, for criminal purposes or for political purposes ... they want to expose something. But often you hack because you're challenged. Because it's exciting. It is a very big challenge for a couple of 18-year-olds working on a basic PC to link directly to a very powerful machine that they've completely penetrated. It was great fun and it's a wonderful feeling and that's why we did it.

We never thought about the legal side of it. My parents knew that the phone bill was horrendous and that I spent an awful lot of time in my bedroom on the computer but they didn't know quite what I was doing.

I How did they track you down?

R Well, because we never really tried to cover our tracks. We would boast to our friends, we would boast to girls. That got us known to the police and the computer crime unit. They arrested us. The guy who arrested us, the detective inspector, I'm now quite friendly with. I see him at computer conferences all over the world. But I met him first when he knocked at my door and took away the contents of my bedroom in black plastic bags.

I Now you're helping companies to avoid people like you.

R Yes, if you want to protect your systems it's a good idea to talk to people like myself rather than big city consultants ... because I know the ways in which I would try to break into your system.

I Do you hackers know each other? Is there a competitive element to all this? Is there a kind of rivalry?

R I think in the beginning people did. Er, they would ... sit round ... talking about hacking and sharing passwords but nowadays because of the Internet ... hackers are all over the world and they tend not to know each other and you tend not, because it's so illegal now and so many people are scared of it, people tend not to want to be known.

There is rivalry. Everyone wants to be the first to hack into a really powerful system. The Pentagon gets something like 200 attempts a day to break into their systems.

I Movies sometimes feature hackers.

R I don't go much for the Hollywood ... hacker. They show hackers coming into your system via the Internet and stealing all your data. That's not generally what happens. In reality about 75% of all hacks into company computers are done by current staff who are simply misusing the privileges you've given them ...

I A recent survey found that four out of ten UK consumers are reluctant to use credit cards for Internet purchases. How risky is it really?

R Some people are nervous about giving their credit card number on the Internet. We've seen in the press, partly due to hackers, partly due to the incompetence of people who are running websites, that you can get databases of credit card numbers. But usually it's the retailers, not the buyers, who get done by people using fake or stolen cards.

Using your credit card on the Internet is no more dangerous than giving your credit card number down the phone or paying at the supermarket with a credit card, throwing the receipt away where somebody can pick it up and then they've got your credit card number and a copy of your signature. The Internet is not as dangerous as that.

My advice is, if you want to buy things on the Internet, get a separate credit card. Ask for a small limit. Then if it gets misused, you've cut your losses. You can buy a pre-paid charge card for small purchases. Long term, smart cards are probably the answer but you would need a reader on your PC.

UNIT 21

Software Engineering

Analyst If I could find out what you do at present. What kind of system do you have at the moment?

Hotel owner Well, we introduced erm a computerised system about five years ago but I'm not very happy with it. What we've got is erm, just a system that allows us to enter bookings as they come in.

A So is everything computerised or ... ?

H No, it's only the reservations system.

A So what features would you like to add to this?

H Well, there are a number of things. I'd like a more sophisticated system that would allow me to link reservations and invoicing. I'd like the system to handle invoices also.

A OK. Now the output. What kind of output are you looking for from this?

G Erm, well there are a number of things I'd like. One is of course the total invoice, a bill for the guests. I'd like it also to display room bookings so that if someone phones up it's easy for the reception staff to identify quickly which rooms are occupied and which are available.

A Is that on the screen?

H Yes, I would like it to be on the screen if possible. A sort of room chart on the screen.

A And the invoices, is it pre-printed forms you use?

H Would pre-printed forms be useful?

A Well, if you have a coloured logo, it's better to have the forms pre-printed.

H Yes, I'd like that. And of course I want the invoice to have details of all expenditure so if the guest has a drink at the bar, extra meals at the restaurant, anything of that nature, it's all detailed. I'd also like the system to generate lists of previous guests so I can send them news of special offers.

A Has the system to print out addressed envelopes?

H If it could, that would be very useful.

A Now, who's going to be inputting the information?

H Right, the main users would be the reception staff. They would be dealing with bookings, largely by phone but some by fax or letter. The accountant, of course, would be using the system to create bills. And, erm, bar and restaurant staff would have to enter sales.

A Are the staff experienced in using computers or would they need a lot of training?

H Reception staff are quite experienced, however, our accountant would need some training as she's used to a paper system.

A What about the bar and restaurant staff?

H Well, I suppose they would be entering only very restricted information on sales.

A Hm. What computer hardware do you have at the moment?

H Er, we've got one PC at reception and one in the office. What would I need?

A One for the accountant, one in the bar and restaurant. And they would have to be networked.

H If they're networked together, that doesn't mean that people can get into the accounts, does it?

A No, it would be password-protected. And the printers?

H I don't want anything too noisy.

A Laser printers tend to be quieter. Now, it would be useful to talk to the receptionist to get details of the input for the guest records and to the accountant to find out what she needs.

H Great, I'll set up meetings for you. What's the next step?

A I'll come back to you with a plan and we'll check through to make sure it has all the features you want. Then we'll create a program and try it out. We'll have to keep adapting it depending on how well it works. And once you're happy with it, we'll put it into service and I'll fix some training for the staff.

H Thanks very much.

UNIT 24

The Future of IT

Speaker A To recreate human intelligence we need speed, we need memory capacity to match the human brain and we need the right hardware. We'll have all this by 2020 but these things aren't enough. We also need to capture the complexity, range and richness of human intelligence. That's more difficult ... but we will do it. And we'll do it by reverse engineering of the human brain. What I mean is that we'll explore the human brain from the inside and find out how it works, how it's connected, how it's wired up. We're already well on the way to this. With brain scanning we can see inside the brain. But by 2030 we'll have another instrument for exploring the brain. We'll be able to send tiny scanning robots along blood vessels to map the brain from the inside. This will give us all the data on how the brain is connected and all the features which enable it to perform as it does. When we know how the brain works, we'll be able to recreate its operation using the powerful computers which will've been developed even before this date.

Speaker B The most important difference at the moment between computers and brains is that computers work in serial and brains work in parallel. This means that we can do incredible amounts of processing compared to what a computer can achieve running for weeks, or even months. What's interesting is not so much that the brain is fast, it's the fact that it operates in parallel. If you look at the way a signal flows down neurons, they don't move extraordinarily quickly. But there are billions of them doing it all at once, whereas in a computer everything has to be done one thing after another.

Many people say we will never have an intelligent computer. They say it's not possible to have a computer that thinks. My own view is that it is possible but not with computers as they are today. If we start having parallel computers, only then I feel will we even start to approach the kind of computing power necessary to begin to make a start to reproducing some of the higher functions of the human brain. But we'll never be able to program in human emotions, moral responsibility and the uniqueness of the individual.

Speaker C What people really don't realise is the accelerating speed of change. They think that a hundred years from now we'll have made a hundred years of progress at today's rate. But we'll see a hundred years of progress at today's rate in twenty-five years because the speed of technical progress is accelerating. Right now we're doubling the rate of technical progress every decade so the next decade will mean twenty years of progress; and the following decade will be like forty. We'll make two thousand years of progress at today's rate this century. Things are changing faster and faster.

Erm, we already have computers that run factories and computers which help to build other computers. It's only a matter of time before these artificial children of ours are able to outdo us. They will think faster than we do. They will make smarter decisions than we do. Who then will be the masters – us or the machines? If we play it right, machines will look after us. If we get it wrong, machines may replace us. And it could happen sooner than we imagine.

UNIT 25

Electronic Publishing

1 Telecommunications engineer
I need information quickly; it's a vital part of my life. Every technology book in my specialism is out of date before it gets printed so I don't buy technical books. I go straight to the research groups who publish on the Web. Electronic books make good sense to me. Publishing something like a laser printer manual is just a waste of paper. What we need is an electronic version available anywhere and updated regularly.

2 Author
What I like about it is my books are available all over the world. They're available in countries where English-language books are hard to get. It doesn't matter if you live in Beijing or Buenos Aires, people can read my books anywhere.

3 An e-publisher
It's much cheaper to publish electronically than to print. It means we can take risks. We can publish books a traditional publisher wouldn't publish because they have a smaller readership. By 2005 ten per cent of titles will be published electronically. And by 2025 electronic publishing will have caught up with traditional publishing.

4 Developer of an ebook reader
Our reader is the size of a paperback. It holds about 200 books at a time. You can download books over the Internet in a few minutes and you can read for twenty hours before recharging the battery. There's a back light so you can read in any lighting conditions. The print size can be adjusted to any size you like. Pop it in a plastic bag, and you can read it in the bath. I'm confident it will replace all the throwaway books we read when we travel, textbooks that date very quickly, technical books that are out-of-date as soon as they're printed. It's just right for schools. Children have to carry far too many books. An ebook can hold about 150,000 pages of text so you could have all of your schoolbooks for a year in a paperback-sized package.

5 Keen reader
I've tried it, it's not complicated. I paid a dollar for the first chapter of Stephen King's book and another dollar because I wanted to read the next chapter. But then I thought ... there's the time on the Internet trying to get to the site, there's time taken to download it and all that time I'm paying just for being on the Internet. Then there's the printing costs because I don't like reading off a computer screen. It's not cheap. And besides I like the look and the feel of books and the fact that you can take them anywhere and who's going to steal a paperback?

And another thing. Paper lasts from 50 to 500 years. Most electronic storage media are obsolete in ten to twenty years. Magnetic tape stretches, CDs delaminate. Printed books are still the best way to preserve knowledge.

Glossary
of computing terms and abbreviations

(Microsoft) Access /'ækses/ noun U [5] a database program developed by the Microsoft Corporation

account /ə'kaʊnt/ noun C [12,13,14,20] a registration for a user of a network system. It is used for controlling access to the system.

active window /'æktɪv ˌwɪndəʊ/ noun C [7] the window in a WIMP system that is currently being used. It is usually on top of any other open windows.

address bus /ə'dres bʌs/ noun C [2] the set of conductors that carry the memory address signals between different parts of a computer system

ADSL /ˌeɪ diː es 'el/ noun U [16,23] abbreviation for asymmetric digital subscriber line. A form of DSL that has a different bandwidth for the upstream and the downstream.

AGP /ˌeɪ dʒi: 'pi:/ noun U [2] abbreviation for accelerated graphics port. A video bus interface that allows the use of a fast video card and allows the use of three-dimensional graphics.

AI /eɪ 'aɪ/ noun U [3,23,24] abbreviation for artificial intelligence

algorithm /'ælgərɪðm/ noun C [2,9] a set of precise rules or instructions for solving a problem

Alt (key) /'ælt, 'ɒlt ki:/ noun C [7] the alternative key on a computer keyboard that changes the function of the other keys when it is held down

ALT text caption /ˌælt, ˌɒlt 'tekst ˌkæpʃn/ noun C [14] text displayed in a webpage as an alternative to a graphic when the facility for displaying graphics is not available or is switched off

AltaVista /ˌæltə'vɪstə/ noun U [13] the name of a well-known search engine website

analogue signal /'ænəlɒg ˌsɪgnəl/ noun C [11,16] a type of signal that can take any value between a maximum and a minimum

analyst programmer /'ænəlɪst ˌprəʊgræmə(r)/ noun C [22] a person whose job is a combination of systems analysis and computer programming

anorak /'ænəræk/ noun C [20] a slang term for an eccentric socially inept person with little or no fashion sense and having an obsessive interest in a hobby or subject

anti-static /ˌænti 'stætɪk/ adj [12] prevents the build up of static electricity

anti-virus (program or software) /ˌænti 'vaɪrəs/ noun C/U [12,19,20] a computer program or set of programs

used to detect, identify and remove viruses from a computer system

Apple /'æpl/ noun U [25] the common name for Apple Computer Incorporated, a well-known producer of computers that introduced the WIMP interface on computers such as the Apple Macintosh

Apple Macintosh /ˌæpl 'mækɪntɒʃ/ noun C [6,25] a family of personal computers produced by Apple Computer Inc.

applet /'æplət/ noun C [23] a very small self-contained computer program

application /ˌæplɪ'keɪʃn/ noun C [3,5,6,18,21,22,25] see applications program

application layer /ˌæplɪ'keɪʃn ˌleɪə(r)/ noun C [11] the only part of a network communications process that a user sees. It prepares a message for sending over a network by converting the message from human-readable form into bits and attaching a header identifying the sending and receiving computers.

application port /ˌæplɪ'keɪʃn pɔ:t/ noun C [12] a path available for a particular type of application data to enter or leave a network system

application service provider /ˌæplɪˌkeɪʃn 'sɜ:vɪs prəˌvaɪdə(r)/ noun C [8] a company that makes applications programs available over the Internet usually charging a fee for access to programs

applications (program or software) /ˌæplɪ'keɪʃnz/ noun C/U [6,8,22] a computer program designed to be used for a particular purpose, e.g. a wordprocessor spreadsheet or database program

applications programmer /ˌæplɪ'keɪʃnz ˌprəʊgræmə(r)/ noun C [22] a person who writes applications programs using a computer language

architecture /'ɑ:kɪtektʃə(r)/ noun C [5] the general specification of a system

archive bit /'ɑ:kaɪv bɪt/ noun C [19] a digital bit stored with a file indicating if the file has been backed up since it was last edited

archiving system /'ɑ:kaɪvɪŋ ˌsɪstəm/ noun C [19] a system used for storing infrequently-used data in a way that does not provide the user with immediate access

artificial intelligence /ˌɑ:tɪfɪʃl ɪn'telɪdʒəns/ noun U [3,21,23,24] an area of computing concerned with developing computer programs that perform tasks that can normally only be done using human intelligence

ASCII /'æski/ noun U [11,18] acronym for American Standard Code for Information Interchange. A standard character encoding scheme.

ASP /ˌeɪ es 'pi:/ noun C [8,22] abbreviation for application service provider

assembly language /ə'sembli ˌlæŋgwɪdʒ/ noun C [21] a low-level computer language that uses mnemonics rather than only numbers making it easier than machine code for humans to read and write

asymmetric /ˌeɪsɪ'metrɪk/ adj [16,23] having a different signal bandwidth in each direction, i.e. the bandwidth for sending is different from the bandwidth for receiving

asynchronous /'eɪˌsɪŋkrənəs/ adj [11,12] not synchronised, i.e. occurring at irregular intervals

AT&T /ˌeɪ ti: ən 'ti:/ noun U [6] abbreviation for American Telephone and Telegraph Company. One of the world's largest IT suppliers

ATI (Technologies) /ˌeɪ ti: 'aɪ/ noun U [17] the name of a well known company that produces computer graphics cards

ATM /ˌeɪ ti: 'em/ noun C [2,3,16,19] common abbreviation for automatic teller machine. The type of machine used by banks for enabling customers to withdraw money from their bank accounts.

authentication /ɔ:ˌθentɪ'keɪʃn/ noun U [18] a process that checks the identity of a user or an object

avatar /'ævətɑ:(r)/ noun C [23] a graphical icon that represents a real person in a cyberspace system

B

B channel /'bi: ˌtʃænəl/ noun C [16] the common name for a bearer channel in an ISDN system

back up /bæk 'ʌp/ verb [5,19] to store a copy of data on a storage device to keep it safe

backbone /'bækbəʊn/ noun C [11,15] the main transmission path handling the major data traffic connecting different LANs together

backend /'bækend/ noun C [14] the server part of a client-server configuration that provides a service on a network at the request of a client

backup /'bækʌp/ noun C [11,17,19,20,24,25] the process of storing a copy of data on a storage device to keep it safe / the term used for the copied data

bandwidth /'bændwɪdθ/ noun C [8,13,16,20,23,24] the range of frequencies that can be transmitted over a communications channel

barcode /'bɑːkəʊd/ noun C [2,3,10,23] a sequence of vertical parallel lines used to give items a unique identification number

barcode reader /'bɑːkəʊd ˌriːdə(r)/ noun C [10] an optical input device that uses the reflection of a light beam to read barcode labels

BASIC /'beɪsɪk/ noun U [22,25] acronym for Beginners' All-purpose Symbolic Instruction Code

batch mode /'bætʃ məʊd/ noun U [13] a process in which all the data is collected and processed together in a batch rather than one at a time as they become available

BBC micro /ˌbiː biː siː 'maɪkrəʊ/ noun C [25] the name of one of the first microcomputers produced in the United Kingdom and used in schools. Its development was sponsored by the British Broadcasting Corporation.

bearer channel /'beərə ˌtʃænəl/ noun C [16] the common name for the part of an ISDN line that carries the data

Beginners' All-purpose Symbolic Instruction Code /bɪˌɡɪnəz ɔːl ˌpɜːpəs sɪmˌbɒlɪk ɪn'strʌkʃn kəʊd/ noun U [21] a simple high-level computer language often used for teaching programming

B-frame /'biː freɪm/ noun C [9] the common name for a bi-directional frame in an MPEG compressed file

bi-directional frame /baɪ dəˌrekʃənl, dɪ-, daɪ- 'freɪm/ noun C [9] a type of image frame used in MPEG compression. It is situated between I and P frames and stores the differences in the image compared with the I or P frame both before and after it.

binary /'baɪnəri/ noun U [5,9] a number system that only uses two digits, i.e. 1 and 0

biometric device /ˌbaɪəmetrɪk dɪ'vaɪs/ noun C [16,19] a security device that measures some aspect of a living being, e.g. a fingerprint reader or an eye scanner

BIOS /'baɪɒs/ noun C [15] acronym for Basic Input Output System. A part of the operating system stored on a ROM chip that controls the input and output of data to peripherals

biotechnology /ˌbaɪəʊtek'nɒlədʒi/ noun U [24] the industrial application of biological science techniques

bit /bɪt/ noun C [2,9,11,12,13,18,23] a small unit of storage capacity. One of the eight binary digits that make up a byte. The term comes from an abbreviation of binary digit.

bitmap compression /'bɪtmæp kəmˌpreʃn/ noun C [9] a way of reducing the size of a stored image where different digital bits or collections of bits are used to describe each element of an image

(data) block /blɒk/ noun C [11,17] a collection of data stored together and treated as a single unit

Bluetooth /'bluːtuːθ/ noun U [23,24] the name of a high-speed microwave wireless network system developed by a group of companies consisting of Ericsson, IBM, Intel, Nokia and Toshiba. It is used with portable equipment.

bookmark /'bʊkmɑːk/ verb [13] to store a link to a webpage to make it easier to find in the future

boot /buːt/ verb [5] to copy a part of the operating system into memory to allow a computer to start up

boot sector virus /buːt ˌsektə 'vaɪrəs/ noun C [18] a self-replicating program that stores itself in the part of a disk containing the programs used to start up a computer

bracketing /'brækətɪŋ/ verb [11] to set the boundaries of a message or part of a message by marking its beginning and its end with special control bits

bridge /brɪdʒ/ noun C [11,15] a hardware and software combination used to connect the same type of networks or to partition a large network into two smaller ones

broadband /'brɔːdbænd/ adj [8,16,23] able to carry signals transmitted over a wide range of frequencies

broadcast /'brɔːdkɑːst/ verb [16,19] to transmit signals that can be picked up by a large number of receivers

browse /braʊz/ verb [14,16] to move from webpage to webpage using a Web browser program

(Web) browser /'braʊzə(r)/ noun C [7,9,13,14,17,20,21] a program used for displaying webpages

BT /ˌbiː 'tiː/ noun U [24] abbreviation for British Telecom. The organisation that provides the telephone system in Great Britain.

buffering /'bʌfərɪŋ/ noun U [13] a process of temporarily storing data from a fast source so that it can be fed at a steady rate to a slower system

bug /bʌɡ/ noun C [6,20] a fault in a system

bulletin board /'bʊlətɪn bɔːd/ noun C [15,16] an electronic noticeboard

system that enables users to display messages for other users to read

bus /bʌs/ noun C [2,5] a set of conductors that carry signals between different parts of a computer

byte /baɪt/ noun C [2,9,11,17,18,25] a unit of storage capacity. A byte is made up of eight bits and stores one character, i.e. a letter, a number, a space or a punctuation mark.

C

C /siː/ noun U [21,22] a general purpose computer programming language that was originally designed for writing Unix systems programs

C drive /'siː draɪv/ noun C [10] the first hard disk in a personal computer

C++ /ˌsiː plʌs 'plʌs/ noun U [5,21,22] an object-oriented superset of the C programming language commonly used for writing applications programs for the Microsoft Windows operating system

cache /kæʃ/ verb [2] to temporarily store frequently-used data in fast memory so that it can be accessed more quickly

cache /kæʃ/ noun C [2,13] fast memory used to temporarily store frequently-used data to allow it to be accessed more quickly

cache coherency /kæʃ kəʊ'hɪərənsi/ noun U [2] a system that ensures that any changes written to main memory are reflected within the cache and vice versa

cache controller /'kæʃ kənˌtrəʊlə(r)/ noun C [2] the set of electronic logic circuits that control the operation of cache memory

cache hit /kæʃ 'hɪt/ noun C [2] the process of successfully finding the required data stored in cache memory

callback system /'kɔːlbæk ˌsɪstəm/ noun C [19,20] a system that automatically disconnects a telephone line after receiving a call and then dials the telephone number of the system that made the call to reconnect the line. It is used in remote access systems to make sure that connections can only be made from permitted telephone numbers

cathode ray tube /ˌkæθəʊd reɪ 'tjuːb/ noun C [16] a display device that uses an electron gun to fire a beam of electrons at a phosphor-coated screen

CCNA /ˌsiː siː en 'eɪ/ noun U [22] abbreviation for Cisco Certified Network Associate. A starting level networking qualification offered by Cisco, a major network equipment vendor.

CD (-ROM) (disk) /si: 'di:/ noun C [1,2,8,9,12,19,22,25] abbreviation for compact disk read only memory. A read only storage device in the form of a disk that is read using laser light.

CD-ROM drive /ˌsi: di: 'rɒm draɪv/ noun C [9,11] a storage device for reading CD-ROM disks

CD-RW (drive) /ˌsi: di: ɑ: 'dʌbl ju:/ noun C [2] abbreviation for compact disk rewritable. A storage device use for reading from and writing to a special type of CD known as a re-writeable CD.

cellphone /'selfəʊn/ noun C [23] the common name for a cellular phone

cellular network /'seljələ ˌnetwɜ:k/ noun C [16] a radio communications systems that divides a region into cells so that each region becomes a network with every point connected to a local transmitter within the cell

cellular phone /ˌseljələ 'fəʊn/ noun C [23] a cellular telephone. A mobile telephone that communicates with a local transmitter located within a small geographic area called a cell.

central processing unit /ˌsentrəl 'prəʊsesɪŋ ˌjuːnɪt/ noun C [6] the electronic processor at the centre of a computer. The term is sometimes used to refer to the combination of the processor and the main memory.

channel /'tʃænəl/ noun C [16,23] a path for the transmission of data

chat room /'tʃæt ruːm/ noun C [12,23] a virtual space on a website where on-line discussions organized around specific interests are held in real-time by users typing text messages

check data /'tʃek deɪtə/ noun U [17] information written to disks in a RAID system which is used to restore data if one of the array drives fail

checksum /'tʃeksʌm/ noun C [11] a calculated value that is stored with data to detect any errors that may occur when the data is copied or transmitted

chip /tʃɪp/ noun C [1,2,5,19,23,24] common name for a microchip. An electronic integrated circuit in a small package.

Cisco /'sɪskəʊ/ noun U [22] the name of a company that makes networking system hardware such as that used to operate the Internet

class /klɑːs/ noun C [21] the term used for a collection of objects in object oriented programming

cleanse /klenz/ verb [3] a term used in data mining meaning to remove duplicate information and erroneous data

(left) click /klɪk/ verb [1,7,13,14,15] to press and release the (left-hand) button on a mouse

client /'klaɪənt/ noun C [6,11,15,16,18] a network computer used for accessing a service on a server

client-server application /ˌklaɪənt 'sɜ:vər ˌæplɪˌkeɪʃn/ noun C [6] a program that is accessed from a client computer but most of the processing is carried out on a server computer

clipart /'klɪpɑ:t/ noun U [1,15] professionally-prepared graphical images stored on a computer system

Clipboard /'klɪpbɔ:d/ noun U [7] the name used in Microsoft Windows for the section of memory that temporarily stores data while it is being copied and pasted

clock /klɒk/ noun C [2] the set of electronic circuits used to control the timing of signals and synchronise different parts of a computer system

cluster /'klʌstə(r)/ noun C [3] a term used in data mining meaning a group of data that has similar features or is based on a limited data range

clustering /'klʌstərɪŋ/ noun U [3] a method used in data mining that divides data into groups based on similar features or limited data ranges

CMC /ˌsi: em 'si:/ noun C [12] abbreviation for computer mediated communication, i.e. the transfer of messages using a computer system

CNE /ˌsi: en 'i:/ noun U [22] abbreviation for Certified Novell Engineer. A qualification aimed at people interested in installing and planning the rollout of Novell based networks.

coax(ial) (cable) /'kəʊæks/ noun C [16] a type of shielded cable for carrying signals. It is often used with radio frequency and video signals.

COBOL /'kəʊbɒl/ noun U [5,21,22,25] acronym for Common Business-Oriented Language

code /kəʊd/ noun U [16,18,21,22] a piece of program text written in a programming language

code /kəʊd/ verb [21,23] to write the text of a program or part of a program using a computer language

COM program /'kɒm ˌprəʊɡræm/ noun C [18] a DOS program with a .com filename extension that loads and runs in 64 kilobytes or less of memory

command interpreter /kə'mɑ:nd ɪnˌtɜ:prɪtə(r)/ noun C [6] the part of an operating system that processes commands that are part of a program or are input using a keyboard

Commodore 64 /ˌkɒmədɔ: ˌsɪksti 'fɔ:(r)/ noun U [8] the model name of one of

the first popular personal computers to be made available in the United Kingdom. It had a very good graphics system and was particularly suited to running computer games programs.

Common Business-Oriented Language /ˌkɒmən ˌbɪznɪs ˌɔ:rientɪd 'læŋɡwɪdʒ/ noun U [21] a high-level computer programming language. It is the principle transaction processing language used to process the records of large organisations on mainframe computers.

compatible /kəm'pætəbl/ adj [6,14] able to operate on the same type of system or run the same software

compile /kəm'paɪl/ verb [6,22] to convert a program written in a high-level language into machine code using a compiler

compiler /kəm'paɪlə(r)/ noun C [5] a program that converts the whole of a program into machine code before the program is used

compress /kəm'pres/ verb [11] to reduce to a much smaller size

compression (scheme) /kəm'preʃn/ noun C [9,11] the process used for reducing a file to a much smaller size

computer /kəm'pju:tə(r)/ noun C [1,2,3,4,5,6,7,8,9,10,11,12,13,15,17,20,22,23,24,25] a general purpose machine that can be programmed to process data in a variety of ways

computer consultant /kəm'pju:tə kən'sʌltənt/ noun C [22,25] a person who is paid to advise on computing system issues

computer engineer /kəm'pju:tər endʒɪˌnɪə(r)/ noun C [17,22] a person who designs and develops computer systems

computer lab /kəm'pju:tə læb/ noun C [19] a room full of computers used for study

computer language /kəm'pju:tə ˌlæŋɡwɪdʒ/ noun C [22] a language used for writing computer programs

computer operator /kəm'pju:tər ˌɒpəreɪtə(r)/ noun C [18] a person whose job it is to operate part of a computer system

computer salesperson /kəmˌpju:tə 'seɪlzpɜ:sn/ noun C [22] a person whose job it is to sell computers

computer science /kəmˌpju:tə 'saɪəns/ noun U [5] the study of computers and their use

computer services engineering technician /kəmˌpju:tə ˌsɜ:vɪsɪz endʒɪ'nɪərɪŋ tekˌnɪʃn/ noun C [22] a person who provides a service of maintaining and troubleshooting computers

computer-aided design /kəmˌpjuːtər ˌeɪdɪd dɪˈzaɪn/ noun U [22] the process of designing using a computer program

computer-aided manufacture /kəmˌpjuːtər ˌeɪdɪd mænjəˈfæktʃə(r)/ noun U [22] the process of manufacturing goods using a computer

computerised /kəmˈpjuːtəraɪzd/ adj [21,22] changed so that it can be operated or controlled using a computer

computer-mediated communication /kəmˌpjuːtə ˌmiːdieɪtɪd kəˌmjuːnɪˈkeɪʃn/ noun C [12,16] a process of transferring messages using computers

computing /kəmˈpjuːtɪŋ/ noun U [5,22] the theory and practice of computers

computing science /kəmˈpjuːtɪŋ ˈsaɪəns/ noun U [22] see computer science

computing support /kəmˈpjuːtɪŋ səˈpɔːt/ noun U [5,17,22] a field of work that provides a service including setting up, maintaining and troubleshooting computing systems and providing technical advice to users

computing support officer /kəmˈpjuːtɪŋ səˈpɔːt ˌɒfɪsə(r)/ noun C [10] a person whose job it is to provide support to computer users including setting-up, maintaining and troubleshooting computer systems and giving technical advice

configure /kənˈfɪɡə(r)/ verb [12,17,22] to adjust the settings

connectivity /ˌkɒnekˈtɪvəti/ noun U [16] the characteristic of being connected

control bit /kənˈtrəʊl bɪt/ noun C [11] a data bit used to mark parts of a transmitted signal so that the transmission can be controlled, e.g. a 'start' bit marks the beginning of a character and a 'stop' bit marks its end

control bus /kənˈtrəʊl bʌs/ noun C [10] the set of conductors that carry the control signals between the Control Unit and other parts of a computer

corrupt /kəˈrʌpt/ verb [18] to damage in such a way that prevents normal use

cp /siː ˈpiː/ noun U [6] a Unix command for copying a file

CPU /ˌsiː piː ˈjuː/ noun C [2,5] abbreviation for central processing unit

crack /kræk/ verb [18,19] to break into a computer system in order to steal information or cause damage

crash /kræʃ/ verb [17,19] to fail suddenly and completely usually referring to the failure of a hard disk

CRT /ˌsiː ɑː ˈtiː/ noun C [24] abbreviation for cathode ray tube

Ctrl + Alt + Del /kənˌtrəʊl plʌs ˌælt (ɒlt) plʌs dɪˈliːt/ noun U [10] set of symbols that signify pressing the combination of the control-alternative and delete keys on a computer keyboard at the same time

cursor /ˈkɜːsə(r)/ noun C [2,10] a symbol on the monitor screen that indicates the point on the screen that is being used

cut and paste /ˌkʌt ənd ˈpeɪst/ verb [7] to remove some data from a file and temporarily store it in the computer's memory then insert a copy of the data in another position in the same or in another file

cyberbabe /ˈsaɪbəbeɪb/ noun C [23] a digital image of an attractive female that is used in programs on the Internet

cybernetics /ˌsaɪbəˈnetɪks/ noun U [23] the study of control and communication in animals and machines. It is used in the design of robots.

cyberspace /ˈsaɪbəspeɪs/ noun U [20,24] the combination of all the data on all the computer networks throughout the world accessed using the Internet

cyborg /ˈsaɪbɔːɡ/ noun C [23] a man-machine system or a person made superhuman by a machine or external system that changes the way the body functions

D

D channel /ˈdiː ˌtʃænəl/ noun C [16] the common name for a data channel in an ISDN system

data /ˈdeɪtə/ noun U [1,2,5,6,12,15,17,18, 19,21,22,23] the information processed by a computer

data bank /ˈdeɪtə bæŋk/ noun C [23] a large collection of data that can be accessed by many users and enables them to copy or store data on a particular topic

data bus /ˈdeɪtə bʌs/ noun C [2] the set of conductors that carry the data signals between different parts of a computer

data centre /ˈdeɪtə ˌsentə(r)/ noun C [8] a facility for storing large amounts of information

data channel /ˈdeɪtə tʃænəl/ noun C [16] the common name for the part of an ISDN line that carries signalling and supervisory information to the network

data communications /ˌdeɪtə kəmjuːnɪˈkeɪʃnz/ noun U [5] the transmission and reception of data signals using a communications network and appropriate protocols

data integrity /ˌdeɪtər ɪnˈtegrəti/ noun U [17,19] a measure of how resistant a system is to causing corruption in data while it is being stored or transferred

data mart /ˈdeɪtə mɑːt/ noun C [3] a storage system that archives large amounts of data in a way that makes it easy to access

data mining /ˈdeɪtə ˌmaɪnɪŋ/ noun U [3] a process of analysing a large amount of stored data to find new useful information

data stream /ˈdeɪtə striːm/ noun C [9] the flow of data

data warehouse /ˌdeɪtə ˈweəhaʊs/ noun C [3] a computing centre that provides a large collection of data gathered from different sources for data mining

database (program) /ˈdeɪtəbeɪs/ noun C [1,3,5,8,15,17,19,20,21,22,23,24] a type of applications program used for storing information so that it can be easily searched and sorted

data-delivery system /ˌdeɪtə dɪˈlɪvəri ˌsɪstəm/ noun C [12] a system for transmitting data from one computer to another

data-link layer /ˈdeɪtə lɪŋk ˌleɪə(r)/ noun C [11] the part of a network communications system that supervises the transmission. It confirms the checksum then addresses and duplicates the packets. This layer keeps a copy of each packet until it receives confirmation from the next point along the route that the packet has arrived undamaged.

date /deɪt/ noun U [6] a Unix and MS-DOS command for displaying the current date

debug /ˌdiːˈbʌɡ/ verb [21] to find and fix faults in a program or system

DEC VAX /ˈdek væks/ noun U [6] a range of computers produced by the Digital Equipment Corporation using their Vax range of processors

decipher /dɪˈsaɪfə(r)/ verb [18] to change coded information into normal text

decision table /dɪˈsɪʒn ˌteɪbl/ noun C [21] a type of grid used in computer program design to show what actions should be taken by the program under different conditions

decision tree /dɪˈsɪʒn triː/ noun C [3] an AI technique used in data mining that separates data into subsets then further divides the subsets into smaller subsets until the subsets are small enough to allow the mining process to find interesting patterns and relationships within the data

decode /ˌdiːˈkəʊd/ verb [9] to decide what a program instruction means

decompress /ˌdiːkəmˈpres/ verb [9] to remove the compression, i.e. to expand to its original size

decrypt /ˌdiːˈkrɪpt/ verb [11,18] to recover the original text from an encrypted message

defacing /dɪˈfeɪsɪŋ/ noun U [18] a computer crime that involves changing the information shown on another person's website without permission

default /dɪˈfɒlt, -fɔːlt/ noun C [10] an initial setting that can be changed by the user

denial of service attack /dɪˌnaɪəl əv ˈsɜːvɪs əˌtæk/ noun C [18] a type of computer crime that involves swamping a server with large numbers of requests

desktop /ˈdesktɒp/ noun C [3,5,6,7,9,11] the main graphical user interface background screen that displays icons for other programs

desktop (PC)/(computer) /ˈdesktɒp/ noun C [1,2,3,5,6,13,22] a personal computer that is designed to be used on an office desk

desktop application /ˌdesktɒp ˌæplɪˈkeɪʃn/ noun C [22] a computer program designed to be used on a desktop computer

desktop organiser /ˌdesktɒp ˈɔːgənaɪzə(r)/ noun C [1] a small computer providing a variety of tools for organising work, e.g. a calendar, to do list, diary, address list, calculator, etc.

development life cycle /dɪˌveləpmənt ˈlaɪf ˌsaɪkl/ noun C [5] the phases a software product goes through from when it is first thought of until it becomes obsolete. This typically includes: requirements analysis, design construction, testing (validation), installation, operation, maintenance and retirement.

DHTML /ˌdiː eɪtʃ tiː em ˈel/ noun U [22] abbreviation for dynamic hypertext markup language. A development of HTML that allows the creation of more dynamic and user-interactive web pages.

dial-up networking /ˌdaɪl ʌp ˈnetwɜːkɪŋ/ noun U [12,17] a communications system that allows computers to connect together using a telephone line

differential backup /ˌdɪfəˌrenʃl ˈbækʌp/ noun C [19,25] a type of backup that copies all the selected files on a system that have been changed since the last time a full backup was carried out

digital /ˈdɪdʒɪtəl/ adj [9,11,16,18,19,23] an electronic system that has only two states, e.g. off or on

digital camera /ˌdɪdʒɪtəl ˈkæmərə/ noun C [1,3,5,13,23] an input device for taking pictures. It has an electronic lens and uses electronics for storing the images rather than chemical film.

digital cash /ˌdɪdʒɪtəl ˈkæʃ/ noun U [19] electronic currency that is stored on electronically sensitive cards or exists in cyberspace and is used for making electronic purchases over the Internet

digital certificate /ˌdɪdʒɪtəl səˈtɪfɪkət/ noun C [18] an electronic message used to show a transaction is trustworthy. It contains information about the company processing the transaction including their public key and is electronically 'signed' by a trusted digital-certificate issuer.

digital subscriber line /ˌdɪdʒɪtəl səbˈskraɪbə laɪn/ noun U [16] a broadband communications system that allows digital signals to be transferred across an ordinary analogue telephone line

directory /dəˈrektəri, dɪ-, daɪ-/ noun C [6,19] a storage area used for grouping files so that they can be easily located. A directory is sometimes called a folder.

disk /dɪsk/ noun C [6,17,19] a flat circular storage device

disk drive /ˈdɪsk draɪv/ noun C [6,17] a storage device for reading from and writing to disks

divider /dɪˈvaɪdə(r)/ noun C [10] a vertical bar that divides a Windows Explorer window into two parts. One part shows the drive folders and the other part shows the filenames of the files in the selected folder.

DNS /ˌdiː en ˈes/ noun C [13] abbreviation for domain name system

domain name /dəˈmeɪn neɪm/ noun C [15,20] an identifier used on the Internet in place of the numerical Internet address. It identifies the host, the type and the country code, e.g. holyrood.ed.ac.uk

domain name server /dəˈmeɪn neɪm ˌsɜːvə(r)/ noun C [13] a network server computer used for operating and controlling the domain name system

domain name system /dəˈmeɪn neɪm ˌsɪstəm/ noun C [13] a system of associating the name of a device on a network such as the Internet with its numerical address so that the name can be used by the user and the numerical address can be used by the network system

dot-matrix printer /dɒt ˈmeɪtrɪx ˌprɪntə(r)/ noun C [8] a printer that prints by hammering pins onto an inked ribbon

double click /ˌdʌbl ˈklɪk/ verb [7] to press and release the left-hand button on a mouse two times in rapid succession

download /ˌdaʊnˈləʊd/ verb [1,8,12,13, 15,16,17,20,23,25] to copy a file from a server to a client computer in a network

download /ˈdaʊnləʊd/ noun C [13,16,23] a process of copying a file from a server to a client computer in a network

downstream /ˈdaʊnstriːm/ noun U [16] the signal path for receiving communications from a server to a client computer in a network

drag and drop /ˌdræg ən ˈdrɒp/ verb [7,10,21] to move data from one location to another with a mouse. Holding down the mouse button while moving the mouse moves the selected data. Releasing the mouse button drops the data in the new location.

drive array /ˈdraɪv əˌreɪ/ noun C [17] a set of hard disks that are used in a RAID system

driver /ˈdraɪvə(r)/ noun C [15,17] a systems program that controls a peripheral device

DSL /ˌdiː es ˈel/ noun U [16] abbreviation for digital subscriber line

DTP /ˌdiː tiː ˈpiː/ noun U [8] abbreviation for desktop publishing. A process of designing documents for publishing using a computer system.

dumb terminal /ˈdʌm ˌtɜːmɪnəl/ noun C [11] a network device with a keyboard and display screen that is used for sending and receiving data but does not do any processing

duplex /ˈdjuːpleks/ adj [16] able to transfer data in both directions, i.e. can send and receive data

DVD (-ROM) /ˌdiː viː ˈdiː/ noun C [2,9,11] abbreviation for digital versatile disk read only memory. An optical disk storage device that can hold a large amount of video data.

E

EAN /ˌiː eɪ ˈen/ noun U [3] abbreviation for European Article Number system. The European price and item codes commonly used in barcode systems

earphone /ˈɪəfəʊn/ noun C [24] sound output device that fits into the ear of the user

earth /ɜːθ/ noun U [12] a common name for an electrical ground point or zero voltage point

ebook /ˈiːbʊk/ noun C [25] common name for an electronic book

ebook reader /ˈiːbʊk ˌriːdə(r)/ noun C [25] common name for an electronic book reader

e-business /'i:bɪznɪs/ noun U [14] common term for electronic business, i.e. business that is carried out using the Internet

e-cash /'i:kæʃ/ noun U [24] common name for electronic cash

ECC memory /ˌi: si: si: 'meməri/ noun U [2] abbreviation for error code correcting memory. A type of memory often used in server computers that automatically fixes simple memory errors without requiring the rebooting of the computer

e-commerce /'i: kɒmɜ:s/ noun U [8,14,22,23] the business of buying and selling goods and services on the Internet

editor /'edɪtə(r)/ noun C [5,25] a computer program for making changes to text in computer programs or data

edutainment /ˌedjʊ'teɪmmənt/ noun U [1] a system that has both educational and entertainment value

EIDE /ˌi: aɪ di: 'i:/ noun U [2] abbreviation for extended integrated device electronics. A type of hard disk control system where most of the control electronics is built into the drive itself. Extended IDE allows the use of multiple drives of more than 528 megabytes.

electronic (book) reader /elek,trɒnɪk 'ri:də(r)/ noun C [18,25] a computing device that displays the text and images of an electronic book

electronic book /elek,trɒnɪk 'bʊk/ noun C [25] a book that is displayed using a computing device instead of being printed on paper

electronic cash/money /elek,trɒnɪk 'kæʃ, 'mʌni/ noun U [24] data that represents real money that is stored and transferred on computing devices connected to the Internet in e-commerce systems

electronic publisher /elek,trɒnɪk 'pʌblɪʃə(r)/ noun C [25] an organisation that produces ebooks

electronic virtual assistant /elek,trɒnɪk ,vɜ:tʃʊəl ə'sɪstənt/ noun C [23] a computer program represented by an animated screen image that is used to help the user perform particular tasks such as searching the Internet for useful data

email /'i:meɪl/ noun C [1,5,7,8,12,13,14, 15,16,17,18,20,23,24] the common name for an electronic mail message, i.e. a text message sent electronically using a computer

email /'i:meɪl/ verb [1,23] to send an email message

email address /'i:meɪl ə,dres/ noun C [12,18] the unique address code used to contact someone using electronic mail

email attachment /'i:meɪl ə,tætʃmənt/ noun C [1,15,19] a file that is attached to an email message

email program /'i:meɪl ,prəʊgræm/ noun C [13] a computer program used for reading and sending email

email service /'i:meɪl ,sɜ:vɪs/ noun C [20] an Internet service that allows user to send and receive emails

encapsulation /en,kæpsjʊ'leɪʃn/ noun U [21] a key feature of object-oriented programming that bundles data and program instructions into modules called objects

encode /,en'kəʊd/ verb [9,11,14,18] to write information in a coded form

encoder /,en'kəʊdə(r)/ noun C [9] a computer program that converts WAV files into MP3 files or vice versa

encrypt /,en'krɪpt/ verb [11,18,19] to transform data into coded form to make it secure

encryption /,en'krɪpʃn/ noun U [18,20,23,24] the transformation of data into coded form to make it secure

Enter (key) /'entə(r)/ noun C [10,13] another name for the RETURN key on a computer keyboard. Pressing the ENTER key inserts the data into the memory of the computer.

enterprise resource planning tool /,entəpraɪz rɪ,zɔ:s 'plænɪŋ tu:l/ noun C [8] a type of computer program for planning and organising business functions in an enterprise. It can help companies manage everything from sales and marketing to human resources.

EPOS till /'i:pɒs tɪl/ noun C [3] acronym for electronic point-of-sale till. A computerised cash register that edits records in sales and stock control databases.

e-publishing /'i: ,pʌblɪʃɪŋ/ noun U [25] the production of ebooks

erasable optical disk /ɪ,reɪzəbl ,ɒptɪkl 'dɪsk/ noun C [19] a CD that allows data to be deleted and new data to be recorded on it

ERP /ˌi: a: 'pi:/ noun U [22] abbreviation for enterprise resource planning

e-solution /'i: sə,lu:ʃn/ noun C [22] common term for electronic solutions, i.e. ways of solving a problem or providing a service using the Internet

ethernet /'i:θənet/ noun U [2,11,12] a widely-used local area network standard that broadcasts packets of data that are addressed to particular devices on the network. Each device on the network reads the address and passes it on to the correct device.

(Microsoft) Exchange /ɪks'tʃeɪndʒ/ noun U [7,22] a Microsoft Windows program that includes an email program, a calendar task list and address list

exe program /,eks'i: ,prəʊgræm/ noun C [18] an MS-DOS executable program that has an .exe filename extension. It can use more than 64 kilobytes of memory and can be located anywhere in the memory.

executable /,eksɪ'kju:təbl/ adj [21] containing instructions that can be run or executed by the processor

execute /'eksɪkju:t/ verb [6,18,21] to perform a computer operation by processing a program instruction

expansion card /ɪk'spænʃn ka:d/ noun C [1,10] an electronic circuit board used for adding facilities to a computer

expansion slot /ɪk'spænʃn slɒt/ noun C [2] a long thin connector that is used for adding additional electronics in the form of expansion cards

expert system /'ekspɜ:t ,sɪstəm/ noun C [1] an artificial intelligence program that collects and uses human expertise to allow non-experts to solve specialised problems

extensible /ɪk'stensəbl/ adj [14] able to be added to, e.g. in an extensible language a developer can add their own terms

extensible markup language /ɪk,stensəbl 'ma:k ʌp ,læŋgwɪdʒ/ noun U [14,16,21] a metalanguage that allows developers to create their own set of customised tags that identify the meaning and structure of data. It is used for creating files that are program-independent, platform-independent and able to be used with different languages.

F

FAQ /,ef eɪ 'kju:/ noun C [14,17] acronym used on websites for frequently-asked question

fault tolerance /'fɒlt ,fɔ:lt ,tɒlərəns/ noun U [17] a computer's ability to recover from hardware errors

fetch /fetʃ/ verb [21] to go and get the next instruction or piece of data from memory

field /fi:ld/ noun C [13] a section of a database where an item of data is stored

file /faɪl/ noun C [5,6,12,15,18,19,22, 23,24] a computer program or data stored on a storage device

file server /'faɪl ,sɜ:və(r)/ noun C [8,11,17,22] a main computer that provides a storage area for data files on a network

file transfer protocol /ˌfaɪl ˌtrænsfɜː
ˈprəʊtəkɒl/ noun U [12] an Internet
service that allows users to transfer
files from one computer to another

file virus /ˈfaɪl ˌvaɪrəs/ noun C [18] a
virus that attaches itself to a program
file

filestore /ˈfaɪlstɔː(r)/ noun C [5] a
collection of computer files stored
centrally on a network server

firewall /ˈfaɪəwɔːl/ noun C [19,20] a
combination of hardware and software
used to control the data going into and
out of a network. It is used to prevent
unauthorised access to the network by
hackers.

flag /flæg/ verb [2] to mark in a way that
indicates that a particular condition
has occurred

flat file database /ˌflæt faɪl ˈdeɪtəbeɪs/
noun C [3] a simple database in which
all the data is stored in one table
which is not related to any other table

floppy (disk) /ˈflɒpi/ noun C [4] a
magnetic storage device in the form of
a small plastic disk. Also known as a
diskette.

floppy (disk) drive /ˈflɒpi draɪv/ noun C
[2,4,10,11] a common magnetic
storage device that reads and writes
data on a floppy disk. Also known as a
diskette drive.

flowchart /ˈfləʊtʃɑːt/ noun C [21] a kind
of diagram used by programmers to
show the logical steps in a program or
by systems analysts to show logical
steps in the design of a system

folder /ˈfəʊldə(r)/ noun C [7,13] see
directory

FORTRAN /ˈfɔːtræn/ noun U [21,22]
acronym for Formula Translator. A high-
level computing language that was
designed by scientists in 1954 and is
oriented toward manipulating formulas
for scientific, mathematical and
engineering problem-solving
applications.

forward /ˈfɔːwəd/ verb [13] to pass on
without changing the content, e.g. a
received email can be passed on to or
forwarded to another address

frame /freɪm/ noun C [14] a section of a
webpage that acts as an independent
browser window. Clicking on a link in
one frame can cause a webpage to be
displayed in another frame, e.g. a
menu in one frame can provide links to
webpages that are displayed in
another frame.

Free Software Foundation /ˌfriː ˌsɒftweə
faʊnˈdeɪʃn/ noun U [6] an organisation
that is dedicated to producing software
that can be used by anyone who wants
to use it at no cost. It depends on the

voluntary effort of a large number of
programmers throughout the world
creating and improving programs and
making their work freely available to
others.

free up /ˌfriː ˈʌp/ verb [5] to make space
available, e.g. by deleting files on a
hard disk

freeware /ˈfriːweə(r)/ noun U [15]
computer programs that are made
available to anyone who wants to use
them at no cost to the user

frequency band /ˈfriːkwənsi bænd/ noun
C [23] a set of frequencies that are
used together to provide a path for the
transmission of signals

frequency display /ˈfriːkwənsi dɪˌspleɪ/
noun C [9] an electronic device for
showing the frequency of a signal

frequency hopping /ˈfriːkwənsi ˌhɒpɪŋ/
noun U [23] a process of changing
frequencies within a fixed bandwidth
during a transmission so that other
transmissions can use the same
bandwidth at the same time without
interfering with each other

FTP /ˌef tiː ˈpiː/ noun U [12,20]
abbreviation for file transfer protocol

full backup /fʊl ˈbækʌp/ noun C [19] a
type of backup that copies all the
selected files on a system whether or
not they have been edited or backed
up before

full-duplex /ˈfʊl ˌdjuːpleks/ adj [11,23]
able to transfer data in both directions
simultaneously, i.e. data can be
transmitted and received at the same
time

futurologist /ˌfjuːtʃəˈrɒlədʒɪst/ noun C
[24] a person who studies and predicts
what technology will be like and what
effects it will have in the future

G

games console /ˈgeɪmz ˌkɒnsəʊl/ noun
C [23] an electronic device used for
playing computer games

gateway /ˈgeɪtweɪ/ noun C [11,12,13,
15,18] an interface that enables
dissimilar networks to communicate
such as two LANs based on different
topologies or network operating
systems

Gb/GB /ˈgɪgəbaɪt/ noun C [2,9,11]
abbreviation for a gigabyte

geek /giːk/ noun C [20] although it was
originally a derogatory term used for
an expert lacking in social skills, it is
now used in computing to mean a
dedicated expert

general packet radio service /ˌdʒenrəl
ˌpækɪt ˈreɪdiəʊ ˌsɜːvɪs/ noun U [16] a
GSM data transmission technique that
transmits and receives data in packets

general-purpose language /ˌdʒenrəl
ˌpɜːpəs ˈlæŋgwɪdʒ/ noun C [21] a
computer language that can be used to
write different types of programs

get listed /get ˈlɪstɪd/ verb [15] to
register the Web address of a website
on an Internet search engine

GHz /ˈgɪgəhɜːts/ noun C [2,23]
abbreviation for gigahertz

gigabit /ˈgɪgəbɪt/ noun C [23] a unit of
storage capacity equal to 1 073 741
824 bits

gigabyte /ˈgɪgəbaɪt/ noun C [2] a unit of
storage capacity equal to 1 073 741
824 bytes

gigahertz /ˈgɪgəhɜːts/ noun C [3] a unit
of frequency equal to one thousand
million hertz (cycles every second)

global positioning system /ˌgləʊbl
pəˈzɪʃnɪŋ ˌsɪstəm/ noun C [16] a
system that determines the user's
location by comparing radio signals
from several satellites

Gnome /gəˈnəʊm/ noun U [6] a project to
build a complete user-friendly Unix-like
desktop system based entirely on free
software. It is part of the GNU project
and part of the OpenSource movement.

GNU /gəˈnuː/ noun U [6] a freely
distributed portable Unix compatible
software system

GPRS /ˌdʒiː piː ɑːr ˈes/ noun U [16]
abbreviation for general packet radio
service

GPS /ˌdʒiː piː ˈes/ noun C [16,20]
abbreviation for global positioning
system

graphic equalizer /ˌgræfɪk
ˈiːkwəˌlaɪzə(r)/ noun C [9] an electronic
device that uses slider controls to
adjust the frequency response of an
audio system

graphical (user) interface /ˌgræfɪkl
ˈɪntəfeɪs/ noun C [6,7,21] the part of an
operating system that allows the user
to interact with a computer using
graphic images and a cursor

grep /grep/ noun U [6] a Unix command
for searching through one or more text
files for a specific text string

GUI /ˈguːi/ noun C [7] acronym for
graphical user interface

H

hack /hæk/ verb [6,20,23] to gain
unauthorised access to a network
system

hacker /ˈhækə(r)/ noun C [18,20] a
skilled programmer who attempts to
gain unauthorised access to a network
system

half-duplex /ˈhɑːf ˌdjuːpleks/ adj [11]
able to transfer data in both directions
but only in one direction at a time, i.e.

data can be transmitted or received but not at the same time

handheld (computer) /'hændheld/ noun C [1,7,16] a small portable computer that can be held in one hand

hang /hæŋ/ verb [17] to suddenly and unexpectedly stop processing during the execution of a program

hard (disk) (drive) /hɑːd (dɪsk) (draɪv)/ noun C [1,2,5,8,15,17,18,19] a common magnetic storage device that reads and writes data on metal disks inside a sealed case

hardware /'hɑːdweə(r)/ noun U [1,5,6,16,17,19,21,22,23,24] the physical components of a computer system

(disk drive) head /hed/ noun C [2] the part of a disk drive that reads and writes data to the disk

header /'hedə(r)/ noun C [11,13] the first section of a message that contains information about the content and transmission of the message including the sending and destination addresses

headphone /'hedfəʊn/ noun C [23] sound output device that fits over the ears of the user

help-desk/helpline /'helpdesk, 'helplaɪn/ noun C [12,22] a telephone service for helping users solve problems that occur on computer systems

hierarchical storage management /haɪəˌrɑːkɪkl 'stɔːrɪdʒ ˌmænɪdʒmənt/ noun U [19] a system of automatically moving files to different storage media depending on how often the files are used, i.e. the least used files are gradually archived. The less a file is used the more difficult it becomes to access it in the archive.

high-end package /ˌhaɪ 'end ˌpækɪdʒ/ noun C [8] a set of computer programs with a wide variety of complex features

Higher National Certificate /ˌhaɪə ˌnæʃnl səˈtɪfɪkət/ noun U [5] a British college qualification that can be gained through part-time or full-time study. It is usually obtained before studying for an HND.

Higher National Diploma /ˌhaɪə ˌnæʃnl dɪˈpləʊmə/ noun U [5] a British college qualification that usually requires a period of full-time study. It is more advanced than an HNC and not as advanced as a degree.

high-level language /ˌhaɪ ˌlevl 'læŋgwɪdʒ/ noun C [21] a programming language closer to human language than low-level computer languages such as machine code or assembly language

high-level program /ˌhaɪ ˌlevl 'prəʊgræm/ noun C [12] a computer program written using a high-level language

highlight /'haɪlaɪt/ verb [10,15] to select by marking on the display screen

hijacking /'haɪdʒækɪŋ/ noun U [18] a computer crime that involves redirecting anyone trying to visit a certain website elsewhere

HNC /ˌeɪtʃ en 'siː/ noun U [22] abbreviation for Higher National Certificate

HND /ˌeɪtʃ en 'diː/ noun U [22] abbreviation for Higher National Diploma

Home button /'həʊm ˌbʌtən/ noun C [13] the button icon on a Web browser program that takes you to the starting webpage

homepage /'həʊmpeɪdʒ/ noun C [20] the main start page of a website

host /həʊst/ noun C [13,18] a computer that provides a service on a network / a program that carries a virus

hot plug /'hɒt plʌg/ verb [2] to attach a device to a system without switching the system off and without causing problems to the system

hover /'hɒvə(r)/ verb [7] to hold a cursor over an icon for a short period of time

HSM /ˌeɪtʃ es 'em/ noun U [19] abbreviation for hierarchical storage management

HTML /ˌeɪtʃ tiː em 'el/ noun U [6,13,14, 16,21,22,25] abbreviation for hypertext markup language. A page description language that uses a system of tags for creating web pages.

hub /hʌb/ noun C [11,15] an electronic device at the centre of a star network topology

humanoid /'hjuːmənɔɪd/ noun C [23] a robot with human characteristics

hyperlink /'haɪpəlɪŋk/ noun C [7,13,20] a text or image in a webpage that causes a related webpage to be displayed or another program to be started when the user clicks on the hyperlink using the mouse

hypertext markup language /ˌhaɪpətekst 'mɑːkʌp ˌlæŋgwɪdʒ/ noun U [14,16,21] a page description language that has a set of tags that can be inserted into a document to make it act as a webpage. The tags determine how the document is displayed on the screen and marks the position of hyperlinks.

I

I/O /aɪ 'əʊ/ noun C [17] abbreviation for input/output

IBM /ˌaɪ biː 'em/ noun U [6,22,23,25] abbreviation for International Business Machines, the largest computer company in the world. It launched the first personal computer called the IBM PC which quickly became the standard.

IC /aɪ 'siː/ noun C [12] abbreviation for integrated circuit. A complete electronic circuit built on a single silicon chip.

icon /'aɪkɒn/ noun C [7,21] a small picture used in a WIMP system to represent a program folder or file

IEEE 802.11 /ˌaɪ iː iː 'iː ˌeɪt əʊ ˌtuː pɔɪnt wʌn 'wʌn/ noun U [23] a wireless networking system standard approved by the American regulating organisation called the Institute of Electrical and Electronic Engineers

I-frame /'aɪ freɪm/ noun C [9] the common name for an intra frame in an MPEG compressed file

image editor /'ɪmɪdʒ ˌedɪtə(r)/ noun C [8] a computer program that allows the user to make changes to images

image map /'ɪmɪdʒ mæp/ noun C [14] a graphic image with separate areas that contain hyperlinks to different parts of a website

IMAP /'aɪmæp/ noun U [13] acronym for Internet mail access protocol

inbox /'ɪnbɒks/ noun C [13] the folder in an email program where emails are stored when they are first received

incremental backup /ˌɪnkrəˌmentəl 'bækʌp/ noun C [19] a type of backup that copies all the selected files that have been changed since the last full differential or incremental backup

industrial scientific and medical band /ɪnˌdʌstriəl ˌsaɪəntɪfɪk ənd 'medɪkl bænd/ noun U [23] a set of radiowave frequencies centred around 2.45GHz used for industrial scientific and medical devices and for Bluetooth devices

information superhighway (the) /ˌɪnfəˌmeɪʃn 'suːpəˌhaɪweɪ/ noun U [1,24] an informal term for a global high-speed network providing communication services that are freely available to everyone, i.e. a highly-developed Internet system

information technology /ˌɪnfəˌmeɪʃn tekˈnɒlədʒi/ noun U [22,23,24,25] the study and practice of techniques or use of equipment for dealing with information

inheritance /ɪnˈherɪtəns/ noun U [21] a key feature of object-oriented programming that allows specific instances of a class to inherit all the properties of the class, e.g. squares are a specific instance of rectangles and inherit all the properties of rectangles

in-house /ˈɪn haʊs/ adj [22] done by employees of an organisation rather than people outside the organisation

initialise (the hard disk) /ɪˈnɪʃəlaɪz/ verb [18] to reboot or restart the computer

input /ˈɪnpʊt/ verb [2,4,6] to put data into a system

input /ˈɪnpʊt/ noun U [2,6,7,21,23] data put into a system

input device /ˈɪnpʊt dɪˌvaɪs/ noun C [2,7] a piece of equipment used for putting data into a system

instruction /ɪnˈstrʌkʃn/ noun C [18,21] one line of a computer program

integrated services digital network /ˌɪntɪɡreɪtɪd ˌsɜːvɪsɪz ˌdɪdʒɪtəl ˈnetwɜːk/ noun U [16] a broadband network communications system that allows the ordinary analogue telephone system to carry digital signals including voice, data, text, graphics and video

Intel /ˈɪntel/ noun U [2,23,25] the American company that designs and produces the electronic processors used in most of the computers in the world

intelligent agent /ɪnˌtelɪdʒənt ˈeɪdʒənt/ noun C [7,24] a computer utility program that uses artificial intelligence to perform tasks for the user such as retrieving and delivering information and automating repetitive tasks

interactive /ɪntəˈræktɪv/ adj [21,24] allows two-way communication so that the user can respond or interact with the system

interface /ˈɪntəfeɪs/ noun C [6,7,9,11,16,24] the hardware or software that connects two systems and allows them to communicate with each other

Internet (protocol) address /ˈɪntənet əˌdres/ noun C [12,13] a 32-bit code number assigned to every node on the Internet. It consists of a series of numbers that identify the major network and the sub-networks to which a node is attached and provides a path that gateways can use to route information from one machine to another.

(Microsoft) Internet Explorer /ˌɪntənet ɪkˈsplɔːrə(r)/ noun U [17] a free browser program developed by the Microsoft Corporation

Internet mail access protocol /ˌɪntənet ˌmeɪl ˌækses ˈprəʊtəkɒl/ noun U [13] a set of standards for accessing email messages stored on an email server. Initially only message headers are retrieved. Users can then organise or delete messages on the server and download individual messages.

Internet protocol /ˌɪntənet ˈprəʊtəkɒl/ noun U [12] the basic set of standards for enabling computers to communicate over the Internet

Internet service provider /ˌɪntənet ˈsɜːvɪs prəˌvaɪdə(r)/ noun C [14,23] an organisation that provides Internet connections for a fee

Internet (the) /ˈɪntənet/ noun U [1,5,6,11,12,13,14,15,16,17,18,20,21,22,23,24,25] the connection of computer networks across the world

interpreter /ɪnˈtɜːprɪtə(r)/ noun C [5] a program that converts other programs into machine code line by line as the programs are being used

intra frame /ˈɪntrə freɪm/ noun C [9] a type of image frame used in MPEG compression which contains only information in the picture itself

intranet /ˈɪntrənet/ noun C [7,23] a computer network that is internal to an organisation and uses the TCP/IP protocol in the same way as the Internet

IP /aɪ ˈpiː/ noun U [12] abbreviation for Internet protocol. A part of the TCP/IP protocol used on the Internet.

IP address /ˌaɪ ˈpiː əˌdres/ noun C [13] abbreviation for Internet protocol address

IP-layer /ˌaɪ ˈpiː ˌleɪə(r)/ noun C [12] the IP part of a TCP/IP system

IRC /ˌaɪ ɑː ˈsiː/ noun U [12,20] abbreviation for Internet relay chat. An Internet service that allows user to have a conversation by sending text messages to each other in real-time.

iris recognition /ˈaɪrɪs rekəɡˌnɪʃn/ noun U [16] a process of identifying a user by scanning their eyes

IS Manager /ˌaɪ ˈes ˌmænɪdʒə(r)/ noun C [22] an abbreviated form of information systems manager. A person who manages a computer-based service that provides information that is useful to a particular organisation

ISDN /ˌaɪ es diː ˈen/ noun U [16] abbreviation for integrated services digital network

isolation adapter /ˌaɪsəˈleɪʃn əˌdæptə(r)/ noun C [11] an electronic device that isolates a network system from high voltages and allows it to use the mains electricity cables for connecting computers together and transferring data

ISP /ˌaɪ es ˈpiː/ noun C [12,13,14,20] abbreviation for Internet service provider

IT /ˌaɪ ˈtiː/ noun U [5,8,22,23,24] abbreviation for information technology

iteration /ɪtəˈreɪʃn/ noun C [21] a process that is repeated as long as certain conditions remain true

J

Java /ˈdʒɑːvə/ noun U [21,22,23] an object-oriented computer programming language that was developed by Sun Microsystems in the mid 1990s. Programs written in Java can be used on a wide range of operating systems. It is widely used for developing interactive applications for the Internet.

JavaScript /ˈdʒɑːvəskrɪpt/ noun U [22] a scripting language that allows simple programs to be embedded into HTML documents

JPEG /ˈdʒeɪ peɡ/ noun U [9] abbreviation for joint photographic expert group the committee that devised a common standard for image file format and compression. JPEG compression is commonly used for photographic images in webpages because it creates very small files.

jukebox /ˈdʒuːkbɒks/ noun C [19] informal name for an optical disk drive that stores many optical disks. The disks are loaded into the drive when required by the host computer.

JUMP command/instruction /ˈdʒʌmp kəˌmɑːnd, ɪnˌstrʌkʃn/ noun C [18] a programming instruction that causes a program to change its normal sequence

junk email /dʒʌŋk ˈiːmeɪl/ noun U [12] unwanted and unsolicited email that is normally advertising or trying to sell something

K

Kb/KB /ˈkɪləbaɪt/ noun C [2] abbreviation for a kilobyte. A unit of storage capacity equal to 1024 bytes.

Kbit/s /ˈkɪləbɪts/ noun C [16,23] abbreviation for kilobits per second. A unit of signal speed equal to 1024 bits every second. A more common form is kbps.

kbps /ˌkɪləbɪts pə ˈsekənd/ noun C [23] abbreviation for kilobits per second. A unit of signal speed equal to 1024 bits every second.

KDE /ˌkeɪ diː ˈiː/ noun U [6] a graphical user interface used with the Linux operating system

kernel /ˈkɜːnəl/ noun C [6,24] the lowest level layer at the core of an operating system. It deals with allocating hardware resources to the rest of the operating system and the application programs.

keyboard /'kiːbɔːd/ noun C [1,2,6,11,16, 19,23,24] the main electronic input device that has keys arranged in a similar layout to a typewriter

keystroke /'kiːstrəʊk/ noun C [18] the process of pressing and releasing a key on a keyboard

keyword /'kiːwɜːd/ noun C [13] a word used to categorise documents or records in a file. Keywords can be used by a search engine to find relevant links on the Internet.

kHz /'kɪləhɜːts/ noun C [9] abbreviation for kilohertz. A unit of frequency equal to 1000 cycles every second.

killer application /'kɪlər ˌæplɪˌkeɪʃn/ noun C [23] an application program that is particularly useful and popular, making a computer system very successful

knowledge base /'nɒlɪʤ beɪs/ noun C [17,22] a collection of information that can be easily modified, revised and manipulated to enable the user to solve particular problems

L

LAN /læn/ noun C [5,8,11,15,17,23] acronym for local area network

language processor /'læŋgwɪʤ ˌprəʊsesə(r)/ noun C [5] software that performs computer language translation

laptop (computer) /'læptɒp/ noun C [23] the largest type of portable computer

laser printer /'leɪzə ˌprɪntə(r)/ noun C [8,16,17,21,25] a printer that prints using toner powder and laser light on a photosensitive drum

LCD /ˌel siː 'diː/ noun C [10] abbreviation for liquid crystal display. An electronic display device that uses liquid crystal cells to control the reflection of light.

leased line /ˌliːst 'laɪn/ noun C [8] a cable connection that is rented for use in a communications system

library /'laɪbrəri/ noun C [21,22] a set of programmed functions that are made available for use by any program

line driver /'laɪn ˌdraɪvə(r)/ noun C [11] an electronic circuit that provides high currents or voltages to other electronic circuits

line size /'laɪn saɪz/ noun C [2] the amount of data transferred each time there is a transfer between the main memory and cache memory

link /lɪŋk/ noun C [13,14,15] a common term used for a hyperlink, i.e. the connection of a webpage to another webpage or file

Linux /'laɪnʌks/ noun U [6] a clone of the Unix operating system created by Linus Torvalds for use on personal computers

Linux distribution /'laɪnʌks dɪstrɪˌbjuːʃn/ noun C [6] the Linux-user term for a complete operating system kit complete with the utilities and applications needed to make it do useful things, e.g. command interpreters, programming tools, text editors, typesetting tools and graphical user interfaces

load /ləʊd/ verb [6,18] to copy a program from a storage device into the computer's memory

local area network /ˌləʊkl ˌeəriə 'netwɜːk/ noun C [8,11] computers connected together over a small area such as a company department

log /lɒg/ verb [11] to record the time that an event happened

log /lɒg/ noun C [20] a record of when an event happened

log on /lɒg 'ɒn/ verb [6,12,18,19,20,23] to connect to a network system account normally using a password

logic bomb /'lɒʤɪk bɒm/ noun C [18,20] destructive code introduced into a program that is triggered by some event taking place on the computer system at a later time

logic circuit /'lɒʤɪk ˌsɜːkɪt/ noun C [2] a digital electronic circuit that compares two or more inputs and gives an output according to a particular rule of logic

look-up table /'lʊk ʌp ˌteɪbl/ noun C [12,13] a method by which a program uses two sets of related records to find a required value. It is quicker than calculating the value using a formula but takes up more memory space.

loop structure /'luːp ˌstrʌktʃə(r)/ noun C [21] see iteration

low-level language /ˌləʊ levəl 'læŋgwɪʤ/ noun C [22] a computer language such as machine code or assembly language that is closer to the form that a computer understands than to that of a human language

loyalty card /'lɔɪəlti kɑːd/ noun C [2] an electronic card that gives the owner discount on purchases at a particular store depending on how much they spend

lpr /ˌel piː 'ɑː(r)/ noun U [6] a Unix command for printing a file

ls /el 'es/ noun U [6] a Unix command for displaying a list of files in a directory

LVD /ˌel viː 'diː/ noun U [2] abbreviation Low Voltage Differential. The interface used in Ultra2 and Ultra3 SCSI.

M

m /em/ noun C [23] abbreviation for metre. An international unit for distance.

mA /'mɪliæmp/ noun C [23] abbreviation for milliamp. A unit of current equal to one thousandth of an amp.

(Apple) Mac /mæk/ noun C [7] the common name for the Apple Macintosh range of computers. A type of personal computer manufactured by Apple Computer Incorporated.

MAC /mæk/ noun C [18] acronym for message-authentication code

machine code /mə'ʃiːn kəʊd/ noun C [22] a computer language that consists entirely of a combination of 1s and 0s

machine intelligence /mə,ʃiːn ɪn'telɪʤəns/ noun U [24] another name for artificial intelligence

Mac OS /ˌmæk əʊ 'es/ noun C [6] the family of operating systems used on the Apple Macintosh range of computers

macro virus /'mækrəʊ ˌvaɪrəs/ noun C [18] a virus program in the form of a macro program

magnetic tape /mæg,netɪk 'teɪp/ noun U [19,24,25] a magnetic storage medium in the form of a thin plastic ribbon wound on a reel or a cassette. It is commonly used for backing up data.

mail bombing /'meɪl ˌbɒmɪŋ/ noun U [18] a computer crime that involves inundating an email address with thousands of messages slowing or even crashing the server

mail client /'meɪl ˌklaɪənt/ noun C [13] an email program that connects to an email server to send and receive email

mail server /'meɪl ˌsɜːvə(r)/ noun C [13] a network service that stores email messages and enables email clients to send and receive emails

mailbox /'meɪlbɒks/ noun C [13] a folder used by an email server to store a user's emails

mailmerge /'meɪlmɜːʤ/ noun C [3,8] a wordprocessing facility that causes a mailing list to be automatically combined with a standard letter to produce a separate copy of the letter addressed to each person on the mailing list

main memory /ˌmeɪn 'meməri/ noun U [2] the electronic memory that holds the programs and data being used

mainframe (computer) /'meɪnfreɪm/ noun C [2,5,6,21,22] the largest and most powerful type of computer. It is operated by a team of professionals.

mains line /'meɪnz laɪn/ noun C [11] the main electricity supply

man /mæn/ noun U [6] a Unix command for viewing the online manual pages on a Unix system

markup language /'mɑːkʌp ˌlæŋgwɪdʒ/ noun C [14] a set of tags that can be inserted into a document to indicate its layout and appearance

massively parallel /ˌmæsɪvli 'pærəlel/ adj [24] being part of a system in which an application is processed by up to 200 or more processors at the same time. Each processors using its own operating systems and memory and working on a different part of the program.

Mb/MB /'megəbaɪt/ noun C [2,12] abbreviation for a megabyte

Mbit/s /ˌmegəbɪt pə 'sekənd noun C [23] abbreviation for megabit per second. A unit of signal speed equal to 1 048 576 bits every second.

Mbps /ˌmegəbɪts pə 'sekənd/ noun C [23] abbreviation for megabits per second. A unit of signal speed equal to 1 048 576 bits every second.

megabyte /'megəbaɪt/ noun C [2,9,17] a unit of storage capacity equal to 1 048 576 bytes

megahertz /'megəhɜːts/ noun C [2] a unit of frequency equal to 1 million cycles every second

megohm /'megəʊm/ noun C [12] a unit of electrical resistance equal to 1 million ohms

memory /'meməri/ noun U [2,5,6,11,15, 18,19,24] the electronic part of a computer system that is used for temporarily storing the programs and data that are being used by the processor

menu /'menjuː/ noun C [2,7,21] a list of options displayed on a computer screen

menu bar /'menjuː bɑː(r)/ noun C [10,16] a row of icons on a display screen that open up menus when selected

message-authentication code /ˌmesɪdʒ ɔːˌθentɪ'keɪʃn kəʊd/ noun C [18] a number produced by a message-digest function that is used to make a message tamper-proof and provide message integrity

message-digest function /ˌmesɪdʒ 'daɪdʒest ˌfʌŋkʃn/ noun C [18] a program function that processes a message to produce a number called a message-authentication code. This number is then used to make a message tamper-proof.

message-integrity scheme /ˌmesɪdʒ ɪn'tegrəti skiːm/ noun C [18] a system that allows the receiver of a message

to detect whether someone has tampered with the message in transit

metadata /'metədeɪtə/ noun U [14] data about data in a document

metalanguage /'metəlæŋgwɪdʒ/ noun C [14,21] a language from which you can create other languages

MHz /'megəhɜːts/ noun C [2,23] abbreviation for megahertz

microchip /'maɪkrətʃɪp/ noun C [22] an electronic integrated circuit in a small package

microcomputer /'maɪkrəʊkəmˌpjuːtə(r)/ noun C [6,11] a personal computer. Smaller and less powerful than a mainframe or a minicomputer.

microprocessor /ˌmaɪkrəʊ'prəʊsesə(r)/ noun C [3,16,25] the main electronic chip in a computer. It can be thought of as the 'brain' of the computer because it does the main processing and controls the other parts of the computer. It is sometimes called the CPU.

Microsoft /'maɪkrəsɒft/ noun U [2,5,6,18,20,22,25] the common name for the Microsoft Corporation. The company founded by Bill Gates that developed the MS-DOS and Windows operating systems and a variety of software commonly used on desktop computers.

microwave /'maɪkrəweɪv/ noun C [23] a high-frequency electromagnetic wave used in data communication systems

MIDI /'mɪdi/ noun U [9,17,18] acronym for musical instrument digital interface. A standard for connecting musical instruments to computer systems.

minicomputer /'mɪnikəmˌpjuːtə(r)/ noun C [6] a computer that is slightly less powerful and a little smaller than a mainframe

Minix /'mɪnɪks/ noun U [6] a compact Unix clone written as a teaching aid by Professor Andy Tannenbaum

mirroring /'mɪrərɪŋ/ noun U [17] a technique used in RAID 1 systems where at least two hard disks are paired in such a way that the hard disk controller writes each byte of data to both disks. This ensures that a backup exists should the primary disk drive fail.

misdirection routine /mɪsdə'rekʃn, dɪ-, daɪ- ruːˌtiːn/ noun C [18] the part of a computer virus that enables it to hide itself by altering the normal sequence of instructions in another program

mixing desk /'mɪksɪŋ desk/ noun C [9] an electronic device used in audio recording that allows a number of audio inputs to be mixed together

mkdir /ˌem keɪ 'dɪə(r)/ noun U [6] a Unix and MS-DOS command for creating a directory

MO /'em əʊ/ adj [19] abbreviation for magneto-optical. Used to describe storage devices that use a combination of magnetism and laser light.

mobile phone /ˌməʊbaɪl 'fəʊn/ noun C [15,16,23] a wireless telephone that operates over a wide area

modem /'məʊdem/ noun C [2,5,10,11,12, 16,23] short for modulator/ demodulator. An electronic device that converts signals to enable a computer to be connected to an ordinary telephone line.

modulation /ˌmɒdjʊ'leɪʃn/ noun U [23] a process of combining a data signal with a carrier wave by causing the data signal to modify the amplitude frequency or phase of the carrier wave

monitor /'mɒnɪtə(r)/ noun C [1,2,9,16,17, 18,24] the main output device used to display the output from a computer on a screen. See VDU.

MOO /muː/ noun C [12,16] acronym for multi-user object oriented. An Internet virtual environment developed from multi-user adventure games that allows many users to interact.

motherboard /'mʌðəbɔːd/ noun C [2,5,16] the main electronic circuit board inside a computer that holds and connects together all the main electronic components

mouse /maʊs/ noun C [1,2,7,11,17,21, 23,25] a common cursor control input device used with a graphical user interface. It commonly has two or three button switches on top and a ball underneath that is rolled on a flat surface.

mouse button /'maʊs ˌbʌtən/ noun C [10] a switch on a mouse that is pressed to select an object on the screen

mouse pointer /'maʊs ˌpɔɪntə(r)/ noun C [15] a cursor image in the shape of an arrow that is controlled by a mouse and is used for pointing and selecting icons on the screen

MouseKeys /'maʊskiːz/ noun U [7] a Microsoft Windows operating system feature that changes the function of the numeric keypad keys on a computer keyboard so that they can be used to control the screen cursor

MP3 /ˌem piː 'θriː/ noun U [9,23] abbreviation for MPEG Audio Layer 3. A Motion Picture Experts Group standard for audio compression.

MPEG /'empeg/ noun U [9,23] a standard video compression scheme. The term is an acronym for Motion Picture

Experts Group a committee that develops standards for audio and video file formats and compression.

MS-DOS /ˌem es ˈdɒs/ noun U [6,25] abbreviation for Microsoft disk operating system. The command line operating system that was used in the first PCs.

multimedia /ˌmʌltiˈmiːdiə/ noun U [1,2,13,15,21] the combination of text graphics animation sound and video

multimodal input /ˌmʌltiˌməʊdəl ˈɪnpʊt/ noun U [7] the process of operating a user interface using a combination of types of input, e.g. keyboard and speech recognition

MVS /ˌem viː ˈes/ noun U [6,22] abbreviation for multiple virtual storage. It is the name given to a family of operating systems used on IBM mainframe computers

mW /ˈmɪliwɒt/ noun C [23] abbreviation for milliwatt. A unit of power equal to one thousandth of a watt.

My Briefcase /maɪ ˈbriːfkeɪs/ noun U [7] a Microsoft Windows feature that simplifies the process of copying and synchronising files between a desktop and a portable computer

N

natural-language programming /ˌnætʃrəl ˌlæŋwɪdʒ ˈprəʊɡræmɪŋ/ noun U [21] the process of writing programs using a computer language that is very similar to natural human language

near-line storage /ˌnɪə laɪn ˈstɔːrɪdʒ/ noun U [19] the part of a hierarchical storage management system that stores infrequently-used files in a way that will allow them to be easily retrieved

Net (the) /net/ noun U [12,15,24] the common name for the Internet

NetPC /ˌnet piː ˈsiː/ noun U [11] an industry specification for a low-cost basic Windows PC with an Intel processor designed for use on a multi-user network system. It is managed centrally and has no floppy disk drive CD-ROM drive or hardware expansion slots, i.e. it is a type of thin client.

Netscape Communicator /ˌnetskeɪp kəˈmjuːnɪkeɪtə(r)/ noun U [11,15] a widely used web browser package

NetWare /ˈnetweə(r)/ noun U [6,22] a widely-used LAN operating system produced by Novell Incorporated

network /ˈnetwɜːk/ verb [7,21] to connect a number of computers and peripheral devices together

network /ˈnetwɜːk/ noun C [1,2,3,4,5,6,7, 8,11,12,15,16,17,18,19,20,22,23,24] a combination of a number of computers and peripheral devices connected together

network computer /ˈnetwɜːk kəmˌpjuːtə(r)/ noun C [11] a computer designed using the industry specification from Oracle and Sun Microsystems for a low-cost basic personal computer that can have an Intel processor or another type of processor and can use a Java-based operating system. It is designed for use on a multi-user network system and is managed centrally. It has no floppy disk drive, CD-ROM drive or hardware expansion slots, i.e. it is a type of thin client.

network guru /ˈnetwɜːk ˌɡuːruː/ noun C [22] a person who is an expert in networking and gives talks and advice on the future development of networking

network layer /ˈnetwɜːk ˌleɪə(r)/ noun C [11] the part of a network communications system that forms the data into packets and selects a route for the message

network operating system /ˌnetwɜːk ˈɒpəreɪtɪŋ ˌsɪstəm/ noun C [11] an operating system that is used to administer and control a network allowing computers to share hardware and software while providing file security and backup facilities

neural net(work) /ˈnjʊərəl ˌnet(wɜːk)/ noun C [3,23] an artificial intelligence system that is capable of developing rules from given input so that it learns how to deal with more complex input

newsgroup /ˈnjuːzɡruːp/ noun C [12,14,22] an Internet discussion group that uses a restricted area on a server computer to display messages about a common interest

node /nəʊd/ noun C [11,12] a network terminal or point where a computer is connected to a network

notebook (computer) /ˈnəʊtbʊk/ noun C [23] a portable computer that is about the same size as a piece of writing paper

Novell /nəʊˈvel/ noun U [22] the common name for Novell Incorporated. The American company that designs and produces the Netware network operating system.

numeric keyboard /njuːˌmerɪk ˈkiːbɔːd/ noun C [7] the section of a computer keyboard that includes keys for entering numerical digits (0–9) and mathematical operators (+–,/)

O

object /ˈɒbdʒekt/ noun C [21] an object-oriented programming module that has its own properties created by bundling data and program instructions together

object-oriented programming /ˌɒbdʒekt ˌɔːrientɪd ˈprəʊɡræmɪŋ/ noun U [21] a type of programming where programs are made from combinations of predefined modules that can be used over and over again

OCR /ˌəʊ siː ˈɑː(r)/ noun U [3] abbreviation for optical character recognition

(Microsoft) Office /ˈɒfɪs/ noun U [8,22] a widely-used application package developed by the Microsoft Corporation that includes programs used in a typical office, e.g. a wordprocessor and spreadsheet

office application / suite /ˈɒfɪs æplɪˌkeɪʃn, ˌswiːt/ noun C [5,8] a computer program or set of programs that are used in a typical office, e.g. a wordprocessor spreadsheet and database

offline /ɒfˈlaɪn/ adj [12,19] disconnected from a computer system or the Internet

online /ɒnˈlaɪn/ adj [12,13,14,16,19,22, 23,24] connected to a computer system or the Internet

OOP /ˌəʊ əʊ ˈpiː/ noun U [21] acronym for object-oriented programming

Open Source /ˌəʊpən ˈsɔːs/ adj [6] part of a system of software development where anyone is free to take a copy of the source code and extend develop or fix bugs in it

operating system /ˈɒpəreɪtɪŋ ˌsɪstəm/ noun C [2,5,6,17,18,19,21,22,25] the set of programs that control the basic functions of a computer and provides communication between the application programs and the hardware

optical character recognition /ˌɒptɪkl ˌkærɪktə rekəɡˈnɪʃn/ noun U [3] a process that enables a computer to scan and recognise printed characters using the reflection of light

optical fibre /ˌɒptɪkl ˈfaɪbə(r)/ noun C [23] a common name for glass fibre cable used in high speed networks. It enables data signals to be transmitted using laser light.

optical media /ˌɒptɪkl ˈmiːdiə/ noun U [19] data storage material that is written to or read from using laser light

ORACLE /ˈɒrəkl/ noun U [22] a widely used database management system

OS /ˌəʊ ˈes/ noun C [6] abbreviation for operating system

OS X /ˌəʊ es ˈten/ noun U [25] version 10 of the Apple Macintosh operating system. It is a modular OS and has a desktop with a 3-D appearance. It includes support for UNIX-based applications as well as older Mac applications.

OS/2 /ˌəʊ es ˈtuː/ noun U [6] a multitasking desktop operating system for PCs that was marketed by IBM

Outlook Express /ˌaʊtlʊk ɪkˈspres/ noun U [17] a free graphical interface email program integrated into the Internet Explorer browser developed by the Microsoft Corporation

output /ˈaʊtpʊt/ noun U [2,8,21,23] the processed data or signals that come out of a computer system

P

pA /ˈpiːkəʊæmp/ noun C [23] abbreviation for picoamp. A unit of current equal to a millionth of a millionth of an amp.

(software) package /ˈpækɪdʒ/ noun C [6,12,16,22] an application program or collection of programs that can be used in different ways

packet /ˈpækɪt/ noun C [11,12,13] a fixed size unit of data prepared for transmission across a network. Messages are normally divided into packets before transmission.

packet-switching /ˈpækɪt ˌswɪtʃɪŋ/ noun U [23] a method of transferring data across a network by dividing it into packets and transferring the packets individually from node to node then putting the packets together again when they arrive at the destination

page-description language /ˌpeɪdʒ dɪsˈkrɪpʃn ˌlæŋgwɪdʒ/ noun C [21] a type of programming language that uses tags to define the layout of a document, e.g. HTML is a page-description language used to design webpages

pager /ˈpeɪdʒə(r)/ noun C [16,20] a small radio receiver which beeps to alert the wearer of messages or telephone calls. It displays the telephone number of the caller so the wearer can call back. Some pagers can display very short messages.

Palm Pilot /ˈpɑːm ˌpaɪlət/ noun U [11] a popular handheld personal organizer produced by 3Com

palm-size PC /ˌpɑːm saɪz piː ˈsiː/ noun C [7] another name for a handheld IBM compatible computer

palmtop (computer) /ˈpɑːmtɒp/ noun C [16] a portable computer that is small enough to be held in the palm of one hand. See handheld computer.

pane /peɪn/ noun C [10] a subsection of a graphical user interface window

parity data /ˈpærəti ˌdeɪtə/ noun U [17] extra data bits added to the end of units of data before transmission and then checked and added after transmission to see if the data has arrived accurately

Pascal /pæsˈkæl/ noun U [5,21] a high-level structured computer language named after the mathematician Blaise Pascal. It is often used in college computing courses to teach programming.

password /ˈpɑːswɜːd/ noun C [6,12,16,19, 20,21] a secret code used to control access to a network system

paste /peɪst/ verb [21] to insert a copy of data held in a computer's memory at a chosen position

patch /pætʃ/ verb [18] to insert programming code into a computer program to fix or modify it in some way

payload /ˈpeɪləʊd/ noun C [18] the part of a virus that carries out the threat such as displaying a slogan on the screen

payroll package /ˈpeɪrəʊl ˌpækɪdʒ/ noun C [8] a set of computer programs used for calculating pay cheques

PC /piː ˈsiː/ noun C [1,2,5,6,17,19,21,23, 25] abbreviation for an IBM type of personal computer

PC-DOS /ˌpiː siː ˈdɒs/ noun U [6] an operating system for desktop PC computers that is similar to MS-DOS

PCMCIA /ˌpiː siː ˌem siː aɪ ˈeɪ/ noun U [2] a type of interface for connecting credit-sized electronic upgrade cards to portable computers. Devised by the Personal Computer Memory Card International Association.

PDA /ˌpiː diː ˈeɪ/ noun C [2,23] abbreviation for personal digital assistant. A small handheld computer providing a variety of tools for organising work, e.g. a calendar, to do list, diary, address list, calculator, etc.

pen-based computer /ˌpen beɪst kəmˈpjuːtə(r)/ noun C [2,6] a small computer that has a pen input device instead of a keyboard

Pentium /ˈpentiəm/ noun C [2,17,25] a family of processors produced by the Intel Corporation

peripheral /pəˈrɪfərəl/ noun C [2,15,16, 23] a piece of equipment that is connected to the central processing unit of a computer system

personal computer /ˌpɜːsənl kəmˈpjuːtə(r)/ noun C [1,7,22,23,25] a computer designed to be used by one person at a time

personal organiser /ˌpɜːsənl ˈɔːgənaɪzə(r)/ noun C [23] see PDA

P-frame /ˈpiː freɪm/ noun C [9] the common name for a predicted frame in an MPEG compressed file

Photoshop /ˈfəʊtəʊʃɒp/ noun U [23] an image-editing computer program produced by Adobe Systems Inc.

physical layer /ˈfɪzɪkl ˌleɪə(r)/ noun C [11] the part of a network communications system that encodes the packets into the medium that will carry them and sends the packets along that medium

piconet /ˈpiːkəʊnet/ noun C [23] a set of very small low power wireless links consuming only picoamps of electricity that are set up between Bluetooth devices when they are within 10 metres of each other

piggybacking /ˈpɪgibækɪŋ/ noun U [18] a computer crime that involves using another person's identification code or using that person's files before he or she has logged off

PIM /pɪm/ noun C [8] acronym for personal information manager. A computer program that provides a variety of tools for organising work, e.g. a calendar, to do list, diary, address list, calculator, etc.

PIN /pɪn/ noun C [16] an acronym for personal identification number. A unique number used by electronic systems to indicate who a person is.

platform /ˈplætfɔːm/ noun C [14,22] a distinctive type of computer system that needs software to be written specifically for it, e.g. PC, Apple Mac, etc.

PlayStation /ˈpleɪsteɪʃn/ noun U [8] a games console developed by the Sony Corporation

pointer /ˈpɔɪntə(r)/ noun C [7] an arrow-shaped cursor

polymorphism /ˌpɒliˈmɔːfɪzm/ noun U [21] a key feature of OOP programming by which different objects can receive the same instructions but deal with them in different ways

POP /pɒp/ noun U [12,13,14] acronym for post office protocol

port /pɔːt/ verb [6] to convert for use in another operating system or computer platform

port replicator /ˈpɔːt ˌreplɪkeɪtə(r)/ noun C [2] a device that connects to a portable computer to make it easier to connect peripheral devices

portable (computer) /ˈpɔːtəbl/ noun C [2] a computer that is small and light enough to be carried from place to place. It can usually be powered by batteries.

post /pəʊst/ verb [12] to display a message in a computer newsgroup or bulletin board

post office protocol /ˌpəʊst ˌɒfɪs ˈprəʊtəkɒl/ noun U [13] a message-retrieval protocol used by many mail clients to get messages from a server. It only allows you to download all messages in your mailbox at once and works in 'pull' mode, i.e. the receiving PC initiating the connection.

predicted frame /prɪˈdɪktɪd freɪm/ noun C [9] a type of image frame used in MPEG compression. A predicted frame only stores the differences in the image compared to the previous I frame or P frame.

presentation layer /ˌprezənˈteɪʃn ˌleɪə(r)/ noun C [11] the part of a network communications system that ensures the message is transmitted in a language that the receiving computer can interpret

primary disk drive /ˈpraɪməri dɪsk draɪv/ noun C [17] the main disk drive in a computer. In a PC this is usually a hard disk known as the C drive.

Print Screen (key) /prɪnt ˈskriːn/ noun C [7,10] the computer keyboard key that copies the current display screen image to memory or to the printer

printed circuit board /ˌprɪntɪd ˈsɜːkɪt bɔːd/ noun C [22] an electronic board that holds and connects the components of an electronic circuit

printer /ˈprɪntə(r)/ noun C [1,2,5,6,17,21,23] a common output device used for printing the output of a computer on paper

private key /ˌpraɪvət ˈkiː/ noun C [18] secret code known only to the owner that is used for encrypting and decrypting messages

procedural language /prəˈsiːdʒərəl ˌlæŋgwɪdʒ/ noun C [5] a computer programming language that enables programs to be written using sections of code known as procedures. Each procedure performs a specific task.

processor /ˈprəʊsesə(r)/ noun C [2,7,11,17,23,25] the part of a computer that processes the data

program /ˈprəʊgræm/ noun C [1,2,5,6,18, 21,22,23,24,25] a set of instructions written in a computer language that control the behaviour of a computer

program /ˈprəʊgræm/ verb [1,6,11,16, 20,21,23] to write a set of instructions for controlling a computer using a computer language

programmer /ˈprəʊgræmə(r)/ noun C [4, 5,6,8,18,19,21,22,25] a person who writes computer programs

programming /ˈprəʊgræmɪŋ/ noun U [5,21,22] the processes of writing a computer program using a computer language

programming language /ˈprəʊgræmɪŋ ˌlæŋgwɪdʒ/ noun C [21] a computer language used for writing computer programs

protocol /ˈprəʊtəkɒl/ noun C [12,13,23] a set of agreed standards

pseudocode /ˈsjuːdəʊkəʊd/ noun C [21] a way of writing a description of a computer program using a mixture of natural language and computer language code

public domain /ˌpʌblɪk dəˈmeɪn/ noun U [19] a condition in which there is no copyright on a work such as a computer program allowing it to be freely copied and used

public key /ˌpʌblɪk ˈkiː/ noun C [18] a secret code the owner makes available to others so that they can encrypt messages they are sending to the owner

public-key cryptography /ˌpʌblɪk kiː krɪpˈtɒgrəfi/ noun U [18] a method of coding messages using public and private keys to prevent others from reading them

pull mode /ˈpʊl məʊd/ noun U [13] a type of communication where the receiving computer initiates the connection

pull-down menu /ˌpʊl daʊn ˈmenjuː/ noun C [14] a list of choices that appear below a menu title on a display screen when the user clicks on the menu title using a mouse

push operation /ˈpʊʃ ɒpəˌreɪʃn/ noun U [13] a communication where the sending computer initiates the connection

R

radar /ˈreɪdɑː(r)/ noun U [3,15] a system of using the reflection of radio waves to detect an object and determine its location

radio button /ˈreɪdiəʊ ˌbʌtən/ noun C [13] one of a set of mutually exclusive options in a dialog box, i.e. the user can only select one, causing the others to be deselected

RAID /reɪd/ noun U [2,17] acronym for redundant array of inexpensive disks

RAID level /ˈreɪd ˌlevl/ noun C [17] a particular arrangement of RAID array disks. Each RAID level is given a number with higher numbers indicating more elaborate methods for ensuring a computer can recover from hardware errors. The best known are RAID 0 to RAID 5.

RAM /ræm/ noun U [2,17] acronym for random access memory

Rambus memory /ˈræmbʌs ˌmeməri/ noun U [2] a fast memory architecture commonly known as DRDRAM (or RDRAM) that is a possible future successor to SDRAM. It was originally developed by Rambus Inc.

random access memory /ˌrændəm ˈækses ˌmeməri/ noun U [2] a type of memory that can be accessed in any order. RAM is the main electronic memory of a personal computer and is used for storing the programs and data being used.

raw data /rɔː ˈdeɪtə/ noun U [24] data that has not been processed

RDBMS /ˌɑː diː biː em ˈes/ noun C [22] abbreviation for relational database management system. A database system that links files together as required.

RDRAM /ˌɑː diː ˈræm/ noun U [2] abbreviation for Rambus dynamic random access memory. A new RAM technology capable of very high-speed transfer of data. See Rambus memory.

real-time /ˈriːl taɪm/ noun U [12,23,24] the immediate processing of computer data enabling interactive applications

reboot /ˌriːˈbuːt/ verb [17] to restart a computer operating system

record /ˈrekɔːd/ noun C [8,19,21] a section of a database made up of related database fields

recorder (program) /rɪˈkɔːdə(r)/ noun C [9] a computer program that allows the user to create their own audio CDs with a writeable CD-ROM drive

Recycle Bin /ˌriːˈsaɪkl bɪn/ noun U [7] the folder in Microsoft Windows operating systems where deleted files are stored

redundant array of inexpensive disks /rɪˌdʌndənt əˌreɪ əv ˌɪnɪkˌspensɪv ˈdɪsks/ noun U [17] a storage system consisting of a set of hard disks that can be combined in different arrangements to store data in such a way that the data can be recovered if one or more of the disks fail

reliable stream service /rɪˌlaɪəbl ˈstriːm ˌsɜːvɪs/ noun U [12] a data management system provided by the TCP protocol to ensure that data is transferred across a network correctly. It structures and buffers the data flow, looks for responses, and takes action to replace missing data blocks.

resident /ˈrezɪdənt/ adj [6,18] is kept in the computer's memory

resistor /rɪˈzɪstə(r)/ noun C [12] an electronic component that reduces the flow of current in a circuit

resolution /ˌrezə'luːʃn/ noun C [2,24] a measure of the quality of a display screen in terms of the amount of graphical information that can be shown on the screen. This partly depends on the number of dots that make up the image.

resolution protocol /ˌrezə'luːʃn 'prəʊtəkɒl/ noun U [12] a set of standards for software used with internal look-up tables in a TCP/IP network for routing data through a gateway between networks

restore /rɪ'stɔː(r)/ verb [17,19] to put data back into its original location

reverse engineering /rɪˌvɜːs endʒɪ'nɪərɪŋ/ noun U [24] to take an object apart to discover how it was originally designed and put together

RF /ɑːr 'ef/ noun U [23] abbreviation for radio frequency

right click /raɪt 'klɪk/ verb [7,21] to press and release the right-hand button on a mouse

ring main /'rɪŋ meɪn/ noun C [23] the main electrical supply circuit in a building

rip /rɪp/ verb [9] to extract songs from a CD and turn them into WAV files

ripper /'rɪpə(r)/ noun C [9] a program that extracts songs from a CD and turns them into WAV files

rm /ɑːr 'em/ noun U [6] a Unix command for deleting a file

rmdir /ˌɑːr em 'dɪə(r)/ noun U [6] a Unix and MS-DOS command for deleting a directory

robot /'rəʊbɒt/ noun C [16,21,23,24] a mechanical device controlled by a computer

robotics /rəʊ'bɒtɪks/ noun U [23] the study of robot systems

rocket science /'rɒkɪt ˌsaɪəns/ noun U [24] something requiring great intelligence or technical ability

ROM /rɒm/ noun U [2] acronym for read only memory

route /ruːt/ noun C [11,12] the path that is used to transfer data in a network

route /ruːt/ verb [9,11,12] to move data from node to node on a network

router /'ruːtə(r)/ noun C [11,13,15,20] an electronic device that links different networks or parts of a network. It determines the path that a signal should take to reach its destination.

rpm /ˌɑː piː 'em/ noun C [2] abbreviation for revolutions per minute

rule /ruːl/ noun C [3] the name given to patterns found in data when using neural networks

run /rʌn/ verb [5,6,17,18] to execute a program, i.e. to get a program to process the data

rwho /ɑː 'huː/ noun U [6] a Unix command for displaying a report of who is currently logged in to the local network

S

s/w /'sɒftweə(r)/ noun U [22] abbreviation for software

salami shaving /sə'lɑːmi ˌʃeɪvɪŋ/ noun U [18] a computer crime that involves manipulating programs or data so that small amounts of money are deducted from a large number of transactions or accounts and accumulated elsewhere

SAP /sæp/ noun U [8,22] a widely used enterprise resource planning tool program

save /seɪv/ verb [1,10,15,18] to copy a program or data to a storage device

scan /skæn/ verb [1,3,16,19] to copy text or graphics using a scanner

scanner /'skænə(r)/ noun C [2,3,19] an optical input device that uses the reflection of light to copy text or graphics into a computer

(monitor)(display) screen /skriːn/ noun C [1,2,7,11,16,17,18,21,24,25] a computer output device used for displaying text and graphic images

scroll /skrəʊl/ verb [16,17] to move through displayed information smoothly on the screen either horizontally or vertically

scrollbar /'skrəʊlbɑː(r)/ noun C [14] the part of a graphical user interface window that allows the user to move through a document by clicking or dragging with the mouse

SCSI /ˌes siː es 'aɪ/ noun U [2] acronym for small computer systems interface. A standard way of connecting peripheral devices to a personal computer system. It is often used to connect hard disks and CD-ROM drives in server computers.

SDRAM /ˌes diː 'ræm/ noun U [2] abbreviation for synchronous dynamic random access memory. A type of fast memory that uses a separate clock signal in addition to the normal control signals.

search engine /'sɜːtʃ ˌendʒɪn/ noun C [1,6, 13,14,15,23] a program designed to find information on the World Wide Web according to data entered by the user. Search engines are usually accessed from special websites.

sector /'sektə(r)/ noun C [2,17] a formatted section of a circular magnetic track used for storing data on a disk

seek time /'siːk taɪm/ noun C [17] the amount of time taken by a disk drive to find a particular track on a disk

segment /'segmənt/ noun C [11] a subdivision of data created by a network communications transport layer for which a checksum is generated

serial /'sɪəriəl/ adj [24] designed to transfer data sequentially, i.e. one data bit after another

serial number /'sɪəriəl ˌnʌmbə(r)/ noun C [17] a number that uniquely identifies a product

serial port /'sɪəriəl pɔːt/ noun C [12] the small connector at the back of the system unit of a personal computer that is used to connect a serial device such as a serial mouse or a modem. Two serial ports labelled COM1 and COM2 are usually provided on a PC.

server /'sɜːvə(r)/ noun C [6,8,11,12,13, 15,17,18,22] a main computer that provides a service on a network

service tag number /'sɜːvɪs tæg ˌnʌmbə(r)/ noun C [17] a number used to identify a computer for maintenance agreements

session layer /'seʃn ˌleɪə(r)/ noun C [11] the part of a network communications system that opens communications and has the job of keeping straight the communications among all nodes on the network. It sets boundaries for the beginning and end of a message and establishes whether the messages will be sent half-duplex or full duplex.

SGML /ˌes dʒiː em 'el/ noun U [14] abbreviation for Standard Generalized Markup Language

shareware /'ʃeəweə(r)/ noun U [15,19] software that is distributed freely and only paid for if the user decides to keep it

shell /ʃel/ noun C [6] a graphical user interface for an operating system

shell script /'ʃel skrɪpt/ noun C [22] a text file that contains a sequence of commands for a UNIX-based operating system. In DOS operating systems a shell script is called a batch file.

shift key /'ʃɪft kiː/ noun C [7] the computer keyboard key that is held down to produce uppercase letters

sign up /saɪn 'ʌp/ verb [12,14] to register with a service

SimCity /sɪm'sɪti/ noun U [18] a well-known computer simulation game in which the users control various aspects of running a virtual city

simple mail transfer protocol /ˌsɪmpl meɪl 'trænsfɜː ˌprəʊtəkɒl/ noun U [12,13] a set of standards for sending email from an email client and transferring email between server computers on the Internet

simulation /ˌsɪmjʊˈleɪʃn/ noun C [12] a programmed virtual environment that imitates a real or planned system

site /saɪt/ noun C [11,12,13,15,18] a common name for a website

site map /ˈsaɪt mæp/ noun C [14,15] a webpage that is used to show the overall layout of a website

skin /skɪn/ noun C [9] a computer program that is used to change the interface of another program, e.g. to change the screen display on an MP3 player program

SM band /es ˈem bænd/ noun U [23] common name for the Industrial Scientific and Medical frequency band

smart card /ˈsmɑːt kɑːd/ noun C [1,3,19,20] a plastic card containing a processor and memory chip. It can be used to store large amounts of confidential data.

smart card reader /ˈsmɑːt kɑːd ˌriːdə(r)/ noun C [19] a device used for reading smart cards

smart device /ˈsmɑːt dɪˌvaɪs/ noun C [1] a device that contains an embedded processor and memory

smart phone /ˈsmɑːt fəʊn/ noun C [24] a telephone that contains an embedded processor and memory and can process data, e.g. translate English into German, Japanese and French in real time

SMS /ˌes em ˈes/ noun U [16] abbreviation for Short Message Service. A method of sending text messages that are 160 characters in length or shorter over a mobile phone.

SMTP /ˌes em ti: ˈpiː/ noun U [12,13] abbreviation for simple message transfer protocol

software /ˈsɒftweə(r)/ noun U [1,2,5,6,14, 17,18,19,21,22,23,24,25] the programs and data used in a computer

software engineering /ˈsɒftweər endʒɪˌnɪərɪŋ/ noun U [21] the discipline of designing high quality software solutions

software house /ˈsɒftweə haʊs/ noun C [25] a company that designs and produces software

software piracy /ˈsɒftweə ˌpaɪrəsi/ noun U [18] a computer crime that involves unauthorised copying of a program for sale or distributing to other users

soundcard /ˈsaʊndkɑːd/ noun C [2,9] the electronic circuit expansion board in a computer that is used to process audio signals and connect to and control a microphone loudspeaker or headphone

source code /ˈsɔːs kəʊd/ noun C [6] programming code that has to be processed by a compiler or translator to make object code for use in a computer

spam /spæm/ noun U [12] unsolicited email sent to large numbers of people indiscriminately usually advertising or trying to sell a product

speaker /ˈspiːkə(r)/ noun C [9,11] common term for a loudspeaker. An output device for providing sound output.

spectrum analyzer /ˈspektrəm ˌænəlaɪzə(r)/ noun C [9] an instrument that plots a graph of frequency parameters for a complete frequency band

splitter-based service /ˈsplɪtə beɪst ˌsɜːvɪs/ noun C [16] a DSL system that separates the data signal from the phone line as it enters a building and sends it to a DSL modem

spoofing /ˈspuːfɪŋ/ noun U [18] a computer crime that involves tricking a user into revealing confidential information such as an access code or a credit card number

spread spectrum /ˈspred ˌspektrəm/ noun U [23] a radiowave system that switches rapidly between different frequencies in a frequency band allowing a number of devices to share the same frequency band without interfering with each other

spreadsheet (program) /ˈspredʃiːt/ noun C [5,6,8,16,17] a type of application program with an array of cells that is used for calculating formulas

SQL /ˌes kjuː ˈel/ noun U [22] abbreviation for structured query language. A language used for searching databases.

standalone /ˈstændələʊn/ adj [5,9] not connected to a network

standard generalized markup language /ˌstændəd ˌdʒenrəlaɪzd ˈmɑːkʌp ˌlæŋgwɪdʒ/ noun U [14] the complex metalanguage from which both HTML and XML were created

Start (button) /stɑːt/ noun C [10] an icon on the bottom left corner of Microsoft Windows operating system desktops that allows the user to access programs and data and to close down the system

start bit /ˈstɑːt bɪt/ noun C [11] a data bit that marks the beginning of a data block in a network transmission

Start menu /ˈstɑːt ˌmenjuː/ noun C [10] the list of choices that opens up on the display screen when the user clicks the Start button in a Microsoft Windows desktop

start-stop transmission /ˌstɑːt ˌstɒp trænzˈmɪʃn/ noun C [11] another name for asynchronous transmission where data is sent one byte (or character) at a time

static earthing band /ˌstætɪk ˈɜːθɪŋ bænd/ noun C [12] a strip of material that is wound round the wrist of a repair technician and connected to earth to prevent the build up of static electricity which could destroy electronic components

status bar /ˈsteɪtəs bɑː(r)/ noun C [10] a narrow band displayed across the bottom of a window in a Microsoft Windows application to display useful information for the user, e.g. number of pages in a document

stealth virus /ˈstelθ ˌvaɪrəs/ noun C [18] a type of virus that hides itself making it hard to detect

stop bit /ˈstɒp bɪt/ noun C [11] a data bit that marks the end of a data block in a network transmission

storage device /ˈstɔːrɪdʒ dɪˌvaɪs/ noun C [2] a piece of equipment used for reading from and writing to a storage medium

storage medium /ˈstɔːrɪdʒ ˌmiːdiəm/ noun C [19] a material used for storing programs and data

streaming /ˈstriːmɪŋ/ noun U [13,16] a process of downloading and storing the next part of a data signal while the first part is being used. In this way the data signal, e.g. an audio or video is fed to the slower destination device at a steady rate.

string /strɪŋ/ noun C [6,11] a series of data characters which can be a mixture of letters or numbers

striping /ˈstraɪpɪŋ/ noun U [17] a process where data is spread across all drives in a RAID array rather than filling up one disk with data before writing to the next disk in the array

structured language /ˌstrʌktʃəd ˈlæŋgwɪdʒ/ noun C [21] a computer programming language that requires the programmer to write programs made up of self-contained units or procedures

structured programming /ˌstrʌktʃəd ˈprəʊgræmɪŋ/ noun U [21] the process of writing a program using a structured programming language

subfolder /ˈsʌbˌfəʊldə(r)/ noun C [10] a storage area that provides a subdivision of a folder so that stored files can be organised into smaller groups

submenu /ˈsʌbˌmenjuː/ noun C [7] a list of choices that is displayed when the user clicks on an item in a menu

sub-network /'sʌb ,netwɜːk/ noun C [12] a self-contained part of a larger network

subpage /'sʌbpeɪdʒ/ noun C [14] a webpage that gives further detailed information about part of the information on a main webpage

sub-program /'sʌb ,prəʊgræm/ noun C [22] a small program that performs a specific function and is part of a larger program

subset /'sʌbset/ noun C [3] a small group of related data that is part of a larger set of data

supercomputer /'suːpəkəm,pjuːtə(r)/ noun C [2,24] the most powerful type of mainframe computer

superset /'suːpəset/ noun C [21] a larger group of objects that include a smaller set of objects

supervisor (program) /'suːpəvaɪzə(r)/ noun C [6] the most important program in the operating system. It is resident and controls the entire operating system. It loads other operating system programs into memory when they are needed.

support analyst /sə'pɔːt ,ænəlɪst/ noun C [22] a person who provides help to computer users by studying their requirements and designing systems to provide for their needs

support engineer /sə'pɔːt endʒɪ,nɪə(r)/ noun C [22,25] a professional who provides help for computer users by designing, building, and maintaining computer systems

support line /sə'pɔːt laɪn/ noun C [12] a telephone line that can be used to get help with hardware or software problems. See helpdesk/helpline.

support technician /sə'pɔːt tek,nɪʃn/ noun C [22] a person who maintains and troubleshoots problems with computers

surf /sɜːf/ verb [15,23] to browse webpages on the Internet in an unplanned way

surge protector /'sɜːdʒ prə,tektə(r)/ noun C [19] an electronic device that protects equipment from damage due to sudden high voltage or current in the power supply

SVGA /,es viː dʒiː: 'eɪ/ noun U [2] abbreviation for super video graphics array. A video screen display standard that provides 1024X768 or 1280X1024 pixel resolution with up to 16.7 million colours

swipe card /'swaɪp kɑːd/ noun C [2] a plastic card with a magnetic strip running across it containing confidential data

SXGA /,es eks dʒiː: 'eɪ/ noun U [2] abbreviation for super extended graphics array. An IBM video screen display standard similar to SVGA that provides 1024X768 or 1280X1024 pixel resolution with up to 16.7 million colours

synch byte /'sɪŋk baɪt/ noun C [] a start or stop bit pattern that marks the beginning or end of a transmitted data block

synchronise /'sɪŋkrənaɪz/ verb [11,21,23] to cause different processes to occur at the same time

synchronous /'sɪŋkrənəs/ adj [2,11,12, 15] occurring at regular intervals and in step with other systems usually controlled by an electronic clock circuit

synthesiser /'sɪnθə,saɪzə(r)/ noun C [9] a device that uses electronic circuits to generate sounds

system bus /'sɪstəm bʌs/ noun C [2] the sets of connectors that carry signals between system components such as the processor and memory in a computer

system tray /'sɪstəm treɪ/ noun C [7,10] a section at the far right of a Microsoft Windows task bar that holds icons for the clock and other programs that run constantly in the background

systems administrator /'sɪstəmz əd,mɪnəstreɪtə(r)/ noun C [19] a person who maintains a multi-user computer system

systems analysis /'sɪstəmz ə,næləsɪs/ noun U [5,22] the study of a system to determine how it can be computerised

systems analyst /'sɪstəmz ,ænəlɪst/ noun C [21,22] a person who designs or modifies information systems to meet users' requirements. This includes investigating feasibility and cost-producing documentation and testing prototypes of the system.

systems manager /'sɪstəmz ,mænɪdʒə(r)/ noun C [20,22] a person who manages a computer system

systems program / software /'sɪstəmz ,prəʊgræm, ,sɒftweə(r)/ noun C/U [5,6,21,22] a program or set of programs that is used to control the basic functions of a computer system, e.g. operating system programs

systems programmer /'sɪstəmz ,prəʊgræmə(r)/ noun C [21,22] a person who specialises in writing systems software such as operating system programs

systems programming /'sɪstəmz ,prəʊgræmɪŋ/ noun U [22] the writing of systems programs

T

TA /tiː 'eɪ/ noun C [16] abbreviation for terminal adapter

tab /tæb/ noun C [8] a dialog box component that is used to switch between different sets of data

tab (key) /tæb/ noun C [7] the computer keyboard key that is used to move the cursor to the next tabulation point in a wordprocessor program so that data can be spaced evenly on the screen

tag /tæg/ noun C [9,14] a label used in a markup language such as HTML. It is attached to a piece of text to mark the start or the end of a particular function.

tape /teɪp/ noun U [19] a magnetic storage medium commonly used for storing backup files

tape changer /'teɪp ,tʃeɪndʒə(r)/ noun C [19] a backup device that allows different magnetic tapes to be used when required during a backup operation

taskbar /'tɑːskbɑː(r)/ noun C [7,10] a Microsoft Windows desktop component that indicates what programs are currently being used and allows the user to switch between them

TCP /,tiː siː 'piː/ noun U [12] abbreviation for transfer control protocol. A part of the TCP/IP protocol used on the Internet.

TCP/IP /,tiː siː piː 'aɪ piː/ noun U [12,22] abbreviation for transmission control protocol/Internet protocol. The official set of standards for determining the form of the signals used for transmitting data on the Internet.

technophobic /teknə'fəʊbɪk/ adj [24] having a fear or strong dislike of technology and technological devices

telecomms /'telikɒmz/ noun U [24] common term for telecommunications

telecommunications /,telikəmjuːnɪ'keɪʃnz/ noun U [5,22] branch of technology concerned with communications over long distances

telecommunications engineer /,telikəmjuːnɪ'keɪʃnz endʒɪ,nɪə(r)/ noun C [25] a person who works with systems concerned with communications over long distances

telecommute /telikə'mjuːt/ verb [1] to communicate with your office by computer, telephone and fax while working a distance from your office, e.g. at home

telephony /tə'lefəni/ noun U [16] the science of audio communication through electric devices. It commonly refers to software that will make a computer act like a telephone.

teleworking /'teliwɜːkɪŋ/ noun U [24] the process of working at home while communicating with your office by computer, telephone and fax. See telecommute.

teller machine /'telə məˌʃiːn/ noun C [25] a machine used for taking payments in large shops and supermarkets

telnet /'telnet/ noun U [12] acronym for teletype network. An Internet service that allows a user to connect to a multi-user server using a computer as a terminal.

terabit /'terəbɪt/ noun C [23] a unit of storage capacity equal to 1 009 511 627 776 bits

terminal /'tɜːmɪnəl/ noun C [11] a network device used to input and output data (usually a basic computer)

terminal adapter /'tɜːmɪnəl əˌdæptə(r)/ noun C [16] a device for connecting an ISDN system to an existing telephone line

text editor /'tekst ˌedɪtə(r)/ noun C [6] a computer program for editing basic data or program text, i.e. like a basic wordprocessor

TFT display /ˌtiː ef 'tiː dɪˌspleɪ/ noun C [2] abbreviation for thin film transistor display. A type of LCD screen display commonly used in portable computers. It uses a separate transistor to control each pixel on the display.

thin client /'θɪn ˌklaɪənt/ noun C [11,15] a low-cost centrally-managed basic computer with a keyboard and display screen processor and memory but no CD-ROM drive, floppy disk drive or expansion slots, e.g. a NetPC or a network computer (NC)

third-generation GSM /ˌθɜːd ˌdʒenəˌreɪʃn ˌdʒiː es 'em/ noun U [23] the third generation of the Global System for Mobile communication standard. It is the standard for mobile users around the world.

throughput /'θruːpʊt/ noun U [17] the amount of data that passes through a system in a given period of time

toggle-box /'tɒɡlbɒks/ noun C [10] a screen icon in Windows Explorer that opens or closes a folder to show or hide its subfolders when the user clicks on it using a mouse

tooltip /'tuːltɪp/ noun C [7] a label that appear on the screen when the user holds the mouse pointer over an icon in a Microsoft Windows system

topology /tə'pɒlədʒi/ noun C [5,11] the physical layout of a network

tower chassis /'taʊə ˌʃæsi/ noun C [2] a personal computer case that stands on end and can be placed on the floor

unlike the normal desktop case that sits flat on a desk under the monitor

track /træk/ noun C [2] a formatted circular magnetic storage area on a computer disk

traffic /'træfɪk/ noun U [11,16] the volume of signals or data that passes through a network system

transaction processing /trænz'ækʃn ˌprəʊsesɪŋ/ noun U [21] the processing of computer transactions by updating the computer file as each transaction takes place rather than storing them until later to be processed as a batch

transistor /træn'zɪstə(r)/ noun C [23] a solid state electronic switch or amplifier

transmission control protocol /trænzˌmɪʃn kənˌtrəʊl 'prəʊtəkɒl/ noun U [12] a set of standards for the delivery of error-free data in communications between computers. It comes into operation once a data packet is delivered to the correct Internet address and application port. It manages the communication exchanges and provides reliable stream service by structuring and buffering the data flow looking for responses and taking action to replace missing data blocks.

transponder /træns'pɒndə(r)/ noun C [23] a device that responds to received coded radio signals by automatically transmitting a different coded signal

transport layer /'trɑːnspɔːt ˌleɪə(r)/ noun C [11] the part of a network communications system that protects the data being sent. It subdivides the data into segments and creates checksum tests. It can also make backup copies of the data.

trapdoor /ˌtræp'dɔː(r)/ noun C [18] a technique used in a computer crime that involves leaving within a completed program an illicit program that allows unauthorised – and unknown – entry

Trojan (horse) /'trəʊdʒən/ noun C [18,20] a technique used in a computer crime that involves adding concealed instructions to a computer program so that it will still work but will also perform prohibited duties. In other words it appears to do something useful but actually does something destructive in the background.

troubleshoot /'trʌblʃuːt/ verb [22] to find and fix faults in a system

troubleshooter /'trʌblˌʃuːtə(r)/ noun C [22] a person who finds and fixes faults in a system

TTS /ˌtiː tiː 'es/ noun U [7] abbreviation for text to speech. A system where a

computer reads text to the user using a speech synthesiser.

tuned /tjuːnd/ adj [11] set to operate on the same frequency

TV (set) /ˌtiː 'viː/ noun C [11,16,23,24] abbreviation for television. A television set is the actual television device used for displaying the video signals.

twisted-pair (cabling) /ˌtwɪstɪd 'peə(r)/ noun U [11,16] a common type of network cable that uses two wires twisted together to reduce interference from external signals

typesetting /'taɪpsetɪŋ/ noun U [6] preparation for printing

U

UDP /ˌjuː diː 'piː/ noun U [12] abbreviation for user datagram protocol

undo /ˌʌn'duː/ verb [10] to restore a file to the condition it was in before the last change was made

unencrypt /ˌʌnen'krɪpt/ verb [18] to remove the encryption from a file

uniform resource locator /ˌjuːnɪfɔːm rɪ'zɔːs ləʊˌkeɪtə(r)/ noun C [13] the unique address of a webpage

uninterruptible power supply /ˌʌnɪntəˌrʌptəbl 'paʊə səˌplaɪ/ noun C [19] a battery backup system that automatically provides power to a computer when the normal electricity source fails

universal mobile telecommunications system /ˌjuːnɪvɜːsl ˌməʊbaɪl ˌtelikəˌmjuːnɪ'keɪʃnz ˌsɪstəm/ noun U [16] a third-generation, broadband, packet-based communications system based on the Global System for Mobile (GSM) communication standard. It provides the same services including the transmission of text-digitised voice video and multimedia to mobile computer and phone users throughout the world.

Unix /'juːnɪks/ noun U [5,6,13,14,21,22, 25] a popular multi-user multitasking operating system originally designed for mainframe computers. A wide variety of versions exist.

update /'ʌpdeɪt/ noun C [5,15,22] a change that provides the latest version

update /ˌʌp'deɪt/ verb [5,15,22] to bring up to date, i.e. to change into the latest version

upgrade /'ʌpgreɪd/ noun C [2] a change that improves the features or performance of a system

upgrade /ˌʌp'greɪd/ verb [2,5,6,16,22] to add components to improve the features or performance of a system

upload /ˌʌpˈləʊd/ verb [5,16,24] to copy a file from a client computer to a server in a network

UPS /ˌjuː piː ˈes/ noun C [2] abbreviation for uninterruptible power supply

upstream /ˈʌpstriːm/ noun U [16] the signal path for receiving communications from a client computer to a server in a network

URL /ˌjuː ɑːr ˈel/ noun C [9,13,20,22] abbreviation for uniform (or universal) resource locator

Usenet /ˈjuːznet/ noun U [12,20] an Internet service that allows users to communicate by means of newsgroups

user /ˈjuːzə(r)/ noun C [1,5,6,18,21,22, 23,25] the person using a computer

user datagram protocol /ˌjuːzə ˌdeɪtəɡræm ˈprəʊtəkɒl/ noun U [12] a set of standards for creating a data address in a TCP/IP message. It is used to indicate what application the message is supposed to contact and provides the final routing for the data within the receiving system.

user-authentication system /ˌjuːzər ɔːˌθentɪˈkeɪʃn ˌsɪstəm/ noun C [18] a system that identifies users. This can be done using digital certificates.

username /ˈjuːzəneɪm/ noun C [19] the network account name assigned to a particular user

utility (program) /juːˈtɪləti/ noun C [6,25] a program included with an operating system that can perform useful common routine tasks or housekeeping operations, e.g. formatting disks or copying files

UTMS /ˌjuː tiː em ˈes/ noun U [16] abbreviation for Universal Mobile Telecommunications System

V

V /vɒlt/ noun C [23] abbreviation for volt, the international unit of voltage

VB /ˌviː ˈbiː/ noun U [22] abbreviation for Visual Basic

VCR /ˌviː siː ˈɑː(r)/ noun C [1] abbreviation for video cassette recorder

VDU /ˌviː diː ˈjuː/ noun C [2] abbreviation for visual display unit. Another name for a computer monitor.

verify /ˈverɪˌfaɪ/ verb [11] to check for accuracy

video /ˈvɪdiəʊ/ noun U [2,9,16,17] signals containing picture information

video (cassette) recorder /ˈvɪdiəʊ rɪˌkɔːdə(r)/ noun C [16,23] a device for recording video signals onto magnetic tape cassettes

video memory /ˈvɪdiəʊ ˌmeməri/ noun U [2] the memory used to store graphics data on a graphics card

videoconferencing /ˌvɪdiəʊ ˈkɒnfərənsɪŋ/ noun U [1,24] a form of communication over a network that uses video cameras so that the people taking part can see and hear each other

virtual /ˈvɜːtʃʊəl/ adj [12,23,24] computer-simulated enabling the user to experience something without needing its physical presence

virtual reality /ˌvɜːtʃʊəl riˈæləti/ noun U [12] a simulated three-dimensional environment that surrounds the user and is generated by a computer

virus /ˈvaɪrəs/ noun C [1,8,10,11,15,17, 18,19,20] a program written with the purpose of causing damage or causing a computer to behave in an unusual way

virus-check /ˈvaɪrəs tʃek/ verb [10,15] to check for viruses

VIS /vɪz/ noun U [2] abbreviation for viewable image size. The actual size of the image that can be seen by the user on a computer display screen.

Visual Basic /ˌvɪʒʊəl ˈbeɪsɪk/ noun U [21,22] a general-purpose programming language with a graphical interface. It is particularly suitable for use by beginners learning how to program.

visualisation technology /ˌvɪʒʊəlaɪˌzeɪʃn tekˈnɒlədʒi/ noun U [24] systems and devices used to create a virtual reality environment

VMS /ˌviː em ˈes/ noun U [6] an operating system used by DEC VAX minicomputers

voice /vɔɪs/ noun C [2] a stored musical instrument sound sample used to produce realistic music output in a wavetable soundcard

voice clip /ˈvɔɪs klɪp/ noun C [21] a short sound recording of the human voice

voice recognition /ˈvɔɪs rekəɡˌnɪʃn/ noun U [7,19] a system that can respond to words spoken by a human being

voice synthesis /ˈvɔɪs ˌsɪnθəsɪs/ noun U [24] the generation of a human-sounding voice using electronic circuits

voice synthesiser /ˈvɔɪs ˌsɪnθəsaɪzə(r)/ noun C [24] an electronic device that generates sounds that represent the human voice

VR /ˌviː ˈɑː(r)/ noun U [23] abbreviation for virtual reality

W

wallpaper /ˈwɔːlpeɪpə(r)/ noun C [9] the background graphics on a Microsoft Windows desktop

Wap /wæp/ noun U [16] acronym for wireless application protocol. A set of standards for allowing users to send emails and access information including video transmissions from the Internet on a mobile phone.

WAV /wæv/ noun U [9] an audio file format

wavetable system /ˈweɪvteɪbl ˌsɪstəm/ noun C [2] a system used in some soundcards for more accurately creating the sound of real musical instruments by reproducing a wide frequency range from a small number of original samples

Web address /ˈweb əˌdres/ noun C [5,13,20] the Internet address of a webpage

Web developer /ˈweb dɪˌveləpə(r)/ noun C [22] a person who is employed to create websites

Web mail /ˈweb meɪl/ noun U [13] an type of email that is accessed from webpages

Web server /ˈweb ˌsɜːvə(r)/ noun C [13] a server computer that stores and provides access to websites

Web space /ˈweb speɪs/ noun U [12,14] disk storage space on a web server used for storing webpages

Web (the) /web/ noun U [1,5,7,12,13,14, 15,16,18,18,19,20,22,23,24,25] common name for the World Wide Web

Webmaster /ˈwebmɑːstə(r)/ noun C [14,22] a person who administers a Web server

webpage /ˈwebpeɪdʒ/ noun C [6,12,13,14,15,16,17,21,22] a hyperlinked document in a web network system

web-ready appliances protocol /ˈweb ˌredi əˌplaɪənsɪz ˈprəʊtəkɒl/ noun U [23] a set of standards for enabling domestic appliances to be connected to the Web and to communicate with each other

website /ˈwebsaɪt/ noun C [1,5,8,12,14, 15,16,17,18,20,21,23,25] a set of related pages on the World Wide Web

wildcard /ˈwaɪldkɑːd/ noun C [13] a symbol used in computer commands and for searching databases. It represents any character or combination of characters, e.g. using an asterisk searching for *ed would find all words ending in ed.

window /ˈwɪndəʊ/ noun C [7] a rectangular screen area containing a program folder or file in a WIMP system

(Microsoft) Windows /ˈwɪndəʊz/ noun U [2,6,12,17,19,22,25] a graphical user interface operating system front-end to MS-DOS developed by the Microsoft Corporation. It has been gradually developed into a full operating system.

Windows Explorer /ˌwɪndəʊz ɪkˈsplɔːrə(r)/ noun U [9] a Microsoft Windows program that allows the user to see the files and folders on all the disks attached to the computer. It can be used for general housekeeping such as moving or deleting files.

Windows Media Player /ˌwɪndəʊz ˈmiːdiə ˌpleɪə(r)/ noun U [9] a Microsoft Windows program for playing multimedia files including audio and video

wipe (a disk) /waɪp/ verb [18] to delete all the files stored on a disk

wirelessly /ˈwaɪələsli/ adj [23] using radio signals without the need for connecting wires or cables

WML /ˌdʌbl juː em ˈel/ noun U [16] abbreviation for wireless markup language. A language similar to HTML used for designing webpages suitable for mobile phones.

(Microsoft) Word /wɜːd/ noun U [1,10,22] a widely-used wordprocessing program developed by the Microsoft Corporation. It is a component of the Microsoft Office package.

wordprocessing /ˌwɜːdˈprəʊsesɪŋ/ noun U [5,6,25] the process of typing and editing text using a wordprocessor

wordprocessor /ˌwɜːdˈprəʊsesə(r)/ noun C [16,18] a type of computer application program used for typing and editing text documents

workstation /ˈwɜːksteɪʃn/ noun C [2,6,22] a powerful desktop computer used by power users for work that requires a lot of processing, e.g. graphic design

World Wide Web (the) /ˌwɜːld ˌwaɪd ˈweb/ noun U [7,13,20,22] an information service on the Internet that allows document pages to be accessed using hyperlinks

WORM /wɜːm/ noun U [19] acronym for write once read many. A standard for optical storage devices that only allows data to be recorded on to a particular optical disk once but allows the data to be read from the disk over and over again. It is commonly used for archiving data.

WRAP /ræp/ noun U [23] acronym for Web-ready appliances protocol. A set of communications system standards that enable web-connected appliances to communicate.

writeable CD-ROM drive /ˌraɪtəbl siː diː ˈrɒm draɪv/ noun C [9] a compact disk drive that allows the user to write data onto a CD as well as read data stored on the CD

write-back cache /ˈraɪt bæk ˌkæʃ/ noun C [2] a buffer storage system where the processor writes changes only to the cache and not to main memory. Cache entries that have changed are flagged as 'dirty' telling the cache controller to write their contents back to main memory before using the space to cache new data.

write-through cache /ˈraɪt θruː ˌkæʃ/ noun C [2] a buffer storage system where the processor writes directly to both the cache and main memory at the same time

WWW /ˌdʌblju: ˌdʌblju: ˈdʌblju:/ noun U [12] abbreviation for the World Wide Web. The Internet service used for connecting to multimedia webpages.

X

X (windowing) (system) /eks/ noun U [6] a windowing system used with different versions of Unix

X.25 /ˌeks ˌtwenti ˈfaɪv/ noun U [12] the International Telegraphic Union packet-switching data communications standard for connecting computers and a public network

XGA /ˌeks dʒiː ˈeɪ/ noun U [2] abbreviation for extended graphics array. An IBM display screen standard with a resolution of 1024X768 pixels and up to 65,536 colours

XML /ˌeks em ˈel/ noun U [7,14,16,20, 21,25] abbreviation for extensible markup language

Y

Yahoo /jæˈhuː/ noun U [15,20] the name of a popular Internet search engine website

OXFORD
UNIVERSITY PRESS

Great Clarendon Street, Oxford OX2 6DP

Oxford University Press is a department of the University of Oxford. It furthers the University's objective of excellence in research, scholarship, and education by publishing worldwide in

Oxford New York

Athens Auckland Bangkok Bogotá Buenos Aires Cape Town Chennai Dar es Salaam Delhi Florence Hong Kong Istanbul Karachi Kolkata Kuala Lumpur Madrid Melbourne Mexico City Mumbai Nairobi Paris São Paulo Shanghai Singapore Taipei Tokyo Toronto Warsaw

with associated companies in Berlin Ibadan

Oxford and Oxford English are registered trade marks of Oxford University Press in the UK and in certain other countries

ISBN 0 19 457375 3

Designed by Shireen Nathoo Design, London

Printed and bound in Spain by Mateu Cromo, S. A. Pinto (Madrid)

Acknowledgements

The authors and publisher are grateful to those who have given permission to reproduce the following extracts and adaptations of copyright material:

p.8 Extracts from Computing in the Information Age (2nd Edition) by Nancy Stern & Robert A. Stern, © John Wiley and Sons Inc. Reproduced by permission; p.16 'Cache memory', PC Plus February 1994 © Future Publishing Limited. PC Plus is a trademark of Future Publishing Limited, a Future Network PLC group company used under licence. All rights reserved. Reproduced by permission; p.17 'How a disk cache works', PC Magazine September 1990. Reproduced by permission of VNU Business Publications; p.22 'Data mining for golden opportunities', Smart Computing Guide Series Vol. 8, Issue 1 January 2000. Reproduced by permission of Copyright Clearance Centre; p.30 'Ready for the bazillion-byte drive' by Thomas Claburn, PC Magazine (American Edition) March 2000. Reproduced by permission of Ziff-Davis Media Inc; p.36 Figure from Understanding Computers: Today and Tomorrow, 1998 Edition by Charles S. Parker, © The Dryden Press. Reproduced by permission of the publisher; p.37 Extracts from Computers and Information Systems by Capron, © Pearson Education Inc, Upper Saddle River, NJ. Reproduced by permission; p.42 'Smooth operator' by Charles Stross, Computer Shopper November 1998. Reproduced by permission of Dennis Publishing; p.50 'User-interfaces' by John Morris, PC Magazine 9 June 1998. Reproduced by permission of VNU Business Publications; p.55 New GPASS Conversion for GP's, © Crown Copyright 1998. Crown copyright material is reproduced with the permission of the Controller of Her Majesty's Stationery Office; p.58 'ASP and you shall receive' by Maggie Williams, PC Direct November 2000. Reproduced by permission of VNU Business Publications; p.61 'Jam on with MP3' by R.V. Schmidt, Smart Computing Guide Series Vol. 8, Issue 1 January 2000. Reproduced by permission of Copyright Clearance Centre; p.66 'The tricks to MPEG's Success', Windows Magazine March 1994. © CMP Media Inc 1994. Reproduced by permission; p.73 'A typical home network set-up', Personal Computer World August 1997. Reproduced by permission of VNU Business Publications; p.78 'Network communications', PC Magazine (American Edition) February 1993. Reproduced by permission of Ziff-Davis Media Inc; p.84 Extracts from PC Explorer March 2000 p.37. Reproduced by permission of Live Publishing International; p.86 'How TCP/IP links dissimilar machines', PC Magazine September 1989. Reproduced by permission of VNU Business Publications; p.94 'Using web-based e-mail' by Jonathan Bennett, PC Magazine November 1999. Reproduced by permission of VNU Business Publications; p.96 'Help web-farers find their way' by Matt Micklewicz, Windows Magazine July 1999. © CMP Media Inc 1999. Reproduced by permission; p.100 'XML takes on HTML', Smart Computing Guide Series Vol. 8, Issue 1 January 2000. Reproduced by permission of Copyright Clearance Centre; p.109 'How the internet phone works' © John Crace, The Guardian 29 February 2000. Reproduced by permission of Guardian Newspapers Ltd; p.111 Guardian text message poems competition winners: 'txtin iz messin' by Hetty Hughes and 'a txt msg pom' by Julia Bird. Appeared in Guardian Online © The Guardian 3 May 2001. Reproduced by permission of Guardian Newspapers Ltd; p.114

'Infrastructure for streaming video', *PC Magazine* July 1999. Reproduced by permission of VNU Business Publications; p.122 'Raiding hard drives', *PC Advisor* 4 January 1996. Reproduced by permission of PC Advisor magazine; p.125 'Overview: Virus protection', *PC Plus* December 1991 © Future Publishing Limited. *PC Plus* is a trademark of Future Publishing Limited, a Future Network PLC group company used under licence. All rights reserved. Reproduced by permission; p.130 'Power user tutor' by Jeff Downey, *PC Magazine* August 1998. Reproduced by permission of VNU Business Publication;. p.132 Extracts from Computing in the Information Age (2nd Edition) by Nancy Stern & Robert A. Stern, © John Wiley and Sons Inc. Reproduced by permission; p.138 'Backup HSM and media choice' by Phil Crewe, *PC Magazine* May 1996. Reproduced by permission of VNU Business Publications; p.140 'Cyberpirates intent on internet celebrity' by Simon Bower, © *The Guardian* 21 August 2000. Reproduced by permission of Guardian Newspapers Ltd; p.152 Extracts from Understanding Computers: Today and Tomorrow, 1998 Edition by Charles S. Parker, © The Dryden Press. Reproduced by permission of the publisher; p.154 Extracts from 'How to become a programming expert' by Dave Jewell, 'How to become a computer consultant' by Jon Honeyball', 'How to become a support engineer' by Mark Stephens and 'How to become an IT manager', from 'A career in computers' by Avril Williams, *PC Pro* August 1997. Reproduced by permission of Dennis Publishing; p.160 'Becoming certified' by David Moss, *PC Pro* November 1997. Reproduced by permission of Dennis Publishing; p.162 Extracts from 'Technology calendar' by Ian Pearson. Reproduced by permission of Gilt Edged Diaries; p.163 'Appliance of science' by M. Bedford, *Computer Shopper* May 2000. Reproduced by permission of Dennis Publishing; p.163 'Talking to the washing' © Chris Partridge / Times Newspapers Ltd 6 December 1999. Reproduced by permission; p.165 'The rise of the robots'. *PC Advisor* March 2000. Reproduced by permission of PC Advisor Magazine; p.170 'Fast forward' by Rupert Goodwins, *PC Magazine* August 1998. Reproduced by permission of VNU Business Publications; p.172 Extracts from 'Our view of the future' by Ian Pearson. Reproduced by permission of Gilt Edged Diaries; p.176 'Futures: Celebrity squares' by Professor Peter Cochrane, *PC Pro* February 1998. Reproduced by permission of Dennis Publishing; p.185 'Lara's looks are a revelation', © Greg Howson, *The Guardian* 3 March 2000. Reproduced by permission of Greg Howson; pp.186, 192 '50 things to do online' by Kyle Shurman, *Smart Computing Learning Series* Vol. 6, Issue 1 January 2000; p.191 'Sim makes it's city slicker' by Jack Schofield, © *The Guardian* 1 June 2000. Reproduced by permission of Guardian Newspapers Ltd.

Illustrations supplied by:

Stefan Chabluk pp.13, 16, 17, 18, 20, 24 (EPOS till), 36, 48, 53, 55, 60, 65, 66, 73, 86, 89, 91, 107, 130, 136, 137, 184, 187, 190, 193.

Mark Duffin pp.10, 11, 23, 24 (inputs/outputs), 52 (game screen), 72, 76, 79, 94, 109, 113.

The publishers would like to thank the following for their kind permission to reproduce photographs and other copyright material:

Ananova Ltd. 2001. p.166 (Ananova); Aura Studios p.15 (opening a computer), p.45 (Mac GUI); Barker Evans, Oxford p.4 (artist), p.32 (former student), p.159 (Paul W Cair); Canon (UK) Ltd. p.25 (camera), p.29 (Canon); Electrolux p.166 (screenfridge); Fuji Photo Film (UK) Ltd. p.29 (Fujifilm); Gemstar eBook Group Ltd. p.179 (lady) (man); ICL p.117 (call centre); John Birdsall Photography p.4 (OU student); McAfee.com Corp. p.135 (anti-virus); Minolta (UK) Ltd. p.29 (Minolta); Olympus Optical Co (UK) Ltd. p.29 (Olympus); Palm p.179 (student); Pentax UK Ltd. p.29 (Pentax); Ricoh UK Ltd. p.29 (Ricoh); Samsung (UK) Ltd. p.29 (Samsung); Science Photo Library p.135 (Volker Steger, Peter Arnold Inc/face recognition, Hank Morgan/voice recognition), p.166 (Peter Menzel/Aibo); Sony UK p.29 (Sony); Stone p.4 (Dan Kenyon/child), p.103 (Daniel Bosler/ webpage creator), p.178 (Daniel Bosler/e-publisher), p.179 (Gandee Vasan/child); The Image Bank p.68 (PS Productions/computing support officer); Topham Picturepoint p.140 (Harold Chapman/ex-hacker); www.educationphotos.co.uk p.4 (John Walmsley/teacher).

Cover: Gemstar eBook Group Ltd. (woman); Photodisk (abstract).

The publishers would like to thank the following for their kind permission to redraw/reproduce copyright material:

De Agostini UK Ltd. p.46 (captions); Dell p.11 (computer); Ericsson p.109 (phone); Future Publishing p.18 (PC Plus Magazine/cache memory), p.45 (Your Imac/captions), p.65 (Computer Music/midi), p.68 (Quick and Easy Windows/captions); Hodder & Stoughton p.20 (EPOS till) Redrawn from 'This is IT, 2' by I. Ithuralde & A. Ramkaran, by permission of Hodder & Stoughton Educational Ltd; Macworld magazine p.91 (video buffering); Microsoft Corporation p.44 (Windows), p.46 (desktop), p.52 (Word Pad, Excel, Calendar, Paint), pp.68–9 (Explorer). Screenshots reprinted by permission from Microsoft Corporation; PC Magazine p.86 (TCP/IP); The Dryden Press p.190 (Visa cards); The Guardian p.101 (XML), p.184 (ATM), p.187 (Love Bug), p.193 (Stealing by stealth); The Mirror p.60 (MP3); University of Edinburgh p.44 (website).

Although every effort has been made to trace and contact copyright holders before publication, this has not been possible in some cases. We apologize for any apparent infringement of copyright and, if notified, the publisher will be pleased to rectify any errors or omissions at the earliest opportunity.

Any websites referred to in this work are in the public domain and their addresses are provided by Oxford University Press for information only. Oxford University Press disclaims any responsibility for the content.